Worth a Thousand Words

Worth a Thousand Words

An Annotated Guide to
Picture Books for Older Readers

Bette D. Ammon
and
Gale W. Sherman

1996
Libraries Unlimited, Inc.
Englewood, Colorado

For Betty Holbrook, a classy librarian and boss who nurtured, taught,
and, most important, let us run with our "wild" ideas!
Love and a thousand thanks.

LIBRARIES UNLIMITED, INC.
P.O. Box 6633
Englewood, CO 80155-6633
1-800-237-6124

Production Editor: Stephen Haenel
Copy Editor: Jan Krygier
Proofreader: Ann Marie Damian
Design: Stephen Haenel & Michael Florman

Library of Congress Cataloging-in-Publication Data

Ammon, Bette DeBruyne.
    Worth a thousand words : an annotated guide to picture books for
older readers / Bette D. Ammon and Gale W. Sherman.
    xv, 210 p. 22x28 cm.
    Includes bibliographical references and index.
    ISBN 1-56308-390-6
    1. Illustrated books, Children's--Bibliography. 2. Picture books
for children--Bibliography. 3. Children--United States--Books and
reading. I. Sherman, Gale W. II. Titlc.
Z1023.A55 1996
011.62--dc20   96-31489
                                                              CIP

 Contents

Acknowledgments

The authors wish to thank the numerous individuals who were incredibly helpful with this project. Yes, we're finally done with this edition and no, Katie, we're not rich yet!

Nancy Spaulding, children's librarian and fine artist, deserves a heartfelt thank-you for her valuable artistic consulting and her ever-ready assistance in recommending and locating a gold mine of picture books.

Kate McClelland responded to a telephone call from a stranger by sharing her vast knowledge of picture books, the fabulous collection she's developed, and prodding us to "Hurry up and finish!"

Though pressed into service because of college vacation time, knowledge of children's literature, and direct bloodline connections, Ashley Sherman helped more than her mother ever expected. She was great at reading shelves, discovering hidden treasures, and giving opinions.

A recent hip replacement didn't keep Harriet Whittelsey, mother and grandmother, from crawling around library floors in pursuit of elusive books on low shelves. Her library card made the collections of many libraries accessible, and her companionship visiting libraries every day for a couple of weeks might have constituted abuse. Must be love.

David Loertscher, thanks for sharing your ideas, helping us refine ours, and encouraging us to tackle such a large project in the beginning.

Additional thanks go to Margie Mickelson for answering art questions and the staff members at Missoula Public Library (Missoula, MT) and Marshall Public Library (Pocatello, ID) for their help with interlibrary loan and other assistance.

A general thanks to the staff members who helped us at other libraries: Boston Public; Cedar Mills Public, Portland, OR; Chicago Public; Ferguson Memorial, Stamford, CT; Greenwich Public, CT; Idaho Falls Public, ID; and Perrot Memorial, Old Greenwich, CT.

If a picture is worth a thousand words, imagine the value of *many* pictures *plus* a thousand words. Pictures plus words (i.e., picture books) can be extraordinary, and picture books for older readers are a resource waiting to be tapped. Traditionally considered the domain of younger children, many picture books today defy that limitation. Even though the picture book format is fairly traditional with text and illustrations presented with a delicate balance, the format alone no longer dictates the age of the audience or the use of the material.

Some picture books are created specifically to deal with difficult subjects or complicated issues. More often than not, these books are designed and intended for an older audience. A classic and contemporary example is the 1995 Caldecott Award winner, Eve Bunting's *Smoky Night* (Harcourt, 1994), illustrated by David Diaz, which depicted the 1992 L.A. riots and their effect on a young boy and his mother who learn the value of getting along with others in their riot-torn neighborhood (entry 93). In his acceptance speech Diaz said he "felt the book could have a positive effect and help erode barriers of prejudice and intolerance. And above all, it was a book that could be a part of the post-riot healing process."

Because this book dealt with such a serious theme, many critics took the Caldecott Committee to task. They believe children are being robbed of an innocent childhood when their books deal with such disturbing themes. Others think that deeply serious issues or historical events (such as riots or the Holocaust) should not be dealt with in picture book format. These objections fail to take into account several issues:

1. Through television and newspapers, children in today's world know a considerable amount about what goes on in city streets and elsewhere. In fact, children live *in* those realities.

2. A picture book can introduce students to a topic or event, providing a frame of reference for further research.

3. Books about serious issues can relieve anxieties and provide opportunities for discussion, healing, and development of critical-thinking skills.

4. Many picture books with these sophisticated themes were never intended for the very young child.

This evolution in picture books is not news to innovative librarians, teachers, and parents who for years have been using picture books with older readers—students in grades four and above, including high school and college students. Those aware of this treasure trove of literature and art have been quick to capitalize on the eye-catching artwork and approachable texts. They know intuitively what recent research suggests—that many students comprehend better when they are reading meaningful text, with meaningful characters and themes. Readers need great stories, written with rich language; books that call out for looking, reading, and discussing. Many of these books are picture books for older readers.

What if there were a tool, an index, that combined distilled examples of concepts, literary devices, and art media along with the picture books that best illustrate them? We know that some teachers, librarians, and parents are using a smattering of picture books for older readers, and sporadic recommended lists appear both online and in professional journals. But until this volume, there has been no single source of comprehensive listings.

The following criteria were used to select the books included in *Worth a Thousand Words*.

1. Artistic and literary quality. The differences between these books and those intended for younger readers center on sophistication, content or subject matter, and length or complexity of art and/or text.

2. Universal themes with value and appeal for a variety of age levels.

3. Important issues that affect older students, dealt with in nonthreatening formats and accessible to multiple learning styles.

4. Publication prior to 1995.

Traditionally a picture book is defined as a story told using two media, a blending of verbal and visual art where the pictures and the text work interdependently to tell a story. The art in these books doesn't merely visualize what the words are saying; instead it goes beyond, giving readers more depth of meaning to the text. One is never too old for many of these books.

Common characteristics shared by most picture books include length (most are 32 pages long, but they can vary from 24 to 64) and format (pictures usually fill the page space and generally the text is brief). This marriage of words and pictures makes the book complete.

The picture book genre is made up of a variety of subgenres and book formats. These include alphabet, concept, wordless, poetry, biographies, historical fiction, nonfiction, and pop-up and toy books. Most of the concept books are geared toward young children, infants through early elementary age. However, even some of these books include complex characteristics such as foreign languages and sophisticated illustrations that will endear them to older readers.

We live in a highly visual environment. Because of television, computers, and movies, most students have well-developed comprehension skills for pictorial and nonlinear narratives. In particular, reluctant readers, English as a Second Language students, and those reading below grade level will learn more readily in a classroom filled with pictures in books. But in reality all students can benefit from the visual/verbal connections provided by powerful picture books.

Whole Language and Literature-Based Reading

Using picture books to explain and expand curriculum is a natural classroom teaching technique. Often picture book language is poetic, simple but eloquent, and teeming with metaphors and other literary devices. Examples of the finest art can be found between picture book covers. The numerous excellent fiction and nonfiction picture books offer countless opportunities for teachers to weave them into nearly every subject.

These short books are perfect to read at the beginning or conclusion of classes. The illustrations and language will often challenge proficient students while at the same time offer the weaker reader access to information presented with simplicity and clarity.

When used as part of a thematic unit, picture books are a natural way to introduce a new topic so that all students can quickly gain information. These books also serve to complement longer books and simplify difficult concepts. Sometimes a good picture book is all that is needed to provide that one clue to help a distracted learner catch on. When teachers combine a picture book along with the study of any subject matter, everybody wins.

Examples of Curricula Supported and Supplemented by Picture Books

Language Arts/Writing

Teachers can use picture books easily in language arts classes to promote writing and fluency. Students can discover elements of plot, setting, character, style, theme, and humor. They can emulate styles, discuss story structures, concretely experience that often nebulous world of literary devices, develop vocabulary, learn story construction devices, and experience conciseness of language. They can notice how both author and illustrator pull them through a piece, controlling the pacing, creating tension, engaging them, and providing resolution.

Poetry

Teachers can help students look with different eyes at poetry interpreted through art in illustrated editions of single poems. Though some would argue against the use of poems accompanied by illustration, there are valid reasons to include these books in poetry studies. Using picture book versions of poems can be a means of introducing poetry to students who think they don't like poetry. Using several illustrated versions of the same poem can help students understand that different interpretations can all be "right." The artistic impact of verse and picture is powerful. But because the individual reader should be allowed space for forming his or her own mental images as suggested by the poetry, we recommend reading the poem before sharing the artist's personal perspective—the illustrations—then encouraging discussion about various interpretations.

Traditional Literature

The study of traditional literature—folktales, fairy tales, myths, fables, etc.—is usually included in every literature curriculum. Older students benefit by being exposed to this literary heritage, and there are virtually thousands of illustrated versions of traditional tales. Because a guide to picture books for older readers in this genre could be a book in and of itself, *Worth a Thousand Words* provides only a representative sample. Teachers should certainly feel free to go beyond the examples included in this book and explore other titles.

Social Studies/Geography

Many picture books present compelling stories inviting students to understand other cultures and lands. Quality illustrations depicting clothing, customs, surroundings, and languages can be a refreshing alternative to videos, filmstrips, and films. Because many nonfiction picture books use maps, students can further develop concepts of world geography.

History

Picture books with text enriched by art can build an understanding of historical context, develop a sense of history, and enable students to discover incidents of humanity in the midst of historical events. Historical events featured in picture books present varied points of view. These can include evocative details about people and places of bygone times, information and pictures of immigration, war, people, places, a particular individual's viewpoint, and depictions of world-altering events. One teacher provides her students with numerous historic picture books and asks them to arrange them in chronological order. By doing so students gain a concrete understanding of the order of historic events.

Math

Many mathematical concepts that are difficult to grasp in the verbal abstract can be understood clearly when defined with pictures.

Drama/Speech

Picture books can provide material suitable for interpretation and study, costume and set ideas, script adaptations, etc. Like plays, the language of many picture books is designed for reading aloud.

Science

The excellent photographs and illustrations found in many picture books provide straightforward, uncomplicated details of biology, geology, astronomy, and other sciences.

Reading Aloud/Literature

The pure pleasure of reading and listening to stories is of paramount importance. Picture book stories are often perfect to read aloud in one session—easing students into a subject area or rewarding and entertaining them.

Art

As you might imagine, picture books can be used across the art curriculum as a rich teaching tool. They can provide examples of styles, techniques, and media; they can provide historical background for artistic trends. Through picture books, art students can learn about some of the great picture book illustrators, gain insight into the relationship between art and text, and learn about creating mood and providing messages. Picture book art can help students understand perspective and enable them to discover the special relationships that occur between story and illustration.

Taking a New Look at Picture Book Collections

Picture books for older readers have earned a place in many libraries and classrooms but are often overlooked by the audience they are produced for when they are shelved in a single picture book collection. So, of course, most library users mistakenly regard all these books as books for young children.

However, strategies for dealing with these particular books are developing. In light of the changes in picture books, professional reviews are creating designations such as "all ages" or "Grade 2 and up." *Horn Book Magazine,* well regarded for many years in the world of children's literature, now designates its picture book review section as books for "Infancy Through Young Adults."

The result is librarians and teachers are taking another look at these books and providing space for special collections of picture books for older readers. These can be placed adjacent to fiction collections or near circulation desks, and identified with a special spine label. The appropriate nonfiction titles can be cataloged with these books.

Bringing these books out of the traditional picture book collection ensures that they will be used and enjoyed by the audience for whom they were intended. Teachers, parents, and librarians can determine creative and innovative uses and promote this special collection of books for all ages.

One public library has pulled together these picture books for older readers and houses them in a collection called "Picture Plus." They have spine labels that read *JP+.* Another public librarian labels these books "Picture Books for All Ages." In a school library one librarian places these books on a shelf close to the novels and puts a star on each spine—she calls them "Gold Star Picture Books."

Another suggestion is to add another line to the call number designating these books as a collection separate from picture books for younger children.

There seems to be no one answer. Each library needs to assess how picture books for older readers can be highlighted in its collection. Computer cataloging allows for the inputting of location information, and special lists and bibliographies are useful and worth compiling.

Worth more than a thousand words, picture books for older readers are worthy of our time, attention, and affection. Although the collection of titles in this book is by no means complete, we believe it is at least a starting point toward bringing the appropriate users to this fascinating and helpful group of books.

Please go beyond what is provided here. Develop other book connections to serve individual classroom needs—and share those ideas with others.

The Top Ten Reasons Why Teachers, Librarians, and Parents Should Provide Picture Books for Older Readers:

10. Themes are often of universal appeal.

9. Talented artists and illustrators are using picture books as public galleries.

8. Many issues dealt with require a maturity level beyond that of young children.

7. The short and appealing format makes picture books easy to incorporate into whole language or literature-based curricula.

6. Students with learning difficulties or those learning English as a second language will be able to make the visual/verbal connections necessary for successful reading and learning.

5. Picture books can serve as models for fine writing and excellent illustration.

4. Picture books can be used to introduce difficult concepts and sophisticated ideas.

3. Students accustomed to learning visually through television and computers will adapt naturally to the picture book format.

2. The language in picture books is succinct and rich—a terrific way to increase vocabulary.

1. Those lucky students who learn to love picture books will receive a lifetime gift and will be forever thankful.

During the last decade the breadth and depth of picture books have changed dramatically. For many it has been exciting to see these changes, but the very nature of change sometimes bring confusion. Some teachers, media specialists, librarians, and parents wonder who the audience is for these books once written almost entirely for the very young. Where do they belong in libraries? How can they be used to their best advantage? How can we get them to their intended audience?

Worth a Thousand Words is a beginning database of picture books intended for, or appropriate to use with, older readers—those in fourth grade and above. The selected main entries are books published through 1994. Out-of-print titles are included because many of these wonderful titles are available in libraries and because books go in and out of print rapidly in today's publishing world.

Worth a Thousand Words can be used in several ways:

- to survey the variety of picture books available for older readers;
- to learn more about an individual title or works by an author or illustrator that may be appropriate to use with older readers;
- to identify books related to a specific area of the curriculum;
- to suggest (and model) uses for books within the curriculum;
- to help educators make connections between picture books and other materials; and
- to help adults match books with readers.

Picture Books

The body of *Worth a Thousand Words* features 645 books recommended for use with older readers. The entries are numbered consecutively and arranged alphabetically by author or editor's last name, or by title if the author is unknown. Each entry includes author, title, publisher, and publication date. Illustrators are listed if they are different from the author.

Each entry is annotated and includes a subject list. This extensive listing includes themes, genres, and subjects selected to enhance the book's potential classroom use, as well as to help match books with readers. Following the annotation are specific suggestions for including each book in the curriculum. These curriculum ideas are accompanied by icons in the margins (see the illustration below).

Extraordinary examples of picture books to use with older readers that include a combination of sophisticated themes, language, and illustrations are marked with an exclamation point (❗). These are also recommended titles for those interested in building a core collection of picture books for this audience. Even though all picture books are intended to be read aloud, some are highly recommended for reading aloud to audiences of older readers for sheer entertainment and are marked with a read-aloud icon (🕯). These exclamation points and read-aloud icons accompany the entry number in the margin.

For convenience and easy reference, three indexes follow the Picture Books section: Author/Illustrator Index, Title Index, and Subject Index.

❗ = Extraordinary!   💡 = Idea   📖 = Further Reading   ✍ = Writing $\frac{2}{+2}{4}$ = Math   ⚛ = Science   📕 = History

🌐 = Geography   🖌 = Art   🎵 = Music   🎭 = Drama   🎤 = Speech   🔍 = Research   🕯 = Read-Aloud

Author/Illustrator Index

Authors and illustrators are listed alphabetically, followed by book entry number(s). Authors and illustrators listed in internal citations are indicated by "n" following the number.

Title Index

The Title Index refers the reader to all the main and internal title citations in this book. Titles are listed alphabetically and are followed by the entry number. Numbers followed by "n" indicate title citations within entry annotations or curriculum ideas.

Subject Index

Each entry includes a subject list, which is the basis of the Subject Index. The Subject Index refers readers to entry numbers for the titles that include that topic.

No list is perfect or complete; a list compiled today will undoubtedly be altered tomorrow. Readers with additions can contact the authors through Libraries Unlimited or e-mail at ammon@mcat.com or gale@poky.srv.net. Suggestions will be considered for future editions.

Bibliography of Picture Book Resources

The following books will be of interest to teachers, media specialists, librarians, and students of children's literature who wish to more thoroughly investigate the world of picture books. These books offer a variety of information such as in-depth views of specific artists and/or analysis of specific books; artistic styles, techniques, and various media used by illustrators; information on book designs; discussions and promotion of visual literacy; guidelines for evaluating picture books; and other ideas for incorporating picture books into the curriculum.

Bader, Barbara. *American Picturebooks from Noah's Ark to the Beast Within* (Macmillan, 1976).

Bang, Molly. *Picture This: Perception and Composition* (Little, Brown, 1991).

Benedict, Susan and Lenore Carlisle, eds. *Beyond Words: Picture Books for Older Readers and Writers* (Heinemann, 1992).

Children's Book Council. *75 Years of Children's Book Week Posters: Celebrating Great Illustrators of American Children's Books* (Alfred A. Knopf, 1994).

Cianciolo, Patricia J. *Picture Books for Children*, 3rd ed. (American Library Association, 1990).

Cummins, Julie, ed. *Children's Book Illustration and Design* (PBC International, 1992).

Hall, Susan. *Using Picture Storybooks to Teach Literary Devices: Recommended Books for Children and Young Adults* (Oryx Press, 1990).

————. *Using Picture Storybooks to Teach Literary Devices: Recommended Books for Children and Young Adults,* Vol. 2 (Oryx Press, 1994).

Harmes, Jeanne McLain and Lucille J. Lettow. *Picture Books to Enhance the Curriculum* (H. W. Wilson, 1995).

Kiefer, Barbara Zulandt. *The Potential of Picturebooks: From Visual Literacy to Aesthetic Understanding* (Merrill, 1995).

Lacy, Lyn Ellen. *Art and Design in Children's Picture Books: An Analysis of Caldecott Award-Winning Illustrations* (American Library Association, 1986).

Lima, Carolyn W. and John A. Lima. *A to Zoo: Subject Access to Children's Picture Books,* 4th ed. (R. R. Bowker, 1993).

Marantz, Sylvia and Kenneth Marantz. *Artists of the Page: Interviews with Children's Book Illustrators* (McFarland, 1992).

————. *Multicultural Picture Books: Art for Understanding Others* (Linworth, 1994).

Marantz, Sylvia S. *Picture Books for Looking and Learning: Awakening Visual Perceptions Through the Art of Children's Books* (Oryx Press, 1992).

Marantz, Sylvia S. and Kenneth A. Marantz. *The Art of Children's Picture Books: A Selective Reference Guide,* 2nd ed. (Garland, 1995).

Moss, Elaine. *Picture Books for Young People 9-13,* 2nd ed. (Thimble Press, 1988).

Nodelman, Perry. *Words About Pictures: The Narrative Art of Children's Picture Books* (University of Georgia Press, 1988).

Richey, Virginia H. and Katharyn E. Puckett. *Wordless/Almost Wordless Picture Books: A Guide* (Libraries Unlimited, 1992).

Roberts, Ellen E. M. *The Children's Picture Book: How to Write It, How to Read It* (Writer's Digest, 1987).

Schwarcz, Joseph H. *Ways of the Illustrator: Visual Communication in Children's Literature* (American Library Association, 1982).

Schwarcz, Joseph H. and Chava Schwarcz. *The Picture Book Comes of Age: Looking at Childhood Through the Art of Illustration* (American Library Association, 1991).

Shulevitz, Uri. *Writing with Pictures: How to Write and Illustrate Children's Books* (Watson-Guptill, 1985).

Society of Illustrators, comp. *The Very Best of Children's Book Illustration* (North Light Books, 1993).

Stewig, John Warren. *Looking at Picture Books* (Highsmith, 1995).

Picture Books

1. Abeel, Samantha. **Reach for the Moon**. Watercolors by Charles R. Murphy (Pfeifer-Hamilton, 1993).

Creative Writing; Disabilities—Learning; Education—Special; Literary Devices; Parents; Poetry; Talents; Teachers

Thirteen years old and learning disabled, Samantha Abeel relates her feelings and experiences through poetry in response to paintings. Though unable to understand mathematical concepts or even tell time when this book was written, Abeel writes with sophistication. Introduction. Essays. Originally published as *What Once Was White* (Hidden Bay, 1993).

This inspiring book is a must to share with learning disabled adolescents. Those who have not yet found their talents can find solace in Abeel's determination, support, and success.

For writing inspiration, students can select paintings or other art that speaks to them on an emotional level. Flexible assignment dates and other adaptations used by Abeel's teacher might inspire students whose creative talents have yet to be tapped. Though Abeel's writing is full of imagery, the techniques used by her teacher can be used for any writing assignment.

2. Abells, Chana Byers. **The Children We Remember** (Greenwillow Books, 1983, 1986).

Children and War; Concentration Camps; Creative Writing; Fear; Holocaust; Jews; Nazis; Museums; Photographs; World War II

With text and photographs, the author briefly describes the fate of Jewish children after the Nazis began to control their lives at the start of the Holocaust.

The United States Holocaust Memorial Museum opened in Washington, D.C., in 1993 to huge crowds and public acclaim. Watch for articles concerning the exhibits and new publications, including the reissue of *I Never Saw Another Butterfly: Children's Drawings and Poems from Terezin Concentration Camp, 1942-1944* edited by Hana Volavková (Schocken Books, 1993) and *Tell Them We Remember: The Story of the Holocaust* by Susan D. Bachrach (Little, Brown, 1994).

The text is a fine example of carefully selected words accompanying, but not describing, evocative photographs. Students can practice similar writing to go along with original photos or artwork.

3. Ada, Alma Flor. **Dear Peter Rabbit**. Ill. by Leslie Tryon (Atheneum, 1994).

Creative Writing; Fairy Tales—Characters from; Letters;

Told through letters, this is a tale of interconnecting relationships between Goldilocks and Baby Bear, and Peter Rabbit and the Three Little Pigs.

Provide other books of letters for further study. All students will be intrigued by the *Jolly Postman* series by Janet Ahlberg and Allan Ahlberg (Little, Brown). High school and college students will enjoy the *Griffin and Sabine* trilogy by Nick Bantock (Chronicle Books).

Revive the lost art of letter writing! Using this book as a model, students can write letters to or from fictional characters.

4. Adkins, Jan. **The Art and Industry of Sandcastles** (Walker, 1994).

Art; Castles; Medieval History; Sandcastles; Sculpture

Originally published in 1971, this delightful book gives specific information about building sandcastles interspersed with historic details about castles and their purposes.

This excellent book will be useful in any study of medieval history or for an in-depth look at castles. For more information consult *The Castle Builder* by Dennis Nolan (Macmillan, 1987) and David Macaulay's *Castle* (Houghton Mifflin, 1977) as well as the excellent PBS documentary narrated by Macaulay, *Castle* (PBS Video, 1983).

Art students will be challenged to create their own sandcastles. Provide the materials and display the results.

5. Adler, David. **Hilde and Eli: Children of the Holocaust**. Ill. by Karen Ritz (Holiday House, 1994).

There is no happy ending to this chronicle of two Jewish children who were among the one and a half million Jewish children who were victims of the Holocaust. Notes.

Children and War; Concentration Camps; Fear; Holocaust; Jews; Nazis; Photographs; World War II

Of particular poignancy are the stories of how the Holocaust affected children. Consult the subject index in this book for other picture books on the Holocaust, and provide novels such as *Number the Stars* by Lois Lowry (Houghton Mifflin, 1989), *Devil's Arithmetic* by Jane Yolen (Viking Kestrel, 1988), *Hide and Seek* by Ida Vos (Houghton Mifflin, 1991), *The Night Crossing* by Karen Ackerman (Knopf, 1994), and *If I Should Die Before I Wake* by Hal Nolan (Harcourt Brace, 1994).

Students can find out more about the United States Holocaust Memorial Museum, which opened in Washington, D.C., in 1993 to huge crowds and public acclaim. Look for articles that deal with the exhibits as well as new publications, including the reissue of *I Never Saw Another Butterfly: Children's Drawings and Poems from Terezin Concentration Camp, 1942-1944* edited by Hana Volavková (Schocken Books, 1993), Chana Byers Abells' *The Children We Remember* (Greenwillow Books, 1983, 1986), and *Tell Them We Remember: The Story of the Holocaust* by Susan D. Bachrach (Little, Brown, 1994).

6. Adler, David A. **A Picture Book of Anne Frank**. Ill. by Karen Ritz (Holiday House, 1993).

This is an illustrated version of the life of Anne Frank, the young Jewish girl who chronicled the years she and her family hid from the Nazis in an Amsterdam attic.

Biographies; Children and War; Courage; Frank, Anne (1929-1944); Jews; Holocaust; Nazis; Netherlands; World War II—Netherlands

This is a perfect introduction to the classic *Anne Frank: The Diary of a Young Girl* (Doubleday, 1967), especially for reluctant readers.

Provide a selection of books detailing various aspects of the Holocaust. Consult the subject index for more picture books on the Holocaust, including *Star of Fear, Star of Hope* by Jo Hoestlandt (Walker, 1995).

7. Adler, David. **A Picture Book of Sojourner Truth**. Ill. by Gershom Griffith (Holiday House, 1994).

Born into slavery in 1797, Sojourner Truth is remembered for her courageous role in the struggle for freedom as an anti-slavery speaker and activist for the rights of Blacks and women. Notes.

Biographies; Courage; Equality; Segregation; Slavery; Speech; Truth, Sojourner (1797-1883); Women's Rights

Use this book as a springboard for further study of Sojourner Truth, including a closer look at her famous "Ain't I a Woman" speech delivered in Ohio in 1852. For more information consult Patricia McKissack and Fredrick McKissack's *Sojourner Truth: Ain't I a Woman?* (Scholastic, 1992).

Encourage speech students to learn Truth's famous speech. It would be timely to present during either February (Black History Month) or March (Women's History Month).

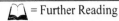

Like Rosa Parks (the freedom fighter who galvanized the Civil Rights movement by refusing to sit at the back of the bus), Sojourner Truth was instrumental in fighting for African American rights. Students can compare these two courageous women, noting the changes that occurred as a result of their actions.

8. Agee, Jon. **The Incredible Painting of Felix Clousseau** (Farrar, Straus & Giroux, 1988).

Adages; Art—Coming to Life; Artists; Creative Writing; Fantasy; Humor; Magic; Puns; Realism

Felix Clousseau is hailed as a genius when his portraits of people and animals actually come alive.

This funny book is a natural to combine with the whimsical novel *A Brush with Magic* by William J. Brooke (HarperCollins, 1993), where in ancient China a boy's drawings become real, and the picture books *The Magic Paintbrush* by Robin Muller (Viking, 1990), *Simon's Book* by Henrik Drescher (Lothrop, Lee & Shepard, 1983), *Liang and the Magic Paintbrush* by Demi (Henry Holt, 1980), and *The Boy Who Drew Cats* by Arthur A. Levine (Dial Books for Young Readers, 1993). Middle school and junior high students can read these books and write about or discuss their feelings about art and what makes it real.

Agee's hilarious portrayal of the old adage "art imitates life" is taken to new heights in this story. Students can write about the "real life" of the people and animals portrayed by Clousseau.

9. Alcorn. Johnny. **Rembrandt's Beret: Or the Painter's Crown**. Paintings by Stephen Alcorn (Tambourine, 1991).

Art—Coming to Life; Artists—Old Masters; Fantasy; Imagination; Museums; Rembrandt, Harmenszoon van Rijn (1606-1669)

The portraits and self-portraits in the "Old Master—Special Admittance Only" hall above the Ponte Vecchio come to life and welcome a visiting boy. Rembrandt is selected to paint the visitor's portrait and lets the boy keep his trademark beret.

A study of Rembrandt's art could include some of the following books: Richard Muhlberger's *What Makes a Rembrandt a Rembrandt?* (Metropolitan Museum of Art/Viking, 1993), Elizabeth Ripley's *Rembrandt: A Biography* (Oxford University Press, 1955), Gary Schwartz's *Rembrandt* (Abrams, 1992), and Pascal Bonafoux's *A Weekend with Rembrandt* (Rizzoli, 1992).

Companion books that feature characters from famous paintings that come to life include *The Girl with a Watering Can* by Eva Zadrzynska (Chameleon Books, 1990) and *The Gentleman and the Kitchen Maid* by Diane Stanley (Dial Books for Young Readers, 1994).

10. Alexander, Lloyd. **The Fortune-Tellers**. Ill. by Trina Schart Hyman (Dutton Children's Books, 1992).

Africa; Cameroon; Folktales—Africa; Fortune-Telling; Humor; Read-Aloud; Responsibility

Set in the country of Cameroon, this modern folktale tells of a young carpenter who has his fortune told with surprising results.

The fortune-teller tells the young carpenter the obvious—he will be happy if he can avoid being miserable. This clever way of making a person responsible for his own fate can be adapted for a school fair or carnival where a student can become a fortune-teller of this sort. Students can create appropriate predictions ahead of time.

Gods and Goddesses;
Mythology—Greek

11. Aliki. **The Gods and Goddesses of Olympus** (HarperCollins, 1994).
Lavishly illustrated pages introduce readers to many characters of Greek mythology.

This eye-catching book will ease students gently into more complete studies of Greek mythology. Use as an introduction to various mythological characters.

Biographies; France—Rulers;
Kings; Louis XIV (1638-1715);
Royalty; Social Life and
Customs—France

12. Aliki. **The King's Day: Louis XIV of France** (Thomas Y. Crowell, 1989).
Aliki presents a day in the life of King Louis XIV of France, focusing on the elaborate ceremonies that took place when he dressed, ate meals, conducted affairs of state, entertained, and prepared for bed. Chronology. Definitions.

Readers learn about life in France during King Louis XIV's rule by observing just one day. To depict life today, students can research, write, and illustrate a day in the life of a teacher, principal, mayor, or other professional worker. For more inspiration present *A Day in the Life of America* (Collins, 1986).

Cooking; England—History;
Feasts; Festivals; History—
Medieval; Royalty; Social Life
and Customs—England

13. Aliki. **A Medieval Feast** (Thomas Y. Crowell, 1983).
A medieval English manor is the setting for the preparations of a feast to entertain royal guests. Intricate illustrations and descriptions provide historical information about the period.

Create *A Medieval Feast* using this book. Students can wear appropriate costumes and cook the type of foods that traditionally would have been served. Excellent secondary resources include *Food & Feasts in the Middle Ages* by Imogen Dawson (New Discovery, 1994), Sarah Howarth's *The Middle Ages* (Viking, 1993), and John D. Clare's *Fourteenth-Century Towns* (Harcourt Brace Jovanovich, 1993).

Africa—Folklore;
Creation Stories; Folklore—
African

14. Anderson, David L. **The Origin of Life on Earth: An African Creation Myth**. Ill. by Kathleen Atkins Wilson, designed by Pete Traynor (Sights Productions, 1991).
Obatela, creator of the earth and human life, climbs to Earth on a golden chain and, upon arriving, plants seeds for vegetation and molds human beings from clay and dust. Glossary.

Use Anderson's creation myth to contrast and compare with other creation stories from a variety of cultures. Some of these are *All of You Was Singing* by Richard Lewis (Macmillan, 1991), *The Woman Who Fell from the Sky: The Iroquois Story of Creation* by John Bierhorst (William Morrow, 1993), *The Fire Children: A West African Creation Tale* by Eric Maddern (Dial Books for Young Readers, 1993), *The Children of the Morning Light: Wampanoag Tales* by Medicine Story and Mary F. Arquette (Macmillan, 1994), and *The Story of the Creation: Words from Genesis* by Jane Ray (Dutton Children's Books, 1993).

Biographies; Courage;
Fears; Modern Art;
Paintings—Modern Art;
Poetry; Read-Aloud

15. Angelou, Maya. **Life Doesn't Frighten Me**. Paintings by Jean-Michel Basquiat (Stewart, Tabori & Chiang, 1993).
First published in 1978, this poem celebrates defiant courage in facing life's real and imagined fears. Includes biographies for both Angelou and Basquiat.

This book is a wonderful introduction to Angelou's poetry. Though Angelou has said "the words 'public' and 'poem' go together like buttermilk and champagne," she has written several poems for very public events: "A Brave and Startling Truth" for the 50th birthday of

! = Extraordinary!   Idea   = Further Reading   = Writing $\frac{2}{4}$ = Math   = Science   = History

the United Nations in 1995, "On the Pulse of Morning," read at the 1993 presidential inauguration for President Bill Clinton and at the historic Million Man March in Washington, D.C., in October 1995. Share both her public and more private poems with students and discuss the ramifications of poetry made public.

Angelou's life, with many early struggles, offers hope to many young adults. Present the brief biography included here as a nice bridge to her acclaimed autobiographies beginning with *I Know Why the Caged Bird Sings* (Random House, 1970).

The Painter's Eye: Learning to Look at Contemporary American Art, a study of 20th-century American art by Jan Greenberg and Sandra Jordan (Delacorte Press, 1991), includes information about Jean-Michel Basquiat's unique art style. Use this information to help explore his paintings featured in *Life Doesn't Frighten Me*.

16. Angelou, Maya. **My Painted House, My Friendly Chicken, and Me**. Photographs by Margaret Courtney-Clarke (Clarkson Potter/Crown, 1994).

Art—Ndebele; Beading; Houses; Murals; Ndebele; Social Life and Customs— South Africa; South Africa

An eight year old tells about growing up in a traditional South African Ndebele village—her peoples' ideas of "good," their famous paint and bead designs, and her family and pet chicken.

This book provides a portrayal of village life in South Africa, which is rarely presented in the media for Americans to see. Include this book in a study of South Africa to provide students with a more balanced presentation.

The traditional bold geometric designs painted on Ndebele houses dominate the photographs. Other groups of people around the world have also decorated the exterior of their homes with their traditional designs, for example, the Pennsylvania Dutch, the Swiss in some regions of the Alps, and the Tlingit and other Northwest Coast tribes. Compare and contrast these designs and investigate their origins.

17. Angelou, Maya. **Now Sheba Sings the Song**. Art by Tom Feelings (E. P. Dutton, 1987).

Black Women—Poetry; Poetry; Portraits; Women—Poetry

Feelings' 84 sepia-toned portraits of Black women are illuminated by Maya Angelou's tribute to the powerful spirit of Black women all over the world. Introduction.

Share this sensuous book with sophisticated and mature students. In Feelings' introduction, the reader discovers the unusual sequence of this book—the art came first and inspired Angelou's poem.

18. Anno, Mitsumasa. **All in a Day** (Philomel, 1986).

Climates; Diversity; Geography—World; Hemispheres; Multiculturalism; Peace; Seasons; Social Studies; Time Zones

Ten internationally known artists from different time zones collaborated to illustrate the similarities and differences between the lives of young people in the United States, England, Russia (referred to as the U.S.S.R.), Japan, China, Australia, Kenya, and Brazil. Emphasizing the communality of humankind, the book is dedicated to peace. Note.

As usual, Anno's books include much more than is originally noticed. The information included here focuses on the scientific principles of the earth's rotation and time zones, as well as hemispheric seasons and climates. Use the notes at the end as a springboard for further study on these topics.

Another book that celebrates diversity on a worldwide scale is Peter Spier's *People* (Doubleday, 1980). Individual stories featuring ethnic groups or individual countries are listed under those terms.

 = Geography   = Art   = Music   = Drama   = Speech   = Research   = Read-Aloud

19. Anno, Mitsumasa. **Anno's Alphabet: An Adventure in Imagination** (Harper, 1975).

20. Anno, Mitsumasa. **Topsy-Turvies: Pictures to Stretch the Imagination** (Philomel, 1970).

21. Anno, Mitsumasa. **The Unique World of Mitsumasa Anno: Selected Works (1968-1977)** (Philomel, 1980).

22. Anno, Mitsumasa. **Upside-Downers: Pictures to Stretch the Imagination** (Philomel, 1988).

Some or all of the paintings and drawings in these books feature Anno's visual delights, consisting of optical illusions in Escheresque perspectives.

Art; Cards; Escher, M. C. (1898-1972); Optical Illusion; Perspective; Point of View; Printmaking; Surrealism

Anno's art falls into three main categories: mathematical, historical, and Escherlike. As an artist, Anno acknowledges the influence of Escher's work on his own. Students can compare some illustrations of the artists: Consider Escher's *Ascending and Descending* with Anno's Plate 5 *The Myth of Sisyphus* and Plate 12 *The Endless Staircase* (in *The Unique World*) and Escher's *Waterfall* with the picture of the river through the town on the last page in *Topsy-Turvies*. Notice the impossible connection between two-dimensional and three-dimensional letters in *Anno's Alphabet* and Escher's *Three Intersecting Planes, Stars,* and *Print Gallery*. Good companion volumes of Escher's works include *The Pop-Up Book of M. C. Escher* (Pomegranate Artbooks, 1991), *M. C. Escher: His Life and Complete Graphic Work* (Harry N. Abrams, 1992), and *M. C. Escher: 29 Master Prints* (Harry N. Abrams, 1983).

23. Anno, Mitsumasa. **Anno's Britain** (Philomel, 1982).

24. Anno, Mitsumasa. **Anno's Italy** (Philomel, 1978).

25. Anno, Mitsumasa. **Anno's Journey** (Philomel, 1978).

26. Anno, Mitsumasa. **Anno's U.S.A.** (Philomel, 1983).

Journeys to different lands incorporate history, literature, art, architecture, popular culture, and famous people.

Geography; History; Journeys; Social Life and Customs— England; Social Life and Customs—Italy; Social Life and Customs—United States; Social Studies; Travel; Wordless Books

These deceptively simple-looking books are filled with sophisticated images relating to history, geography, and social studies. Students can spend hours browsing and looking for the treasures hidden in the pictures and mentioned in the notes in the back of each book. These books can also be used for visual contests (finding clues hidden in artwork) as well as springboards for further research.

27. Anno, Mitsumasa. **Anno's Magical ABC** (Philomel, 1981).

Distorted letters of the alphabet (and representative pictures) can be "seen" with the help of the accompanying silver tube. Instructions.

Alphabet; Anamorphic Art; Literary Recreations; Mathematics; Optical Images; Picture Puzzles; Toy and Moveable Books

Other books with anamorphic drawings (in addition to other distorted images in art) include Carl Sandburg's *Arithmetic* (Harcourt, 1993) and Linda Bolton's *Hidden Pictures* (Dial Press, 1993).

Anno explains how to make anamorphic drawings using polar coordinates so students can create their own. Carry this activity across the curriculum by having students make art books in math class.

---

28. Anno, Mitsumasa. **Anno's Math Games** (Philomel, 1987).

29. Anno, Mitsumasa. **Anno's Math Games II** (Philomel, 1989).

30. Anno, Mitsumasa. **Anno's Math Games III** (Philomel, 1991).

31. Anno, Mitsumasa. **Anno's Mysterious Multiplying Jar** (Philomel, 1983).

32. Anno, Mitsumasa. **Socrates and the Three Little Pigs** (Philomel, 1986).

Abstract Thinking; CD-ROMS; Circuitry; Literary Recreations; Mathematics—Concepts; Puzzles; Topology

The math games, picture puzzles, and simple activities contained in this series of books introduce mathematical concepts through illustrations and a clear text. The first and second *Math Games* books include multiplication, sequence, ordinal numbering, measurement, and direction. *Math Games III* includes abstract thinking, circuitry, geometry, and topology. *Anno's Mysterious Multiplying Jar* visually explores factorials, and *Socrates and the Three Litle Pigs* includes mathematical permutations and combinations. Notes.

$\frac{2}{+2}{4}$ Anno's approach to math is from the perspective of "creative discovery." Work on the puzzles yourself before you present them to students. Once students (gifted or struggling) understand what they are trying to do, you can use these puzzles for extra credit or pure enjoyment. Anno has continued his story and math book combinations with *Anno's Magic Seeds* (Philomel, 1995). Reading "The Picture Books of Anno: A Search for a Perfect World Through the Fascination with Mathematics" (*Children's Literature Education,* 25(3):193+) will be helpful and interesting. *Anno's Learning Games: Math Made Fun and Easy* is a CD-ROM (Putnam New Media, 1994) designed to develop math and logic skills. It is a perfect companion to these books and just might be the experience needed for students having trouble with math.

33. Anno, Mitsumasa. **Anno's Medieval World** (Philomel, 1979).

Astronomy; Copernican Theory; Medical Ethics; Middle Ages; Ptolemaic Theory; Science—Astronomy; Superstitions

This journey through the Middle Ages (from the Dark Ages to the Age of Reason) fosters understanding of the time when people believed the world was flat, pestilence was caused by demons and witches, and scientific thoughts could be considered heresy. Note. Chronology.

The detailed note about the Ptolemaic and Copernican theories along with a chronology concerning these theories throughout world history makes this book perfect for astronomy students at any introductory level, including college. *3-D Galaxy: See the Hidden Pictures in the Stars* (William Morrow, 1994) is an unusual introduction to astronomy and will help beginners find well-known patterns in the stars.

Use this book to instigate a debate about scientific discoveries and new ethical and philosophical questions. Invite a medical ethicist to lead a discussion about current issues and discoveries.

34. Anno, Mitsumasa. **Anno's Twice Told Tales: The Fisherman & His Wife & The Four Clever Brothers** (Philomel, 1993).

Creative Writing; Fairy Tales; Fathers and Sons; Foxes; Literacy; Read-Aloud; Social Issues—Literacy

Freddy the Fox finds a book with two stories that he asks his father, Mr. Fox, to read. The original Brothers Grimm version is told at the top of each page, while Mr. Fox's version is printed at the bottom.

Readers will discover the reason for Mr. Fox's different interpretations—he can't read. Illiteracy among adults continues to be a societal problem in the United States. Literacy Volunteers of America provides services in most communities. Invite a spokesperson to class to discuss opportunities to help in your community; interested students may want to volunteer.

A typical child, Freddy doesn't really mind when his father reinterprets books. According to Anno, "What Freddy really wanted was just to sit on his father's lap and have his father hold him close. . . ." The importance of reading aloud cannot be overemphasized. Use this theme as a springboard for discussion or further projects involving reading aloud. Interested students can develop a read-aloud program for younger children.

Students can use this as a model to retell any story by reinterpreting the illustrations.

35. Anno, Mitsumasa. **In Shadowland** (Orchard, 1988).

Fantasy; Paper Cuttings; Pop-Up Books; Shadows; Sundials; Time; Winter

The watchman, leaving his post in Shadowland to help the poor little match girl, causes chaos to descend on both his world and the parallel "real" world.

Expand upon the topic of shadows by having students research and make sundials as Anno explains. Also provide *Anno's Sundial* (Philomel, 1987), a pop-up book that explores the relationship between the motion of the sun and earth and the use of shadows for telling time.

36. Applebaum, Diana. **Giants in the Land**. Ill. by Michael McCurdy (Houghton Mifflin, 1993).

Conservation; Forests— Old Growth; History (1760-1775); Logging; Naval Power; New England—History; Shipbuilding; Trees

With scratchboard drawings resembling woodcuts, this book describes how the giant pine trees in New England were cut down and transported to be used on the massive wooden ships for the King's navy.

This book can serve to pique interest in naval powers throughout world history. The British Royal Navy ruled the seas during the late 18th century. Provide students with Richard Platt's *Stephen Biesty's Cross Sections: Man-of-War* (Dorling Kindersley, 1993) for superlative information about these first-class British warships.

The absence of old-growth forests in the eastern United States has influenced the wilderness movement in the West. Students can look at all sides of the issue to determine their own point of view.

37. Asch, Frank and Valdimir Vagin. **Here Comes the Cat** (Scholastic, 1989).

Bilingual Books; Cats; Cooperation; Fear; Friendship; Languages— Russian; Mice; Russia

The mice are excited, and worried, about the arrival of a cat.

The limited text, in Russian and English, makes this book ideal for introducing the Russian language.

Since *Here Comes the Cat*, Valdimir Vagin has illustrated another book with Asch, *Dear Brother* (Scholastic, 1992) and also one with Katherine Paterson, *The King's Equal* (HarperCollins, 1992).

This joint project between a Russian and American can help students focus on the theme of cooperative efforts. Joint business ventures between the United States and Russia are becoming commonplace. A group of five U.S. companies has formed a consortium to develop cooperative efforts. Even cross-cultural friendships are being encouraged. For instance, the Samantha Smith Exchange program was promoted by Senator Bill Bradley and funded though the Freedom Support Act to enhance cultural awareness and understanding. What other cooperative efforts between Russia and the United States can your students locate?

 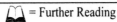

38. Axelrod, Amy. **Pigs Will Be Pigs**. Ill. by Sharon McGinley-Nally (Four Winds Press, 1994).

Addition; Finance—
Personal; Humor;
Mathematics; Money;
Pigs; Restaurants;
Subtraction

The hungry Pig family turn their house upside down looking for enough money to buy dinner. They find dollars and coins everywhere. Note.

$\frac{\begin{array}{r}2\\+2\end{array}}{4}$ Students can add up the amounts the pigs find as they read this story. Other mathematical functions are suggested at the end. As a bonus there are also hidden answers throughout the book.

B

39. Bahr, Mary. **The Memory Box**. Ill. by David Cunningham (Whitman, 1992).

Aging; Alzheimer's
Disease; Families;
Grandparents; Memory;
Old Age; Social
Issues—Aging

With his grandson's help, Gramps (depicted in the early stages of Alzheimer's disease) starts a Memory Box. He hopes it will help his family deal with the disease and keep alive the memories of the times he has shared with them.

The Memory Box is reminiscent of Mem Fox's *Wilfrid Gordon McDonald Partridge* (Kane-Miller, 1989). Both main characters are boys who participate in collecting memorabilia for friends who are losing, or have lost, their memories. This simple positive action can help children build memories with older friends and relatives whether or not Alzheimer's disease or general memory loss becomes a problem.

The causes of Alzheimer's disease are not yet understood. Intermediate students can use books such as Laurie Beckelman's *Alzheimer's Disease* (Macmillan, 1990) and articles in current journals to learn more about it.

40. Baillie, Allan. **Rebel**. Ill. by Di Wu (Ticknor & Fields, 1994).

Burma; Civil
Disobedience; Historical
Fiction; History—Burma;
Military Rule; Myanmar;
Rebellion; Repression;
War

The General, arriving with tanks and clanking medals designed to make the villagers fearful of his military rule, is ridiculed by a brave student. This story is based on a true incident.

"I'm Tipingee, She's Tipingee, We're Tipingee Too" in *The Magic Orange Tree and Other Haitian Folktales* collected by Diane Wolkstein (Alfred A. Knopf, 1978) is an appropriate companion story.

Henry David Thoreau (1817-1862) wrote an essay entitled "Civil Disobedience" (1848), and Martin Luther King Jr. defended his actions in his 1963 "Letter from Birmingham Jail" (see *The Negro in American History* [Encyclopaedia Britannica Educational Corp., 1969]). Both discourses will be of interest to older students.

Students may be familiar with boycotts, hunger strikes, and sit-ins but not realize they are a form of civil disobedience. Study civil disobedience in depth. Examples from the 20th century include Mahatma Gandhi (1869-194 8) and the struggle for independence in India, Martin Luther King Jr. (1929-1968) and his challenge to segregation in America, and the 1990s cyberspace protest of government oppression in Myanmar (formerly Burma).

 = Geography   = Art   = Music   = Drama   = Speech   = Research   = Read-Aloud

Animals; Art—Collage;
Birds; Collage; Hobbies;
Pigeons; Science—
Adaptation

41. Baker, Jeannie. **Home in the Sky** (Greenwillow, 1984).
Light, a banded homing pigeon, is rescued by a young boy after a series of adventures and then set free to find his rightful owner.

 Pigeons are just one of the many species of birds that inhabit cities. Interested students will enjoy Ethan Herberman's *The City Kid's Field Guide* (Simon & Schuster, 1989) and Barbara Bash's *Urban Roosts: Where Birds Nest in the City* (Sierra Club/Little, 1990). Have your student consider this question: Why have some birds adapted so well to urban life?

 Baker's extraordinary multidimensional collages consist of ceramics, wire, clay, litter, pigeon feathers, fabric, and grasses, among other things, and took two years to complete. The final "collage constructions" were exhibited in several art galleries around the world. These sophisticated works can serve as models for art students.

Art—Collage; Australia;
Ecology; Environmental
Action

42. Baker, Jeannie. **Window** (Greenwillow, 1991).
Viewing the area beyond his bedroom window, a boy watches "progress" in action as the lush vegetation of the land changes to a crowded urban area with high-rise buildings, billboards, and litter. Note.

 Baker's note includes statistics concerning humanity's impact on the environment and presents a challenge to readers. She writes, "by understanding and changing the way we personally affect the environment, we can make a difference." This book is a catalyst to use in beginning student discussion on the global aspects of humans' impact on the environment. Local action is a terrific option for student involvement! Books such as Anne Pedersen's *The Kids' Environment Book: What's Awry and Why* (John Muir, 1991) and *Going Green: A Kid's Handbook to Saving the Planet* by John Elkington et al. (Viking, 1990) can be helpful.

Bison; Buffaloes;
Indians of North America;
Legends; Magazines;
Visual Literacy

43. Baker, Olaf. **Where the Buffaloes Begin**. Drawings by Stephen Gammell (Warne, 1981).
Little Wolf's secret adventure to find the sacred lake where the buffaloes began turns into a desperate attempt to save his people by diverting a stampeding herd. Caldecott Honor, 1982.

 Olaf Baker was born in the 1870s in England and then migrated to the United States in 1902. "Where the Buffaloes Begin" was first published in the important children's periodical of the time *St. Nicholas Magazine* (42(4):291+, February 1915). Students might be interested in seeing copies of this early magazine, which is available in book format because many subscribers had their issues bound every six months. Also provide *The St. Nicholas Anthology* edited by Henry Steele Commager (Random House, 1948).

Historically, the lives of the Plains Indians and the buffaloes were intertwined. Students can consult books such as *Buffalo Hunt* by Russell Freedman (Holiday House, 1988), *Buffalo: The American Bison Today* by Dorothy Hinshaw Patent (Ticknor & Fields, 1986), and *Buffalo Woman* by Paul Goble (Macmillan, 1984) for more information and folklore.

 The power of these black-and-white illustrations is evident when reading *Where the Buffaloes Begin*. To enhance visual literacy, expose students to a variety of books done in this style and discuss the artwork. Consult "Black-and-White Magic" by Dilys Evans (*Book Links* 2(1):49-53, September 1992).

---

44. Bang, Molly. **The Grey Lady and the Strawberry Snatcher** (Four Winds, 1980).

Adventure; Creative Writing; Strawberries; Wordless Books

In this eerie wordless adventure, a green skateboard creature follows the grey lady, who is carrying strawberries through the swamp and woods to her home. Caldecott Honor, 1981.

This short wordless book is mysterious, terrifying, and alluring. It provides plenty of grist for creative writing assignments for students of any age in writing their own text to accompany the illustrations.

45. Bartone, Elisa. **Peppe the Lamplighter**. Ill. by Ted Lewin (Lothrop, Lee & Shepard, 1993).

American Dream; Brothers and Sisters; Family Life; Fear of the Dark; Historical Fiction; Immigrants; Italian Americans; Pride; Social Life and Customs—New York City—Early 1900s

Peppe takes a job as a lamplighter to help his family financially but has to face the scorn of his father for taking such a lowly job. Caldecott Honor, 1994.

This book offers students a good look at life in America for immigrants at the turn of the century. The Lower East Side Tenement Museum in New York City pays tribute to those workers. Have students do research to answer this question: Realistically, what were the typical jobs immigrants could get at that time?

What is the American Dream? Is it the same dream now as a 100 years ago? Students can gather information by interviewing immigrants who have lived in the United States for varying amounts of time, as well as lifelong citizens of different ages.

46. Base, Graeme. **Animalia** (Harry N. Abrams, 1986).

47. Base, Graeme. **The Eleventh Hour: A Curious Mystery** (Harry N. Abrams, 1989).

Adventures; Book Games; Clues; Games; Literary Recreations; Mysteries; Picture Puzzles

On the title page of *Animalia,* Base sets the stage for an alphabet adventure in an imaginary world populated by exotic and familiar animals, as well as the author himself. *The Eleventh Hour* mystery story is filled with hidden messages and visual clues.

Notice the games pictured throughout *The Eleventh Hour.* Use this book to launch a game party where students bring in various games to play and share, particularly those pictured in this book. Include chess (the perennial challenge) and Clue™, which has many similarities to this mystery. Rosemary Sutcliff's picture book *Chess-Dream in a Garden* (Candlewick Press, 1993) is an ideal companion book dealing with games.

48. Base, Graeme. **My Grandma Lived in Gooligulch** (The Australian Book Source, 1988).

Animals—Australia; Australia; Grandmothers; Poetry; Science—Wildlife; Speech; Tall Tales

A rollicking poem and lush illustrations describe Grandma and her interactions with the animals of Australia.

Use the excellent illustrations in this book as a springboard to a study of Australian animals and their characteristics.

Students interested in Australia and its distinctive language can use this book to define unfamiliar words. It would also be delightful as an interpretive poem for speech presentations.

49. Bates, Katharine Lee. **America the Beautiful**. Ill. by Neil Waldman (Atheneum, 1993).

Geography—United States; Patriotism; Poetry; Social Studies—United States; Songs—Patriotic; United States

This illustrated 19th-century poem (later set to hymn music) celebrating the beauty of America is a favorite patriotic song. Foreword. Musical score. Notes.

This annotated catalog of panoramas features human-made and natural wonders that are perfect for including in geography and social studies units. For regional geography studies consider using Diane Siebert's *Heartland* (Thomas Y. Crowell, 1989), *Mojave* (Thomas Y. Crowell, 1988), and *Sierra* (HarperCollins, 1991), and Byrd Baylor's four Southwest desert books: *The Desert Is Theirs* (Charles Scribner's Sons, 1975), *Desert Voices* (Charles Scribner's Sons, 1981), *Everybody Needs a Rock* (Charles Scribner's Sons, 1974), and *I'm in Charge of Celebrations* (Charles Scribner's Sons, 1986). Another good resource is Chris Van Allsburg's *Ben's Dream* (Houghton Mifflin, 1982).

50. Baylor, Byrd. **The Desert Is Theirs**. Ill. by Peter Parnall (Charles Scribner's Sons, 1975).

51. Baylor, Byrd. **Desert Voices**. Ill. by Peter Parnall (Charles Scribner's Sons, 1981).

52. Baylor, Byrd. **Everybody Needs a Rock**. Ill. by Peter Parnall (Charles Scribner's Sons, 1974).

53. Baylor, Byrd. **I'm in Charge of Celebrations**. Ill. by Peter Parnall (Charles Scribner's Sons, 1986).

Collections; Creative Writing; Desert Life; Desert People; Read-Aloud; Rocks; Southwest; Writing

These four books feature the Southwest desert environment of the United States. Readers view the desert from the perspective of the animals and people who are at one with the land. *The Desert Is Theirs* was a Caldecott Honor book in 1976.

Be sure to include these books in a social studies unit of the American Southwest. The desert defines both itself and the way humans interact with the environment.

Everybody Needs a Rock is a poetic presentation of the 10 rules for finding a special rock you can keep forever. As a creative writing project, students can develop 10 rules for guiding the development of their collections.

54. Baylor, Byrd. **If You Are a Hunter of Fossils**. Ill. by Peter Parnall (Charles Scribner's Sons, 1980).

Cretaceous Period; Fossils; Geology; Paleontology; Science—Geology; Science—Paleontology; Texas

A fossil hunter describes how the western Texas mountain area must have looked millions of years ago.

Amateur fossil hunters will be pleased with this book, which focuses on a specific area of Texas but also mentions fossil finds in other parts of the country. What kind of fossils are found in your area? What geologic time period are they from? Invite a fossil hound to share stories, artifacts, and information with your students. Rocks have stories to tell, and students can learn to read these stories!

55. Baylor, Byrd. **The Table Where Rich People Sit**. Ill. by Peter Parnall (Charles Scribner's Sons, 1994).

Family Life; Geography; Lists; Nature; Values Clarification; Wealth; Work Ethic

A girl realizes that although her family has little money, they are rich because of their experiences. These include watching the changing colors of the mountains, seeing eagles fly, and hearing the sound of coyotes.

This book is a perfect discussion starter for values clarification classes. Themes include materialism, choices, lifestyles, and personal values.

Students feeling a kinship with nature, like Mountain Girl and her family, would also enjoy Diane Siebert's three poetic celebrations of American landscapes: *Heartland* (Thomas Y. Crowell, 1989), *Mojave* (Thomas Y. Crowell, 1988), and *Sierra* (HarperCollins, 1991).

56. Baylor, Byrd. **The Way to Start the Day**. Ill. by Peter Parnall (Charles Scribner's Sons, 1978).

Comparative Religions; Multicultural Experiences; Nature; Religions— Comparative; Religions— The Sun; Sun—in Folklore; Sun—in Religion; Sun Worship

This story is a celebration of how people throughout the world, in the past and the present, greet the rising sun. Caldecott Honor, 1979.

This stunning book would be a change of pace for older students in comparative religion classes. It certainly is a must for a brief introduction to sun worship. A companion book, *I Sing for the Animals* by Paul Goble (Bradbury Press, 1991), celebrates the Creator and reveals how all nature is connected.

57. Belloc, Hilaire. **Matilda Who Told Lies and Was Burned to Death**. Ill. by Posy Simmonds (Alfred A. Knopf, 1991).

Cautionary Tales; False Alarms; Fire; Humor; Poetry; Speech

An incorrigible liar, Matilda is ignored when her house *really* catches on fire.

Like the legendary "Boy Who Cried Wolf," Matilda's later cries for help are ignored. For student edification and enjoyment, gather several cautionary tales, such as Anthony Browne's *Piggybook* (Alfred A. Knopf, 1986), *The Great White Man-Eating Shark* by Margaret Mahy (Dial Books for Young Readers, 1990), and *Pierre* by Maurice Sendak (Harper & Row, 1962).

A collection of cautionary tales like those listed above may inspire students to write their own cautionary tales based on current events or school happenings.

Matilda would be a great selection for oral interpretation, but be sure to provide students with opportunities to view the delightful illustrations.

 58. Benjamin, Alan. **Appointment**. Ill. by Roger Essley (Green Tiger Press/Simon & Schuster, 1993).

Baghdad—Iraq; Death; Fatalism; Fate; Fear; Maugham, W. Somerset (1874-1965); Read-Aloud; Short Stories

Death (disguised as an old woman) is surprised to see Abdullah in Baghdad as she is supposed to meet him in Samarra. An adaptation of a story by W. Somerset Maugham.

This is the perfect selection for beginning, or complementing, a discussion on predetermination or fatalism. The discussion could include the Greek mythological roots of the Fates, the three daughters of Nyx who controlled the destinies of humankind.

 = Geography   = Art   = Music   = Drama   = Speech   = Research   = Read-Aloud

This picture book adaptation, based on "Appointment in Samarra" from *Sheppy* (Doubleday, 1933), is representative of the short story form Maugham was famous for—"economy of expression, satire, and ironical detachment" (*Benet's Reader's Encyclopedia,* 3rd edition [Harper & Row, 1987], p. 630). Use this book when studying short stories or W. Somerset Maugham specifically.

This haunting picture book, with its surprise ending and dramatic, realistic chalk drawings covering two-page spreads, will capture the attention of reluctant readers.

59. Berenzy, Alix. **A Frog Prince** (Henry Holt, 1989).

Fairy Tales; Folktales—Fractured; Fractured Folktales; Honor; Kindness; Transformations

Treated poorly by a princess he has befriended, a prince of a frog sets off to find "a *true* princess, of a different mind."

Focus student attention on the transformation of the frog into the prince. Find other tales of transformation such as in "East of the Sun and West of the Moon," "Beauty and the Beast," "The Crane Wife," and any one of the many Native American stories featuring transformations between humans and animals.

How does this version differ from traditional tellings of this Brothers Grimm story? As an extension, students can read other fractured folktales indexed in this book.

60. Bernbaum, Israel. **My Brother's Keeper: The Holocaust Through the Eyes of an Artist** (G. P. Putnam's Sons, 1985).

Children; Concentration Camps; Cruelty; Heroism; Holocaust; Jews; Nazis; Photographs; World War II

The artist/author describes the Holocaust and explains how he went about capturing the horrific events of the time with his art. Photographs detailing treatment of the Jews by Nazi soldiers are included.

This title should be included in any study of the Holocaust. Bernbaum's art is based on memory and historic photographs. Use this book's subject index to locate other Holocaust picture books.

Using Bernbaum's style of combining many events and explaining details within paintings as they relate to actual events (such as children with stars on their coats and their hands raised), young artists can depict current or historic events in their communities or worldwide.

61. Berson, Harold. **Charles and Claudine** (Macmillan, 1980).

Drama; Folktales—Fractured; Folktales—French; Frogs; Love; Magic; Read-Aloud; Witches; Writing—Scripts

Charles, a handsome young man, and Claudine, a charming little frog, overcome their differences and, with the help of the witch Grisnel, live happily ever after.

For a dramatic presentation, students can easily write a script for this unusual tale, interspersing this version with a more traditional characterization of the Frog Prince.

62. Björk, Christina. **Linnea in Monet's Garden**. Drawings by Lena Anderson (R & S Books, 1985).

Art; Artists; Biographies; Gardens; History of Art; Impressionism; Internet; Monet, Claude (1840-1926); Museums; World Wide Web

Visiting French impressionist artist Claude Monet's garden is the highlight of Linnea's trip to France. She also tours a museum and learns more about Monet's family and his art. Chronology. Photographs.

Linnea compiles a photographic collection of the flowers she sees in Monet's garden. Students interested in photography can select a subject and compile a photographic record for display in a classroom, library, or museum. Famous photographs taken by a young artist, which might inspire students, can be seen in John Cech's *Jacques-Henri Lartigue: Boy with a Camera* (Macmillan, 1994). A video version of *Linnea in Monet's Garden* is available from First Run/Icarus Films, 1993.

The information about Monet and his art will doubtless inspire some students to learn more about him and the other Impressionists. For references to books and activities related to art, artists, and museums, students should consult "Musing About Museums" by Barbara Fleisher Zucker [*Book Links* 3(2):11-20, November 1993]. Visit more than 1,500 highlights housed at the Smithsonian Museums in Washington, D.C., via a World Wide Web connection: http://www.si.edu or the "mirror" connection site for the West Coast: http://www.si.sgi.com.

63. Björk, Christina. **Linnea's Almanac**. Ill. by Lena Anderson (R & S Books, 1989).

Almanacs; Birds; Calendars; Constellations; Crafts; Gardens; Science— Botany; Seasons

Linnea keeps track of her indoor and outdoor activities all year long by writing her own almanac. She feeds birds, plants flowers, harvests vegetables, dries flowers, builds kites, and learns about the constellations and more.

Students can create their own almanacs (with or without illustrations) portraying the flowers, fauna, weather, and seasons in their area.

Intermediate students can choose one or more of Linnea's activities to do for a science or naturalist project.

64. Björk, Christina. **Linnea's Windowsill Garden**. Ill. by Lena Anderson (R & S Books, 1978).

Gardens; Greenhouses; Plants; Seeds

A young girl grows plants everywhere—in pots, glass jars, and crates— and gives readers tips on gardening and growing.

Planting and nurturing seeds is a wonderful classroom activity for students of all ages. Language arts, music, science, and art activities can all be integrated within the development of an indoor garden. For an extensive bibliography of helpful books, as well as a list of activities and resource addresses, consult "Growing a Garden" by Carolyn Wiseman [*Book Links* 3(4):12-17, March 1994].

65. Blake, William. **The Tyger**. Ill. by Neil Waldman (Harcourt Brace & Company, 1993).

Art; Blake, William (1757-1827); Poetry; Read-Aloud; Tigers

Readers experience the "tyger, tyger, burning bright" in this illustrated version of Blake's well-known poem.

A fine companion book is Nancy Willard's 1982 Newbery winner, *A Visit to William Blake's Inn: Poems for Innocent and Experienced Travelers* illustrated by Alice Provenson and Martin Provensen (Harcourt Brace Jovanovich, 1981). This collection of 18 original lyrical and nonsensical poems (including "The Tiger Asks Blake for a Bedtime Story") was written in tribute to William Blake. Further study should feature Blake's other poetry, including *Songs of Innocence and Experience* (Dover, 1971), with reproductions of his original engravings.

Using this book as an example, illustrate other famous or original poetry. Look at Susan Jeffers' illustrated version of Robert Frost's *Stopping by Woods on a Snowy Evening* (E. P. Dutton, 1978).

 = Geography   = Art   = Music   = Drama   = Speech   = Research   = Read-Aloud

66. Bliss, Corinne Demas. **Matthew's Meadow**. Ill. by Ted Lewin (Jane Yolen Books/Harcourt Brace Jovanovich, 1992).

Bird Calls; Birds; Birdwatching; Hawks; Nature

From ages nine to fifteen, Matthew meets a red-tailed hawk in his grandmother's meadow during blackberry time. There the hawk teaches him about the natural world.

Birdwatching is an enjoyable pastime for people of all ages. Provide books such as *Backyard Birds of Winter* by Carol Lerner (Morrow Junior Books, 1994), Roger T. Peterson's *How to Know the Birds: An Introduction to Bird Recognition* (Gramercy, 1986), Barbara Bash's *Urban Roosts: Where Birds Nest in the City* (Sierra Club/Little, 1990), regional field guides, and videos like *Birds, Birds, Birds: Why Birdwatchers Watch* (Maslowski Wildlife Productions, 1994). These materials can be used to introduce potential bird-watchers to this hobby. Jane Yolen's *Bird Watch* (Philomel, 1990) is a complementary selection for both bird and poetry lovers.

Cassettes such as *Know Your Bird Sounds* (from Nature Sound Studio, Chelsea Green Publishing, Rt. 113, Box 130, Post Mills, VT 05058) will be of interest to students wanting to learn about bird calls. Invite a guest speaker who can demonstrate them. Contact your state or local Audubon Society for additional information.

67. Blos, Joan W. **Old Henry**. Ill. by Stephen Gammell (William Morrow, 1987).

Conformity; Diversity; Individuality; Neighbors; Outcasts; Pride; Read-Aloud; Tolerance

Old Henry's neighbors are unhappy with his dilapidated house and unkempt property. However, after he leaves, they aren't happy with themselves.

Use this book as a focal point for a discussion of the themes of diversity, independence, and individual rights. Excellent companion books include Alice Provensen and Martin Provensen's *Shaker Lane* (Viking Kestrel, 1987) and Jane Yolen's *Letting Swift River Go* (Little, Brown, 1992).

68. Blyler, Allison. **Finding Foxes**. Ill. by Robert J. Blake (Philomel, 1991).

Foxes; Haiku; Picture Puzzles; Poetry—Haiku

The activities and musings of a fox are detailed in Blyler's prose.

Blyler's study of the poet Wallace Stevens and her fondness for haiku inspired her to write this book. Use this book as an introduction to haiku. Use Carolyn Phelan's informative article, "Reading and Writing Haiku" [*Book Links* 1(4):28-29, March 1994] and books such as *In the Eyes of the Cat: Japanese Poetry for All Seasons* translated by Tze-si Huang (Henry Holt, 1992).

69. Bouchard, Dave. **The Elders Are Watching**. Images by Roy Henry Vickers (Fulcrum, 1993).

Conservation; Environment—Human Impact; Indians of North America; Nature; Poetry; Read-Aloud; Wildlife Issues— Salmon Conservation

Beautifully illustrated, simple, and passionate poetry speaks to the issues of conservation and nature from a Native American perspective.

A good companion book is Claire Rudolf Murphy's *The Prince and the Salmon People* (Rizolli, 1993), which addresses issues surrounding salmon conservation.

70. Bowen, Betsy. **Tracks in the Wild** (Little, Brown, 1993).

Animal Tracks; Animals— Habits and Behavior; Hiking; Tracks—Animals; Woodcuts; Woodlands

The woodcuts and wilderness lore presented in this book reveal the tracks, habits, and behavioral mysteries of 13 northwood animals.

 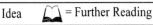

Bowen reveals the story of each animal track. Animal trackers use feces (or scat), footprints, songs and calls, compressed grass, kill sites, rubbed-off fur or teeth, antler marks on trees, and constructions such as dens or nests to identify wildlife and their habitat. Take a wilderness hike with a professional tracker who can help students identify clues. Helpful titles include *Whose Footprints?* by Masayuki Yabuuchi (Philomel, 1985), *Animal Tracks* by Arthur Dorros (Scholastic, 1991), *A Field Guide to Mammal Tracking in Western America* by James C. Halfpenny (Johnson Books, 1986), and *Tracking & the Art of Seeing: How to Read Animal Tracks & Signs* by Paul Rezendes (Camden House, 1992).

71. Bowen, Gary. **Stranded at Plimoth Plantation 1626** (HarperCollins, 1994).

Art—Printmaking; Colonial America; Historical Fiction; Pilgrims; Printmaking; Woodcuts

Christopher Sears' journal is based on historical records and accounts of life at Plimoth Plantation, 1626-27. His entries reveal details of the daily life (foods, customs, farming techniques, hunting, militia training, Puritan laws, worship, etc.) of colonial pilgrims.

Other books that will give students more information about colonial times include *Across the Wide Dark Sea: The Mayflower Journey* by Jean Van Leeuwen (Dial Books for Young Readers, 1995), *Homes in the Wilderness: A Pilgrim's Journal of the Plymouth Plantation in 1620 by William Bradford and Others of the Mayflower Company* by Margaret Wise Brown (Linnet Books/Shoestring Press, 1988), *Penny in the Road* by Katharine Wilson Precek (Macmillan, 1989), and Marcia Sewall's *The Pilgrims of Plimoth* (Atheneum, 1986) and the sequel *People of the Breaking Day* (Atheneum, 1990).

Though the pilgrims in Eve Bunting's picture book *How Many Days to America? A Thanksgiving Story* (Clarion, 1988) arrived more than 350 years after the colonial period, both groups have much in common. Students can list the hopes each group of pilgrims shared (desire for safety and freedom, escape violence and persecution, etc.) and delve further into history by identifying other groups who have faced similar struggles.

 The most common method of printmaking in the 17th century was with woodcuts. Bowen was true to the old craft by cutting the illustrations on cherry and pearwood, and hand coloring the proofs. Provide students with other examples of woodcuts in picture books such as Jean Giono's *The Man Who Planted Trees* (Chelsea Green, 1985), books illustrated by Keizaburo Tejima, and the scratchboard drawings resembling woodcuts in Diana Applebaum's *Giants in the Land* (Houghton Mifflin, 1993). An artist can demonstrate and teach these interesting art techniques (woodcuts and scratchboard), and students can create their own small prints.

 72. Bradbury, Ray. **Switch on the Night**. Pictures by Leo Dillon and Diane Dillon (Alfred A. Knopf, 1993).

Allegory; Fear of the Dark; Friendship; Literary Devices; Loneliness; Metaphor; Perspective; Read-Aloud

Bradbury's story (originally published in 1955) tells the tale of a lonely little boy who is afraid of the dark. But when Dark, portrayed as an African American girl, introduces him to the magic of night, he finds beauty and comfort.

Several of Bradbury's short stories have been republished either with illustrations or in comic format. Examine these with your students, then consider this question: Are these illustrated versions better than the originals, or do they add new perspective? Some of these are *The Veldt* (Creative Education, 1987) and *The Other Foot* (Creative Education, 1987) both illustrated by Gary Kelley, *Fever Dream* illustrated by Darrel Anderson (St. Martin's Press, 1987), and multiple volumes of graphic novels entitled *Ray Bradbury Chronicles* and illustrated by various comic artists (Bantam Books).

The artistic interpretation of this story by the Dillons takes it to a level Bradbury may not have been intended. By painting Dark as an African American girl, the Dillons reveal humankind's propensity toward fearfulness and prejudice of the unknown. Use this as an example of artistic metaphor and invite students to develop similar devices with familiar poems or stories.

Budding artists will want to further examine the interesting perspectives included in nearly every picture of this book. What do these different angles reveal about the boy and his fears? Students can create their own drawings of buildings or rooms, using various perspectives and points of view.

73. Breathed, Berkeley. **Red Ranger Came Calling: A Guaranteed True Christmas Story** (Little, Brown, 1994).

Art Deco; Bicycles; Christmas; Comics; Creative Writing; Faith; Fantasy; Hermits; Loneliness; Read-Aloud; Santa Claus; Writing

This Santa Claus story for nonbelievers is reportedly a retelling of an event that happened to the author's father—a devoted Red Ranger fan hoping to get an "Official Buck Tweed Two-Speed Crime-Stopper Star-Hopper bicycle" on Christmas Eve, 1939.

Berkeley Breathed is the Pulitzer Prize-winning author of the popular *Bloom County* comics. Provide a variety of Breathed's books for thought-provoking, laughter-producing recreational reading.

Another story of enchanted flying is Chris Van Allsburg's *The Wreck of the Zephyr* (Houghton Mifflin, 1983), which tells the story of how a boat came to rest in an impossible location.

So your students still don't believe after you've read the story? Now show them the last page (a photo of a rusted bicycle hanging permanently 10 feet off the ground as part of a rather large tree) and have them write how they think that bike got there.

74. Briggs, Raymond. **The Man** (Douglas & McIntyre, 1992).

Graphic Novels; Hospitality; Little People; Rudeness

A tiny tyrant of a man appears at a boy's house, stays for more than three days, and wears out his welcome.

Literature about miniature people is plentiful and popular. Develop a classroom collection for recreational reading. For junior high and high school students collect *Truckers* by Terry Pratchett (Delacorte, 1990) and *Gulliver's Travels* by Jonathan Swift (NAL, 1975). Middle-grade readers will enjoy *The Borrowers* by Mary Norton (Harcourt, 1953), *The Boggart* by Susan Cooper (Margaret K. McElderry, 1993), *The Indian in the Cupboard* by Lynne Reid Banks (Doubleday, 1980), and *The Castle in the Attic* by Elizabeth Winthrop (Holiday House, 1985).

 = Extraordinary!    = Idea   = Further Reading   = Writing   = Math   = Science   = History

75. Briggs, Raymond. **The Tin-Pot Foreign General and the Old Iron Woman** (Little, Brown, 1984).

Ambition; Battle; Death; Greed; Humanity; War

Fighting over a tiny island, the ambitious Tin-Pot Foreign General and the greedy and violent Old Iron Woman end up killing hundreds of brave men in a meaningless war.

Briggs uses the picture book format with comic-style illustrations to explore a painful and complex issue. Compare with Umberto Eco and Eugenio Carmi's *The Three Astronauts* (Harcourt Brace Jovanovich, 1989) and Umberto Eco's *The Bomb and the General* (Harcourt, 1989), other picture books dealing with a similar theme. Students can also investigate peacekeeping tactics and look at books such as *Ain't Gonna Study War No More* by Milton Meltzer (Harper & Row, 1985), *Some Reasons for War: How Families, Myths and Warfare Are Connected* by Sue Mansfield and Mary Bowen Hall (Harper & Row, 1988), and *The Big Book for Peace* by Ann Durell et al. (Dutton Children's Books, 1990).

76. Briggs, Raymond. **When the Wind Blows: The Story of the Bloggs and the Bomb** (Schocken Books, 1982).

Art—Comic Books; Atomic Bomb; Comic Book Art; Graphic Novels; Nuclear War; War

In comic book format, a retired British couple experience the next nuclear war.

Understanding the history of nuclear war, the proliferation of arms during the Cold War, and the current instability of worldwide peace is not an easy task. The nuclear balance will shift if countries such as Iraq, North Korea, and Iran obtain nuclear hardware and technology from countries such as cash-strapped Russia. Students can study the current balance of nuclear firepower and how it affects the United States and the world. Expect students to have different opinions about the threat of nuclear war and what the position of the United States should be. *Encyclopedia of the Cold War* by Thomas S. Arms (Facts on File, 1994) will be a useful reference book.

The comic style Briggs employs is similar to that used in graphic novels—generally self-contained stories using text and sophisticated comic artwork printed on high-quality paper. Scott McCloud's *Understanding Comics* (Kitchen Sink Press, 1993) is an important and unique reference book on comics and art narrative. Both Michael Foreman's picture book *War Game* (Arcade, 1994) and George Pratt's graphic novel *Enemy Ace: War Idyll* (Warner, 1990) deal with the realities of war. Also provide Mark Twain's "The War Prayer" in *The Portable Mark Twain* (Viking, 1968). These selections provide an abundance of material for mature students to ponder and discuss.

77. Brown, Don. **Ruth Law Thrills a Nation** (Ticknor & Fields, 1993).

Biographies; Cross Country Flying; Flight—History; Law, Ruth (1887-1970); Pilots; Pilots—Women

On November 19, 1916, a young pilot named Ruth Law attempted to fly from Chicago to New York City in one day. Although she wasn't successful in the attempt, she flew 590 miles nonstop and broke all existing flight records.

The only pilots of long ago with which students will probably be familiar are Amelia Earhart and Charles Lindbergh. In a study of flight history include this book, along with *The Wright Brothers: How They Invented the Airplane* by Russell Freedman (Holiday House, 1991) and others listed in the subject index for this book.

78. Brown, Laurene Krasny and Marc Brown. **Visiting the Art Museum** (E. P. Dutton, 1986).

Art; Culture; Families; Museums; Paintings; Pop Culture; Sculpture

A family wanders through an art museum viewing examples of various art styles from primitive times through the 20th century.

This book is an excellent springboard for museum visits or further investigations of any of the variety of artists whose works are viewed by the family.

79. Brown, Ruth. **Alphabet Times Four: An International ABC** (Dutton Children's Books, 1991).

Alphabet; Bilingual Books; Languages—French; Languages—German; Languages—Spanish; Languages—Study of; Word Derivations

A visual introduction to a word for each letter of the alphabet in four different languages—English, Spanish, French, and German—with phonetic pronunciations. Notes.

This approachable introduction to foreign languages is excellent for schools that offer students opportunities to explore several different foreign languages. Use the Note page to illustrate words in different languages that share the same roots. Continue with a study of Latin and other word derivations.

Another picture book that highlights multiple languages (English, Spanish, and Polish) is Leyla Torres' *Subway Sparrow* (Farrar, Straus & Giroux, 1993).

80. Brown, Tricia. **The City by the Bay: A Magical Journey Around San Francisco**. Ill. by Elisa Kleven (Chronicle Books, 1993).

Architecture; California; Cities—San Francisco; Guidebooks; United States— History

Conceived as a fund-raiser by the Junior League of San Francisco, *City by the Bay* is a visual trip around the city, accompanied by explanatory text. Chronology.

A wonderful companion to *The City by the Bay* is *The Great American Landmarks Adventure* booklet (National Park Service/American Architectural Foundation, 1992) created by Kay Weeks with drawings by Roxie Munro. This noncopyrighted book features 43 National Historic Landmarks and is available from the Superintendent of Documents, Government Printing Office, Washington, D.C. 20402-9328 for a nominal fee. It is filled with general information concerning how landmarks are chosen, cared for, etc., as well as specifics about the featured landmarks. A Teacher's Guide is also available. Use this book as a model for a project (such as the following one) or as an additional resource for studying your city or National Historic Landmarks.

Like most cities, San Francisco has recognizable landmarks such as cable cars and the Golden Gate Bridge. Using this book as a model, students can create a visual guide to their own community. Perhaps the local Chamber of Commerce would publish the finished product for distribution.

81. Browne, Anthony. **The Big Baby: A Little Joke** (Alfred A. Knopf, 1993).

Aging; Cautionary Tales; Fountain of Youth; Literary Devices; Puns; Social Issues— Aging; Vanity; Youth

Vain and obsessed with his youthful appearance, Mr. Young drinks a youth elixir that changes him into a baby, except for his adult face.

Sociology classes studying the current fascination with youth culture will find this book of particular interest. Mr. Young tries to look and feel young through his choice of clothes, hairstyle, music, and his den full of "toys." Students will no doubt see in Mr. Young adults they know—perhaps even their parents! Discussion and research can focus on fad diets, pills, and exercise programs that claim to keep adults young—adults who, like Peter Pan, refuse to grow up.

❗ = Extraordinary!   💡 = Idea   📖 = Further Reading   ✍ = Writing   ²⁄₄ = Math   ⚛ = Science   📖 = History

A great companion novel is Natalie Babbitt's *Tuck Everlasting* (Farrar, Straus & Giroux, 1975), a classic cautionary tale concerning the difficulties of living forever. *Stranger in the Mirror* (Houghton Mifflin, 1995) by Allen Say also portrays a negative attitude toward aging and shows the struggle young Sam has coming to terms with his outer and his inner selves.

 The quest for the Fountain of Youth is a tale as old as time. As a topic for discussion and research, students can investigate historical references to the legendary fountain mentioned in folktales and sought by the Spanish explorer Ponce De Leon when he discovered Florida in 1513.

82. Browne, Anthony. **Changes** (Alfred A. Knopf, 1990).

Joseph takes his father's admonition ("things are going to change around here") literally with results that are surprising and most unusual.

Anxiety; Art—Surrealism; Babies; Dali, Salvador (1904-1989); Fantasy; Imagination; Literal Interpretations; Surrealism

 Joseph took what his father said, "things are going to change around here," literally, much like the characters in Fred Gwynne's books. Provide Gwynne's *A Chocolate Moose for Dinner* (Prentice-Hall, 1976), *The King Who Rained* (Prentice-Hall, 1970), *A Little Pigeon Toad* (Simon & Schuster, 1988), and *The Sixteen Hand Horse* (Prentice-Hall, 1980) for further reading.

 Since the early 20th century, surrealism has been used to portray the mysterious and sometimes haunting world of imagination and dreams. Beginning with his first book, *Through the Magic Mirror* (Greenwillow, 1977), much of Browne's art has been surreal and similar to that of the Spanish representational surrealist Salvador Dali. In *Changes,* everyday household items are transformed—the teapot becomes a cat, a slipper becomes a bird, an armchair becomes a huge gorilla. Study surrealism, Browne's art, and that of Salvador Dali. For an added twist, refer to the essay on Dali and his stereographic paintings of the 1960s and 1970s in *Stereogram* (Cadence Books, 1994) edited by Seiji Horibuchi. A fascinating surreal tribute to René Magritte and Salvador Dali can be found in *Dinner at Magritte's* by Michael Garland (Dutton Children's Books, 1995), which is true to the spirit of the original pieces of art by Magritte and Dali and is a fine introduction to the work of these artists.

83. Browne, Anthony. **King Kong** (Turner, 1994).

This is a full-color, graphic, novel-like version of the classic black-and-white film story of King Kong.

Fantasy; Films; Foreshadowing; Greed; Literary Devices; Monsters; Movies—Monsters

 Provide students with a movie treat by showing the classic film version of *King Kong* (RKO, 1933) and/or the remake (Dino de Laurentis, 1976) along with reading this book. A lively discussion of interpretive styles can follow.

Browne makes many references to the fairy tale "Beauty and the Beast." Compare and contrast the story of King Kong and his tragic demise with one or more of the many versions of "Beauty and the Beast."

Browne is a master of illustrative foreshadowing. Astute students can locate the many hints of things to come located throughout the book.

---

84. Browne, Anthony. **Piggybook** (Alfred A. Knopf, 1986).

Cautionary Tales; Chauvinism; Family Relationships; Feminism; Gender Roles; Literary Devices; Read-Aloud; Sociology; Stereotypes

Mr. Piggott and his two sons are decidedly chauvinistic in this modern cautionary tale focusing on gender roles. When Mrs. Piggott leaves home her family actually turn into pigs. Her eventual return brings democracy and order to the household.

Piggybook is perfect for initiating gender role discussions among children or adults.

Piggybook can be included in discussions on cautionary tales and their purposes. Use the subject index of this book to identify others.

Concrete examples of metaphor, irony, foreshadowing, and satire (difficult concepts for some students) are all contained in the illustrations of this short story. Students can locate and identify these literary devices and then apply this knowledge to their writing.

85. Browne, Anthony. **Zoo** (Alfred A. Knopf, 1993).

Animals; Family Dynamics; Fathers; Freedom; Human Condition; Surrealism; Zoos

When this family visits the zoo it becomes hard to know who's looking in through the bars and who's looking out.

Browne challenges the reader with his clever paintings. Although the visiting people are normally clothed, many also match the animals they watch, sporting antlers, tails, and other animal appendages. Students can discuss or write their feelings about Browne's messages concerning families, zoos, or the human condition.

Whether or not zoos should exist is an age-old controversy. Interested students can do further research. What types of animal preserves are kinder to animals? What animal species are protected by zoos?

86. Bruchac, Joseph. **Fox Song**. Ill. by Paul Morin (Philomel, 1993).

Art—Baskets; Basket Weaving; Crafts; Death; Grandmothers; Indians of North America; Nature; Traditions

Jamie finds comfort in her memories of her Indian great-grandmother and all that they shared. Grama Bowman taught her about many wonders of the natural world and passed along important Indian traditions.

As Jamie realizes her connection to all things in this world, she shares an Abenaki song with a fox. In the author's notes Bruchac tells about a similar experience in his own life. Students may have experiences of their own to speak or write about and share.

One activity shared by Jamie and Grama Bowman is basket weaving. Students can learn this ancient craft, perhaps using designs similar to those featured in this book. Invite a basket weaver to class to demonstrate techniques students can use for beginning projects. For more information about baskets and other important aspects of North American Indian culture consult *Turtle Island Alphabet: A Lexicon of Native American Symbols and Culture* by Gerald Hausman (St. Martin's Press, 1992).

87. Bruchac, Joseph and Jonathan London. **Thirteen Moons on Turtle's Back: A Native American Year of Moon**. Ill. by Thomas Locker (Philomel, 1992).

Calendars; Indians of North America; Legends; Lunar Calendar; Moon; Poetry; Seasons; Turtles

This collection of poems celebrates the seasons and pays tribute to the turtle, who carries the mystery of the moon on its upper shell. The 13 poems are based on legends of (and attributed to) different Native American nations.

Begin a Native American study of the 13 tribes represented in this poetry collection. Extend the unit to other tribes by focusing on the poets' "Note about this book." Have the students do research to answer this question: What are some of the legends based in nature from the tribes in the far North and desert Southwest who do not talk about the 12 or 13 moons?

The lunar calendar is just one way humankind has divided the year. Using almanacs and Leonard Everett Fisher's *Calendar Art: Thirteen Days, Weeks, Months and Years from Around the World* (Four Winds Press, 1987), students can investigate other kinds of calendars used throughout history.

88. Buehner, Caralyn and Mark Buehner. **The Escape of Marvin the Ape**. (Dial Books for Young Readers, 1992).

Apes; City and Town Life; Creative Writing; Fantasy; Humor

Marvin (an ape) has wonderful adventures after slipping out of the zoo. Then Helvetica, a hippo, follows.

With his attaché case by his side, Marvin calmly waits to escape, then easily blends into city life. But how will Helvetica fare? Students can write about her adventures or more about Marvin. Illustrations can be a bonus!

89. Bunting, Eve. **Fly Away Home**. Ill. by Ron Himler (Clarion Books, 1991).

Airports; Birds; Fathers and Sons; Freedom; Homeless; Hope; Social Action; Social Issues— Homeless

A busy airport is home for Andrew and his dad as they move from terminal to terminal, trying not to be noticed. When Andrew sees a trapped bird find its freedom, it restores his hope of having a home of his own someday.

Provide students with *We Are All in the Dumps with Jack and Guy: Two Nursery Rhymes with Pictures* illustrated by Maurice Sendak (HarperCollins, 1993). The newspaper headlines featured in Sendak's illustrations, along with Bunting's realistic story, combine to provide ample grist for discussions on the plight of the homeless. Michael J. Rosen's *Home* (HarperCollins, 1992) celebrates the places and things that make up a home and provides some financial support for Share Our Strength (SOS), a nonprofit group established to fight homelessness. Interested students can discover what programs are available to serve the homeless in their communities. For further information about SOS, write to Share Our Strength, 1511 K Street N.W., Suite 600, Washington, D.C. 20005.

90. Bunting, Eve. **How Many Days to America? A Thanksgiving Story**. Ill. by Beth Peck (Clarion Books, 1988).

Boat People; Caribbean; Freedom; Immigration; Refugees; Thanksgiving

Refugees fleeing a Caribbean island at night endure a frightening trip to America in search of freedom.

Although this is a Thanksgiving story, it is appropriate for any time of the year when studying immigration. *Klara's New World* by Jeanette Winter (Alfred A. Knopf, 1992), highlighting a Scandinavian family's boat trip to America; *New Hope* by Henri Sorensen (Lothrop, Lee & Shepard, 1995); and Maxinne Rhea Leighton's *An Ellis Island Christmas* (Viking, 1992) are fine companion volumes. Consult "From Many Shores" by Barbara Elleman [*Book Links* 2(6):11-15, July 1993], which features many books and activities about immigrants coming to America.

91. Bunting, Eve. **The Man Who Could Call Down Owls**. Ill. by Charles Mikolaycak (Macmillan, 1984).

Vengeance comes swiftly to a stranger who stole the power to call down the owls from an old man who was a friend to the birds.

Fables; Good Versus Evil; Nature; Night; Owls; Power; Science— Wildlife; Wildlife Rehabilitation

The Man Who Could Call Down Owls and the main character in Paul Gallico's classic *The Snow Goose* (Alfred A. Knopf, 1992) both perform wildlife rehabilitation on injured birds. Find out if there is an animal rehabilitation specialist in your area. Invite that person (and his or her animals) to your class or school for a visit. Assemble a book collection featuring wildlife rescue to provide further information for interested students.

The old man had befriended many kinds of owls. Begin a study of these night creatures by researching those mentioned in the story. Extend the project to owls indigenous to your area and, perhaps, to all active night creatures. Another owl story, this one illustrated by woodcuts, is *The Owl Scatterer* by Howard Norman (Atlantic Monthly Press, 1986).

92. Bunting, Eve. **Night of the Gargoyles**. Ill. by David Wiesner (Clarion Books, 1994).

The gargoyles that decorate the walls of an art museum come alive and frighten the night watchman.

Architectural Details; Fantasy; Fear; Gargoyles; Horror Stories; Read-Aloud; Sculpture; Supernatural

In medieval times, gargoyles embellished stone walls, balconies, and buttresses because they were thought to repel evil spirits. At the beginning of *Night of the Gargoyles,* the term *gargoyle* is defined as "a waterspout in the form of a grotesque human or animal figure projecting from the roof or eaves of a building." Many buildings or structures feature such decorations. Students can locate, photograph, and research the appearance of gargoyles in their communities.

93. Bunting, Eve. **Smoky Night**. Ill. by David Diaz (Harcourt Brace & Company, 1994).

Daniel worries about his lost cat after looting and rioting disrupt his neighborhood. Caldecott Medal, 1995.

Anger; Fear; Interpersonal Relations; Looting; Neighborliness; Read-Aloud; Riots— California; Social Issues— Violence; Violence

Students can study the causes and effects of riots and street violence. What caused the Los Angeles riots that occurred in 1992? What has the aftermath been? For further references to books about street violence refer to "Street Violence" by Barbara Ellemen [*Book Links* 3(4):6-7, March 1994].

This book, an excellent example of a picture book for older readers, sparked a national discussion on the merit of such reality-based books. Some expressed the view that picture books should not deal with serious issues like riots, the homeless, or war. Students can research the controversy and discuss their feelings and observations. Does this book appropriately address this serious issue? How does the art affect the reader?

94. Bunting, Eve. **Terrible Things: An Allegory of the Holocaust**. Ill. by Stephen Gammell (The Jewish Publication Society, 1989).

The forest animals were content until the Terrible Things came. Even then, the animals stood by as the Terrible Things took away their fellow creatures one by one.

Allegory; Animals; Fear; Graphic Novels; History—World War II; Holocaust; War

---

❗ = Extraordinary!   💡 = Idea   📖 = Further Reading   ✍ = Writing $\frac{2}{4}$ = Math   ⚛ = Science   📚 = History

In a study of the Holocaust use this title in conjunction with other Holocaust picture books such as *Let the Celebrations Begin!* by Margaret Wild (Orchard, 1991), *Rose Blanche* by Roberto Innocenti (Creative Education, 1985), and *The Number on My Grandfather's Arm* by David A. Adler (UAHC Press, 1987).

For a different allegorical presentation geared toward older students, provide them with volumes I and II of *Barefoot Gen* by Keiji Nakazawa (New Society Publishers, 1988) as well as Art Spiegleman's Pulitzer Prize-winning *Maus: A Survivor's Tale* (Pantheon, 1986) and the sequel, *Maus II: And Here My Troubles Began* (Pantheon, 1991). Spiegleman's graphic novels use anthropomorphic mice to relate the horrors of the Holocaust.

95. Bunting, Eve. **The Wall**. Ill. by Ronald Himler (Clarion Books, 1990).
A young boy and his father travel to visit the Vietnam Veterans Memorial in Washington, D.C., and find the name of the boy's grandfather.

Art—Rubbings; Death; Grief; Soldiers; Vietnam Veterans Memorial; Vietnam War; War

As a memento, the boy and his father leave a photograph at the wall. The first memento to appear at the memorial was a Purple Heart tossed into the wet cement of the foundation. Since then more than 30,000 offerings have been left in tribute to those who died in Vietnam. The National Park Service has collected, preserved, and catalogued every item. *Offerings at the Wall* (Turner, 1995) lists each of the 58,183 names engraved plus the mementos left at the site. Provide this book to students to look at and arrange to visit war memorials in your area. A brief glimpse of *Offerings at the Wall* can be found in the magazine article "Offerings at the Wall" by Don Moser [*Smithsonian* 26(2):54-59, May 1995].

Using a piece of paper and a pencil, the boy and his father make a rubbing of the grandfather's engraved name from the wall. As an art project, students can make rubbings of any objects that have raised surfaces. These can include headstones and cornerstones.

96. Burgie, Irving, compiled by. **Caribbean Carnival: Songs of the West Indies**. Ill. by Frané Lessac (Tambourine Books, 1992).
This is a collection of calypso music of the West Indies. Piano and guitar arrangements with words are included. Afterword.

Calypso; Caribbean; Composers—Burgie, Irving; Music—Calypso; Social Life and Customs— Caribbean; Songs— Calypso; West Indies

Lessac's primitive paintings highlight Caribbean island life. Use this book along with his *Caribbean Alphabet* (Tambourine Books, 1994), and *Caribbean Canvas* (J. B. Lippincott, 1987), and John Agard's *The Calypso Alphabet* (Henry Holt, 1989) for students to gain a greater understanding of life in the Caribbean.

Burgie is the composer of the calypso classics "Day-O," "Jamaica Farewell," and others sung by Harry Belafonte and other recording artists. Using Rosa Guy's afterword (featuring information about calypso music, its history and development) students can begin more in-depth research about this type of music, especially the growing popularity of steel drum bands. Be sure to play some classical calypso and steel drum band recordings during this project.

97. Burkert, Nancy Ekholm. **Valentine & Orson** (Farrar, Straus and Giroux, 1989).

This classic story of twins separated at birth is retold as a folk play. Author note. Bibliography.

Artists; Brueghel, Pieter, the Elder (1525?-1569); Drama—Medieval Romance; History of Art; Medieval History—16th Century; Pantomime; Social Life and Customs—Flanders—16th Century; Twins

Burkert was inspired to write this book by a Pieter Brueghel the Elder woodcut, *The Masquerade of Valentine and Orson* (also sometimes called *The Play of the Wild Man*). Study reproductions of this piece, as well as Brueghel's other paintings discussed in the author note, to learn more about Brueghel and his life.

Though straddling the line between a "picture" and an "illustrated" book, this title includes numerous paintings that are perfect for helping to design, costume, and produce this nine-scene pantomime play. The author's note will enhance production of the play, set in 16th-century Flanders.

98. Burleigh, Robert. **Flight: The Journey of Charles Lindbergh**. Ill. by Mike Wimmer (Philomel, 1991).

Charles Lindbergh's remarkable and historic nonstop flight to Paris in 1927 is chronicled in this biography.

Airplanes; Aviation—History; Biographies; Courage; Diaries; History—Aviation; Lindbergh, Charles A. (1902-1974); Pilots

Other picture books about Lindbergh include *View from the Air: Charles Lindbergh's Earth and Sky* (Viking, 1992) by his daughter Reeve Lindbergh and *Lindbergh* by Chris Demarest (Crown, 1993).

Lindbergh kept a detailed diary during the 33-hour trip. Encourage students to keep a diary or journal detailing daily events or personal experiences.

Use this dramatic biography to begin a study of the early days of air travel. Look at other pilots in history, such as Amelia Earhart, the Wright Brothers, and Ruth Law.

99. Burleigh, Robert. **A Man Named Thoreau**. Ill. by Lloyd Bloom (Atheneum, 1985).

Through quotations and explanations, Burleigh describes the inner and outer worlds of Henry David Thoreau. Bibliography. Chronology.

Biographies; Conservation; Environmental Issues—Urban Growth; Nature; Social Action; Thoreau, Henry David (1817-1862); Walden Pond

This simple, eloquent book is an excellent introduction to Henry Thoreau's most famous book, *Walden*. Provide one of the many editions such as *Walden* (Courage Books, 1990) so students can read his own words. Another picture book version of Thoreau's works is *Into the Deep Forest with Henry David Thoreau* by Jim Murphy (Clarion Books, 1995).

As the eastern United States becomes more populous, the ecology of Walden Pond has been threatened. In April 1990, rock star and environmentalist Don Henley founded and organized the Walden Woods Project to save the pond and wood from development. Interested students can explore this topic, noting the current status of Walden Pond.

C

100. Carlstrom, Nancy White. **Goodbye Geese**. Ill. by Ed Young (Philomel, 1991).

Birds—Migration; Creative Writing; Fathers and Daughters; Geese; Migration—Birds; Poetry; Seasons; Winter

A father poetically answers questions about the coming of winter while capturing the magic of the changing season and the majesty of nature.

Students can use the question-and-answer format of this book in their own poetic writing. Young's visual blending of the images makes this a perfect example of the combined power of illustrations and words in a picture book. Students might be inspired to use visual aids to enhance their writings.

101. Carrick, Carol. **Whaling Days**. Woodcuts by David Frampton (Houghton Mifflin, 1993).

Animals—Endangered; Animals—Whales; Conservation; Endangered Animals; Environmental Action; Hunting—Whales; Science—Wildlife; Social Action; Whales; Whaling; Woodcuts

This book surveys the whaling industry from colonial American times to the present and describes current efforts to regulate and control whaling. Glossary. Bibliography. Index.

This detailed book will enhance any study of whales. Interested students can review the current status of such whale species as sperm whales, blue whales, and right whales. The author notes that organizations such as Greenpeace, USA and The World Wildlife Federation are working to save remaining whale species. Concerned students can learn more about conservation activism. Another aspect of study can focus on the whaling industry in Russia, Norway, and Japan.

102. Carroll, Lewis. **Jabberwocky**. Ill. by Graeme Base (Harry N. Abrams, 1987).

Carroll, Lewis (1832-1893); Games; Imagination; Literary Recreations; Picture Puzzles; Poetry; Popular Culture; Speech

Carroll's classic poem is interpreted through Base's artistic talents and imagination. The psychedelic "Jabberwocky" is slain by a young prince in a fantastical medieval world, which is filled with hidden 20th-century objects.

Use this book as an introduction to or an additional interpretation of Carroll's classic nonsense poem.

"Jabberwocky" is perfect for students to deliver in speech interpretation classes.

103. Carson, Jo. **The Great Shaking: An Account of the Earthquakes of 1811 and 1812 by a Bear Who Was a Witness, New Madrid, Missouri**. Ill. by Robert Andrew Parker (Orchard, 1994).

Bears; Earthquakes; Historical Fiction; History—United States—1811-1812; Missouri—History; Natural Disasters; Read-Aloud; Science—Geology

A bear, having survived at the epicenter of the huge New Madrid earthquake, poetically recounts the fear and wonder surrounding this natural phenomenon.

Earthquakes are fascinating and/or of concern to students depending on where they live in the United States. Use this book to spark a study of historical earthquakes and the scientific research surrounding them.

104. Cech, John. **Jacques-Henri Lartigue: Boy with a Camera** (Four Winds Press, 1994).

Art—Photography; Inventions; Lartigue, Jacques (1900-); Photography

Jacques-Henri Lartigue was given a camera for his seventh birthday in 1907. This collection of some of his photographs captures his exploration of the world around him. Biographical note.

There are many excellent photo-illustrated books on a variety of topics for readers of all ages. Provide a sampling of these for student perusal. Include Pam Conrad's biography of a prairie photographer, *Prairie Visions: The Life and Times of Solomon Butcher* (HarperCollins, 1991); *Sand and Fog: Adventures in Southern Africa* by Jim Brandenburg (Walker, 1994); Elizabeth Tayntor Gowell's *Sea Jellies: Rainbow in the Sea* (Franklin Watts, 1993); Suzanne Haldane's *Painting Faces* (E. P. Dutton, 1988); Maira Kalman's *Roarr: Calder's Circus* (Delacorte Press, 1993); and the many published titles by Russell Freedman and Jim Murphy.

Use this book as inspiration for budding photographers. Students can chronicle special events or simply provide a glimpse of their own lives as Lartigue did. Sylvia Wolf's *Focus: Five Women Photographers* (Whitman, 1994) will be of interest.

 105. Cendrars, Blaise. **Shadow**. Ill. by Marcia Brown (Charles Scribner's Sons, 1982).

Africa; Cendrars, Blaise (1887-1961); Languages—French; Poetry; Shadows; Shamans; Storytellers; Tribes—African

A French poem, written by Blaise Cendrars and translated by Brown, provides the text for this haunting book about shadows. Caldecott Medal, 1983.

 Read this poem (in English or French, depending on the class) without showing the illustrations, and then focus a discussion of the poem based on the following quote: "The village storytellers and shamans of an Africa that is passing into memory called forth for the poet Blaise Cendrars an eerie image, shifting between the beliefs of the present and the spirits of the past." Consider including other works of Cendrars for the students to diuscuss. Sharing the book's illustrations after students are attuned to the words will add new depth and images to those they have already imagined!

106. Chall, Marsha Wilson. **Up North at the Cabin**. Paintings by Steve Johnson (Lothrop, Lee & Shepard, 1992).

Creative Writing; Essays—Examples; Imagination; Minnesota; Nature; Summer; Vacations; Writing

A young girl tells about her summer vacation at her grandparents' Minnesota lakeside cabin.

 Reading Chall's book aloud will let students hear the magic of the girl's vacation, which includes her feelings and active imagination. Use this as a model to inspire less factual and more creative prose for the perennial "What did you do this summer?" essay.

107. Cherry, Lynne. **The Armadillo from Amarillo** (Harcourt Brace & Company, 1994).

Armadillos; Concepts; Geography; Map Skills; Spatial Relations; Texas; Travel; Wildlife

A wandering armadillo learns the concept of where he is in relation to his state, continent, world, and planet as he travels through Texas visiting historic sites and geographic features.

Students can trace the armadillo's route on a Texas road map and/or use their own state map to plot a personal journey.

Use along with computer programs such as *Where in the World Is Carmen San Diego?* to further geography study.

108. Cherry, Lynne. **The Great Kapok Tree: A Tale of the Amazon Rain Forest** (Harcourt Brace Jovanovich, 1990).

Amazon; Animals; Brazil; Conservation; Ecology; Logging; Rain Forests—Amazon; Science—Ecology

A community of animals living in one of the Amazon rain forest's great kapok trees convinces a man with an ax to spare their tree. Map.

Cherry's lush watercolors provide a disturbing reminder that rain forests are being destroyed at an alarming rate. Use this book as a discussion starter or a jumping off point for further research into rain forest conservation attempts. Use *Welcome to the Green House* by Jane Yolen (G. P. Putnam's Sons, 1993), a poetic description of tropical rain forests and the abundant life they support; *Here Is the Tropical Rainforest* by Madeleine Dumphy (Hyperion Books for Children, 1994); and *The Tree That Would Not Die* by Ellen Levine (Scholastic, 1995) as companion books.

109. Cherry, Lynne. **A River Ran Wild** (Harcourt Brace Jovanovich, 1992).

Clean Water Act; Ecology; Environment—Human Impact; Environmental Issues—Pollution; Government; Indians of North America; Pollution—Water; Rivers; Science—Ecology; Water Quality

This environmental history of the Nashua River covers its pristine state when first discovered by Indians, its ecologically dead period caused by years of pollution, and Marion Stoddart's successful fight to restore it. Detailed maps and borders. Timeline. Author's note.

Other books that focus on specific waterways include Mary Hoff and Mary M. Rodgers' *Our Endangered Planet: Rivers and Lakes* (Lerner, 1991), George Ancona's *Riverkeeper* (Macmillan, 1990), and Edith McCall's *Biography of a River: The Mississippi* (Walker, 1990). High school students can read John J. Berger's *Restoring the Earth* (Alfred A. Knopf, 1985), which documents 12 environmental success stories and was the inspiration for Cherry's book.

A combined ecology and government project can begin by focusing student attention on the first Clean Water Act, passed by the U.S. Congress in 1965. Does your state have a similar act? In what condition are the waterways in your state? Science research can focus on specific rivers and/or community action projects to help restore rivers, streams, or lakes. Some students may want to get involved directly in such cleanup efforts.

110. Chetwin, Grace. **Box and Cox**. Ill. by David Small (Bradbury Press, 1990).

Drama; Farce; Humor; Vaudeville; Victorian Era

The lives of Box (a printer who works at night) and Cox (a hatter who works by day) are intertwined by Mrs. Bouncer when she rents them the same room and then accepts marriage proposals from both.

Drama students can adapt this book for a stage production. The story is based on a popular Victorian vaudeville routine, and the illustrations are purposely reminiscent of stage settings. Students wishing to learn more about vaudeville will find *The Encyclopedia of Vaudeville* by Anthony Slide (Greenwood, 1994) useful.

111. Children's Book Council. **75 Years of Children's Book Week Posters: Celebrating Great Illustrators of American Children's Books** (Alfred A. Knopf, 1994).

Art—Posters; Artists; Books— Illustrators; Books and Reading; Children's Literature; History of Art; Illustrators; Poster Art

The posters that have promoted literacy and encouraged the reading and enjoyment of children's books during the first 75 years of Children's Book Week are presented. Biographical information about each illustrator is included.

Advanced art students can research the history of poster art, its uses (in propaganda and ideology, product promotions, etc.), art styles, and famous poster artists such as Paul Berthon (1872-1909), Jules Cheret (1836-1932), Henri De Toulouse-Lautrec (1864-1901), and Alphonse Muncha (1860-1939).

Introduce students to poster art with this "coffee table" book featuring children and reading. Students can produce their own posters promoting Children's Book Week, an author's visit, a favorite book, etc.

 = Geography   = Art   = Music   = Drama   = Speech   = Research   = Read-Aloud

*Courage; Farm Life;
Fear; Historical Fiction;
History—United States—
1844; Hudson River Valley;
Landlords and Tenants;
Rebellions; Sharecroppers*

112. Christiansen, Candace. **Calico and Tin Horns**. Paintings by Thomas Locker (Dial Books for Young Readers, 1992).

Hannah, considered too young to participate in a rebellion against the landlords, courageously warns her father and the other farmers of the approaching sheriff and posse. Note.

Calico and Tin Horns is based on an actual event that occurred in the Hudson River Valley in 1844. The rebellion was the result of a broken agreement between the sharecroppers and the landlords that had gone unresolved for generations. Have students look at historic land issues such as sharecropping, development of the National Park system, leasing of public land for grazing, and the forced relinquishment of private land for public projects. What current controversies surround these issues?

*Buildings; Food
Preservation; Historical
Fiction; History—United
States—Late 19th Century;
Horses; Houses; Hudson
River Valley*

113. Christiansen, Candace. **The Ice House**. Paintings by Thomas Locker (Dial Books for Young Readers, 1993).

During the annual ice harvest, Jack remembers his uncle's instructions and acts quickly to save a horse who breaks through the ice and plunges into the frigid water. Note.

The icehouses in this region of New York provided the ice for the residents of New York City. Explore the history of food preservation including the use of drying, canning, salting, and ice blocks.

The discovery of the ruins of an old icehouse prompted the creation of this book, while Crescent Dragonwagon's discovery of an old farmstead near her home inspired *Home Place* (Macmillan, 1990). Are there places in your community where students can go to hunt for signs of earlier habitation? If not, search through newspapers to track the evolution of a specific street or area.

*African Americans;
Comics; Courage; Crime;
Depression; Gangsters;
Historical Fiction;
Jazz; Musicians*

114. Claverie, Jean. **Little Lou** (Stewart, Tabori & Chiang, 1990).

Little Lou, a young and talented musician, has an exciting adventure and a brush with organized crime.

Claverie begins this tale with lush illustrations that develop into a quick-moving, comic-book-style format when the gangster element enters the story. Art students can study this technique, noting how it affects the telling of this story and perhaps employing it in their own work.

Claverie based this story on research he did in Memphis visiting jazz clubs and interviewing people about the 1920s. Use this book along with Alan Schroeder's *Ragtime Tumpie* (Little, Brown, 1989) to initiate a study of jazz and ragtime music. Provide recordings of this music or invite a jazz band to perform.

*Caribou; Drama—
Puppet Shows; Hunting;
Indians of North America;
Inuits; Legends—Canada;
Puppet Shows; Shadow
Puppets*

115. Cleaver, Elizabeth. **The Enchanted Caribou** (Atheneum, 1985).

An evil shaman changes a girl into a white caribou and a brave Inuit hunter saves her.

Cleaver uses her fascination with shadow puppets for the illustrations in this book. Students can follow her instructions, found at the end of the book, for making these puppets and producing shadow plays. Be sure to show students Paul Fleischman's *Shadow Play* (Harper & Row, 1990) to provide them with another example of these puppets.

This legend features an Inuit belief that the white caribou might be an enchanted person. Other Indians of North America believe a white buffalo is special. The birth of a white calf in the summer of 1994 generated much national interest for the same reason. Students can use the *Readers' Guide to Periodical Literature* to research the news coverage of that unusual birth and its potential meaning.

116. Clément, Claude. **The Painter and the Wild Swans**. Pictures by Frédéric Clément (Dial Books for Young Readers, 1986).

Artists; Birds—Swans; Calligraphy; Fairy Tales— Japan; Japan—Fairy Tales; Painters; Photography; Swans

A fine Japanese painter is overcome by the beauty of a passing flock of swans and cannot work until he sees them again.

Clément's story is dedicated to and based on the work of Japanese photographer Teiji Saga. Students interested in photography can learn more about Saga and try to imitate his distinct style.

As an introduction to famous artists provide other picture books based on artists such as Christina Björk's *Linnea in Monet's Garden* (R & S Books, 1985), *The Princess and the Painter* by Jane Johnson (Farrar, Strauss & Giroux, 1994), and Diane Stanley's *The Gentleman and the Kitchen Maid* (Dial Books for Young Readers, 1994).

117. Clément, Claude. **The Voice of the Wood**. Paintings by Frédéric Clément (Dial Books for Young Readers, 1989).

Cellos; Honesty; Music; Musical Instruments; Symbolism; Venice; Violoncello

A magic cello, made from a Venetian instrument maker's beloved tree, can be played only after a famous young musician takes off his mask and plays with honesty and feeling.

The age-old craft of building musical instruments is alive and well throughout the world. Invite an instrument maker to your classroom to demonstrate what is involved. Have students review *Sound Designs: A Handbook of Musical Instrument Building* by Reinhold Banek (Ten Speed Press, 1980) and *Music in the Wood* by Cornelia Cornelissen (Delacorte Press, 1995).

The cello constructed by the old man is magic and thus can only be played by an honest musician who plays with heart. Invite a musician to speak about the feelings that go into composing, playing, or singing music that evokes an emotional response.

Provide students with cello recordings representing the greatest works for cello such as *Cello-Suiten*, the six suites for unaccompanied cello by Johann Sebastian Bach, Haydn's *Concerto in D Major for Cello and Orchestra,* and Beethoven's five *Sonatas for Piano/Klavier and Cello and Piano.*

118. Clement, Rod. **Counting on Frank** (Gareth Stevens, 1991).

Counting; Mathematics; Perception; Size

A youthful narrator presents funny mathematical facts that make his everyday life, with his dog Frank, an adventure. Afterword.

$\frac{2}{\underset{4}{+2}}$ This book is a perfect companion to Jon Scieszka's *Math Curse* (Viking, 1995). Both are witty views of math in the everyday lives of kids. Students can solve some of the mathematical problems and write their own unique story problems for classmates to solve. A classroom math book might be the end result!

 = Geography   = Art   = Music   = Drama   = Speech   = Research   = Read-Aloud

119. Clements, Gillian. **The Picture History of Great Inventors** (Alfred A. Knopf, 1994).

Discoveries; Inventions— History; Inventors; Patents; Science—Inventions

Using numerous detailed illustrations, Clements presents an illustrated, decade-by-decade introduction to 60 major inventors, from the unknown inventor of the wheel to today's developers of virtual reality. Glossary. Index.

Use this book to inspire students to create inventions. Hold a fair and display and demonstrate the finished products. You may also wish to use this as an opportunity to investigate the method of obtaining a patent.

120. Cober, Alan E. **Cober's Choice** (E. P. Dutton, 1979).

Animals; Artists; Audubon, John James (1785-1851); Collections; Drawings; History of Art; Science—Wildlife; Taxidermy

Twenty-three detailed pen-and-ink drawings of animals are accompanied by a brief text. Some of the drawings are done from live animals (rented or observed at the Bronx Zoo), but most were done from dead or stuffed animals collected from antique or taxidermy shops.

Many students will be fascinated by taxidermy. Invite a taxidermist to your class for a demonstration and discussion of taxidermy skills.

Many of Cober's drawings, like those of John James Audubon, were done from dead or stuffed animals. Students can study some of Audubon's prints from his folios, *Birds of America* or the *Quadrupeds*. A study could focus on birds or other animals that live in your region of the country.

121. Coerr, Eleanor. **Sadako**. Ill. by Ed Young (G. P. Putnam's Sons, 1993).

Atomic Bomb; Cancer—Leukemia; Death; Hiroshima; Japan— History; Legends—Japanese; Leukemia; Origami; Peace; World War II—Japan

Ten years after the bombing of Hiroshima, Sadako Sasaki became ill with leukemia. In a race of hope she tried to fold 1,000 paper cranes, which would, according to legend, help her win back her health. This picture book is based on Coerr's earlier novel, *Sadako and the Thousand Paper Cranes* (Putnam, 1977).

Like the statue that stands in Hiroshima Peace Park, Young's luminous pastels illustrate Sadako's struggle for life. The illustrations were originally done for the video *Sadako and the Thousand Paper Cranes*, narrated by Liv Ullman (Center for Informed Democracy, 1989). Consider showing the video.

Study origami as a traditional Japanese art form and provide origami paper and instructions so students can create their own projects. If your school system has an exchange student from Japan who has experience in paper folding, invite that student to demonstrate, teach, and explain Japanese art and culture. Be sure to introduce students to Molly Bang's retelling of an ancient Japanese folktale, *The Paper Crane* (Greenwillow Books, 1985), another picture book featuring origami cranes.

The Hiroshima Peace Park has become a gathering place for peace demonstrations. Explore the history of various peace symbols and peace or anti-war movements. Sheila Hamanaka's *Peace Crane* (William Morrow, 1995), an illustrated poem told from the perspective of a young African American girl, will be of interest.

122. Cohen, Daniel. **Erni Cabat's Magical World of Monsters**. Paintings by Erni Cabat (Cobblehill Books, 1992).

Animals—Mythical; Art; Monsters; Mythology

Legendary monsters are depicted and explained. Featured are Dragon, Griffin, Chimera, Basilisk, Kraken, Cerberus, Medusa, Centaur, Minotaur, Hydra, and Phoenix.

Because many works of poetry and prose refer to historic monsters, students need to have some point of reference for increased understanding. Provide this book for the monster information as well as the visual experience. Do students agree with Cabat's interpretations? Student artists can sketch or paint their own versions.

123. Coleridge, Samuel Taylor. **The Rime of the Ancient Mariner**. Ill. by Ed Young (Atheneum, 1992).

Coleridge, Samuel Taylor (1772-1834); Imagery; Literary Devices; Literature—English; Poetry; Sailors; Superstitions; Tragedy

Young adds paintings and line drawings to Coleridge's classic poem about a sailor who tells of the terrible fate that befell his ship after he shot down an albatross.

 Most students come in contact with this famous poem at some point during their school years; Coleridge's writing endures due to the style, imagery, and versification. In this version, the combination of Coleridge's evocative qualities of the mysterious and the supernatural, along with Young's powerful illustrations, create a riveting literary experience. Have the students initially read the poem without illustrations, and then read it with Young's illustrations. Discuss the poem's power after each reading. Do students have a preference for hearing the poem and seeing the illustrations or hearing the poem and not seeing the illustrations? Do the illustrations change the impact and the meaning of the poem for the students? Discuss individual preferences.

124. Cooper, Susan. **The Selkie Girl**. Ill. by Warwick Hutton (Margaret K. McElderry, 1986).

Folktales—Scottish; Love; Magic; Scotland—Folktales; Seals; Selkies

Donallan falls in love with a beautiful selkie girl and discovers he can keep her forever if he hides her seal skin.

Cooper retells this well-known Scottish tale with poignancy. Collect other versions for comparison. For high school students, the novel *The Selkie* by Rosanne Alexander (Deutsch, 1991) can be used to extend the activity.

125. Craft, Ruth. **Pieter Brueghel's The Fair**. Ill. by Pieter Brueghel (J. B. Lippincott, 1975).

Artists; Brueghel, Pieter, the Younger (1564-1637); Fairs; History of Art; Medieval Period; Paintings

Many details in Brueghel's painting *The Village Fair* are explained through rhyme. Note.

For comparison, note the similarity of the composition and the details in Brueghel's painting with *Anno's Flea Market* by Mitsumasa Anno (Philomel, 1984). Students can learn more about Brueghel's life by reading the end notes and conducting further research with books such as Richard Mühlberger's *What Makes a Brueghel a Brueghel?* (Viking, 1993).

126. Crossley-Holland, Kevin, translator. **Beowulf**. Ill. by Charles Keeping (Oxford University Press, 1982).

Beowulf; Dragons; Epics; Literature—British; Monsters; Read-Aloud; Warriors

The story of Beowulf is retold in prose with illustrations. Pronunciation guide.

This is an accessible prose introduction to the famous Old English epic written by an unknown poet in about 700 A.D. Consider reading it aloud to lessen the degree of anxiety some students might feel before tackling the original.

 = Geography   = Art   = Music   = Drama   = Speech   = Research   = Read-Aloud

127. Cummings, Pat, compiler and ed. **Talking with Artists**. Photographs of and illustrations by various artists (Bradbury, 1992).

Art—Painting and Drawing; Artists— Children's Literature; Biographies; Bookmaking; Careers—Artists; Interviews

The 14 interviews with favorite children's book illustrators reveal that practice, hard work, and a little luck are keys to success. Each biography includes personal information about the artist, a childhood photograph, a current photograph, a sample of their childhood artwork, a reproduction of their current work, and the answers to eight questions kids frequently ask them. Artists featured are Victoria Chess, Pat Cummings, Leo and Diane Dillon, Richard Egielski, Lois Ehlert, Lisa Campbell Ernst, Tom Feelings, Steven Kellogg, Jerry Pinkney, Amy Schwartz, Lane Smith, Chris Van Allsburg, and David Wiesner. Glossary. Bibliographies.

 Students can become published authors and illustrators. Books such as the following can inspire and guide students toward publishing. Consider using the most current edition of Kathy Henderson's *Market Guide for Young Writers: Where and How to Sell What You Write* (Writer's Digest Books, 1993), Michael Kehoe's *A Book Takes Root: The Making of a Picturebook* (Carolrhoda Books, 1993), and David Melton's *Written & Illustrated by. . .* (Landmark Editions, 1985). More serious and mature students will benefit from Ellen E. M. Roberts' *The Children's Picture Book: How to Write It, How to Sell It* (Writer's Digest Books, 1981) and *Writing with Pictures: How to Write and Illustrate Children's Books* by Uri Shulevitz (Watson-Guptill, 1985). Budding comic artists will find *The Art of Making Comic Books* by Michael Morgan Pellowski (Lerner, 1995) very useful.

The answers to why and how these artists became illustrators might inspire talented art students.

Use this book in conjunction with numerous samples of an artist's work as seen in children's books. Discuss that artist's use of media, various techniques, and styles.

D

128. Dabcovich, Lydia. **The Keys to My Kingdom: A Poem in Three Languages** (Lothrop, Lee & Shepard, 1992).

Art—Painting; Bilingual Books; Languages—French; Languages—Spanish; Literary Devices; Metaphor; Painting; Spanish; Visual Perspectives

Paintbrushes are the "keys" to a young girl's kingdom as she travels through her city, town, street, lane, yard, house, and so on, and then back again. The text to this classic rhyme is presented in French, Spanish, and English on each page.

 The world of languages can be made more inviting by introducing students to bilingual books. *The Keys to My Kingdom* goes a step further by presenting three languages. The repetition of words in the texts make this book an excellent choice for ESL classes and/or French and Spanish language programs. For another picture book featuring multiple languages (Spanish and Polish) share Leyla Torres' *Subway Sparrow* (Farrar, Straus & Giroux, 1993).

 The idea of zeroing in on a location by featuring size and perspective ("In that city there is a town; In that town there is a street; In that street . . .") is also explored in Istvan Banyai's wordless companion books *Zoom* (Viking, 1995) and *Re-Zoom* (Viking, 1995) and in *Looking Down* by Steve Jenkins (Houghton Mifflin, 1995).

❗ = Extraordinary!   ⚲ = Idea   📖 = Further Reading   ✍ = Writing $\frac{2}{4}$ = Math   ⚛ = Science   📖 = History

129. Dahl, Roald. **Roald Dahl's Revolting Rhymes**. Ill. by Quentin Blake (Alfred A. Knopf, 1982).

Fairy Tales—Fractured; Fractured Fairy Tales; Humor; Poetry; Read-Aloud; Writing

Consistent with Roald Dahl's inimitable style, this collection features hilarious poetic retellings of six well-known fairy tales peppered with gruesome and violent details as well as surprising endings.

The poem featuring the "Three Little Pigs" (with a surprising appearance by Red Riding Hood) can be used with Jon Scieszka's *The True Story of the 3 Little Pigs by A. Wolf* (Viking Kestrel, 1989) and Eugene Triviza's *The Three Little Wolves and the Big Bad Pig* (Macmillan, 1993) for a feast of pig and wolf tales!

These tales, suitable for the older set, can be read aloud and offered as models of rollicking verse. Students will love these twisted poems.

130. Daly, Niki. **Papa Lucky's Shadow** (Margaret K. McElderry, 1992).

Dancers; Grandfathers; Historical Fiction; Public Access Television; Street Theater; Tap Dancing

Papa Lucky, a great tap dancer in his youth, practices with his granddaughter before dancing in the streets to make some extra money.

Street theater has become a bona fide business for performers in some cities. Students living in areas with street theater actors can document these performances with video or still photography. Consider submitting a video for broadcast on your local public access television station and/or displaying the best photographs in a school gallery.

Invite a tap dancer to demonstrate tap dancing and teach some of the basic moves. Introduce students to the three steps mentioned in this book: the soft-shoe shuffle, the slide, and the Madison.

131. Davidge, Bud. **The Mummer's Song**. Ill. by Ian Wallace (Orchard, 1993).

Canada; Christmas; Costumes; Mummering; Music; Newfoundland; Songs; Traditions

The folk custom of mummering (costumed visitors going into homes for dancing and refreshments after Christmas in rural Newfoundland) is presented through illustrations and the words from a popular regional song. Afterword. Musical score.

Regional customs help younger generations remember or discover their own heritage. Mummering was actually revived by this song, written as a tribute to a custom dating from at least the early 1800s. Is there a regional custom in your area that students can learn more about?

132. Day, David. **The Walking Catfish**. Ill. by Mark Entwisle (Macmillan, 1991).

Contests; Gangs; Humor; Lying Contests; Speech; Storytelling— Contests; Tall Tales

Two gangs of archrivals have a three-day lying contest where the final tale comes true . . . perhaps!

Telling outrageous tall tales is an American storytelling tradition. Sponsor a storytelling contest and provide students with a variety of materials they might like to use for selecting tales. Collections such as Alvin Schwartz' *Whoppers: Tall Tales and Other Lies* (J. B. Lippincott, 1975) complements the many individual tall tales cited in this book.

133. DeFelice, Cynthia C. **The Dancing Skeleton**. Ill. by Robert Andrew Parker (Macmillan, 1989).

Dancing; Fiddles; Folklore—American; Read-Aloud; Storytelling; Supernatural

No one cared much that the mean and ornery Aaron Kelly was dead, including his widow. But Aaron comes back from his coffin and refuses to leave his rocking chair, until the best fiddler in town comes to call on the widow.

Use this book as an introduction to the genre of folktale and supernatural literature. For more great stories consult other collections of ghostly tales of love and revenge that have been passed on for generations.

DeFelice is a professional storyteller and is half of "The Wild Washerwomen" team. Read this story aloud and have students decide what specific storytelling elements (examples of the language, structure, etc.) it contains. Some students may wish to learn this story to share with others.

134. Demi. **Chingis Kahn** (Henry Holt, 1991).

Behavior—Codes of Conduct; Biographies; Kahn, Genghis (1162-1227); Kings and Rulers; Leadership; Monarchs; Mongols; Sports— History; War

Based upon historical resources and folklore, this is Demi's interpretation of the life of Chingis Kahn (Genghis Kahn), a military genius who garnered the greatest contiguous land empire in history.

The sport of polo was invented by the Mongolians. Research a variety of sports to learn their often unusual and historic beginnings. General books like Tim Hammond's *Sports* (Alfred A. Knopf, 1988) will be helpful.

Genghis Kahn created a code of rules called the Yassa, which required loyalty, obedience, and honesty. This was an essential element in his ability to rule and conquer. Have students discuss the question: What other codes of conduct can be found in school, government, or private industry?

135. Demi. **Demi's Dragons and Fantastic Creatures** (Henry Holt, 1993).

Dragons; Chinese—Folklore; Dragons; Folklore—Chinese; Mythical Creatures; Poetry

Lavish illustrations accompany short verses presenting the traditional wisdom of 18 magical, dancing, roaring Chinese dragons and creatures. End notes.

Students studying Chinese customs can use the dragons in this book as models for making or drawing dragon costumes used in a Chinese New Year celebration.

Many people love dragons and dragon lore. In addition to Demi's book, include some of the following in a classroom dragon book collection: *The Flight of Dragons* by Peter Dickinson (HarperCollins, 1979; *A Book of Dragons* by Hosie Baskin and Leonard Baskin (Alfred A. Knopf, 1985); *Dragons and Dreams* by Jane Yolen, Martin H. Greenberg, and Charles G. Waugh (HarperCollins, 1986); *Dragons, Gods and Spirits from Chinese Mythology* by Geraldine Harris (Schocken Books, 1983); *Dragons: Truth, Myth, and Legend* by David Passes (Western, 1993); and *The Truth About Dragons* by Rhoda Blumberg (Four Winds Press, 1980).

 136. Diaz, Jorge. **The Rebellious Alphabet**. Ill. by Oivind S. Jorfald (Henry Holt, 1993).

Censorship; Dictators; Fables; Freedom; Governments—Dictators; Literacy; Reading; Writing

When reading and writing are banned by an illiterate dictator, an old man trains birds to print his liberty poems and leaflets. When these papers are burned by the soldiers, the letters on them form a rebellious alphabet that develops into a black cloud. The rain brings words to the villagers and prison stripes to the general.

Originally written as a play in 1977 (and now a film), students should know that Diaz, a native of Chile, lives in political exile. The sophisticated graphics and subject of this political fable make it an excellent choice for high school government classes. Provide this book along with Umberto Eco's *The Bomb and the General* (Harcourt Brace Jovanovich, 1989) and Raymond Briggs' *The Tin-Pot Foreign General and the Old Iron Woman* (Little, Brown, 1984).

Many groups are vigilant in their protection of freedom of speech and freedom of the press—rights guaranteed by the First Amendment. Librarians, for example, work hard to protect and provide access to a variety of materials, some of which certain groups might prefer to ban. Give students examples of First Amendment infringements and lists of banned books. Novels such as *Westmark* by Lloyd Alexander (E. P. Dutton, 1981), which features freedom of the press as a major theme, and Avi's *Nothing But the Truth* (Orchard, 1991), with the theme of freedom of speech, can spark further discussion and reflection on this important issue. Consult "Studying the First Amendment" by Pat Scales [*Book Links* 5(1):20-24, September 1995] for activities, discussion topics, and related reading references.

137. Dorros, Arthur. **Radio Man: A Story in English and Spanish** (Harper-Collins, 1993).

Bilingual Books; Family Life; Farming; Geography; Grandfathers; Languages—Spanish; Mexican Americans; Migrant Labor; Radios

Diego relies on his radio for companionship and information as he travels with his migrant family from state to state harvesting vegetables.

Anne Sherley Williams' picture book *Working Cotton* (Harcourt Brace Jovanovich, 1992) is an excellent companion book focusing on children of migrant farm workers. Students researching migrant labor should be sure to consult *Voices from the Field: Children of Migrant Farm Workers Tell Their Stories* by S. Beth Atkin (Little, Brown, 1993). Encourage students to seek answers to questions not answered in Dorros' text, such as: What will happen to Grandpa when he is too old to pick? How do migrant children get an education when they keep moving? Another moving picture book about Mexican American labor is Eve Bunting's *A Day's Work* (Clarion Books, 1994). This book highlights a strong relationship between a grandfather and grandson.

Although students listen to music on radio, most have little knowledge about the "golden age of radio" that existed before television. Create a book and tape collection featuring historical information, original broadcasts of famous programs, and modern radio shows modeled on the classics. Consider including books and recordings like the *The Shadow* (Great American Radio Corp., 1992), available as eight episodes of the original broadcast starring Orson Welles and including commercials; *The Lone Ranger* (Radio Spirits, 1992); and *The Green Hornet* (Radio Reruns, 1987). Also available are cassettes of *Radio WOOF: Woof's Greatest Bits,* which is Bill Wellington's fictitious radio station WOOF ("World of Folklore"). This modern-day recording introduces fans to a skateboarder named Gnarly Roadrash, Whine-A-Day Vitamins, and haunted chewing gum. Additionally, many National Public Radio stations feature weekly programs of "Riders in the Sky" on *Rider's Radio Theater. Sounds in the Air: The Golden Age of Radio* by Norman H. Finkelstein (Charles Scribner's Sons, 1993), Roger Barr's *Radios: Wireless Sound* (Lucent, 1994), and, for middle-grade readers, Avi's novel *Who Was That Masked Man, Anyway?* (Orchard, 1992) are books to consider using.

138. Drescher, Henrik. **Pat the Beastie: A Pull-and-Poke Book** (Intervisual Books, 1993).

Artists; Beasts; Books—Toys; Humor; Parodies; Read-Aloud; Reluctant Readers; Satire; Toy and Moveable Books

This tongue-in-cheek parody of the baby classic *Pat the Bunny* (Golden/Western, 1942) features Paul and Judy, owners of a pet named Beastie. "Readers" can pull Beastie's hair, jiggle his eyes, poke his worm boogers, etc.

 = Geography   = Art   = Music   = Drama   = Speech   = Research   = Read-Aloud

Provide this book along with *Pat the Bunny* for sheer entertainment or to generate copycat books from students who are so inclined.

 This unusual moveable book was selected by the American Library Association's Reluctant Teen Reader Committee as a "Quick Pick for Reluctant Young Adult Readers." Since research indicates that the surest way young adult librarians can increase circulation is through class visits, take along this "charmer" and read-aloud as a testament to your sense of humor and openness to these dynamic patrons.

Drescher's unique collage work and illustrations have also appeared in the *New York Times, Rolling Stone,* and in Richard Wilbur's poetry collection *Runaway Opposites* (Harcourt Brace & Company, 1995). Assemble a collection of his work so all can gain a better appreciation of Drescher's talent and style.

Art—China Painting;
China—Folklore;
Creative Writing; Love;
Willow Pattern China

139. Drummond, Allan. **The Willow Pattern Story** (North-South Books, 1992).

Drummond retells a story invented to explain the landscape on willow pattern china. Two Chinese lovers escape a cruel father but are later captured and punished. However, their eternal love transcends their imprisonment. Notes.

Most interesting is the accompanying note describing the author's interest and research in willow pattern china. Students can look further into china painting as an art form, then create their own original paintings and write the story their china tells.

E

Folklore—Switzerland;
Freedom; Independence;
Legends; Switzerland—
History—14th Century;
Switzerland—Legends;
Tyranny

140. Early, Margaret. **William Tell** (Harry N. Abrams, 1991).

The legendary national hero of Switzerland, William Tell (who shot the apple from his son's head) is placed in historical context as the Swiss populace struggles to fight the tyrannical rule of the Austrian emperor, Albert I.

Switzerland was once formed from small countries (Schwytz, Ur, and Unterwalden). Students can research further the history of this country, long considered the bastion of neutrality in the world.

 Art—Collage; Atomic
Bomb; Collage;
Generals; Nuclear Arms;
Nuclear War; Soldiers;
War—Nuclear

141. Eco, Umberto. **The Bomb and the General**. Ill. by Eugenio Carmi (Harcourt Brace Jovanovich, 1989).

A power-hungry, warmongering general is sent off to be a doorman (where he can use his uniform with all the braid) after his failed attempt to launch an atomic war.

 This humorous and deceptively simple story is perfect to begin a discussion about nuclear proliferation of arms. Provide Carl B. Feldbaum and Ronald J. Bee's provocative *Looking the Tiger in the Eye: Confronting the Nuclear Threat* (Harper & Row, 1988) among other books and periodical articles for students to gather information and become better informed for the future.

 = Extraordinary!   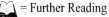 = Idea   = Further Reading   = Writing   = Math   = Science   = History

142. Eco, Umberto and Eugenio Carmi (translated by William Weaver). **The Three Astronauts** (Harcourt Brace Jovanovich, 1989).

Three astronauts from different countries, competing to land on Mars first, meet a Martian and make an amazing discovery about humanity on Earth and in outer space.

Astronauts; Astronomy; Compassion; Competition; Mars; Martians; Peace; Science—Astronomy; Space Exploration; War

Eco writes, "Just because two creatures are different they don't have to be enemies." Do students agree or disagree with this statement? What are some of the complicated issues leading to wars? Students can investigate peacekeeping tactics and look at books such as *Ain't Gonna Study War No More* by Milton Meltzer (Harper & Row, 1985), *Some Reasons for War: How Families, Myths and Warfare Are Connected* by Sue Mansfield and Mary Bowen Hall (Harper & Row, 1988), and *The Big Book for Peace* by Ann Durell et al. (Dutton Children's Books, 1990). Students might also be interested in *War and Peas* by Michael Foreman (Thomas Y. Crowell, 1974), a picture book fable concerning war and peace.

Sending explorers to Mars may become a reality in the early 2000s. Students can research this possibility along with the scientific goals of such a mission. Consult books such as *The Cambridge Encyclopedia of Space* edited by Michael Rycroft (Cambridge University Press, 1990) for more information.

143. Ehlert, Lois. **Moon Rope: Un Lazo Ala Luna** (Harcourt Brace Jovanovich, 1992).

Ehlert adapts a Peruvian folktale in which Fox and Mole attempt to climb up to the moon on a rope woven of grass.

Art; Bilingual Books; Languages—Spanish; Moons—Folklore; Peru—Folklore

Because this book includes both English and Spanish text, it is an excellent choice for beginning Spanish students to read in order to practice their pronunciation and enlarge their vocabulary. Many picture books are available in Spanish such as *Flecha al Sol: Un Cuento de los Indios Pueblo* (*Arrow to the Sun*) by Gerald McDermott. These are perfect for studying Spanish in a literature-based Spanish language program. The annotated reviews periodically published in *School Library Journal*'s "Children's Books in Spanish" section will be helpful in identifying other titles to use in Spanish language classes.

A brief note explains that the vivid illustrations in *Moon Rope* were inspired by "ancient Peruvian textiles, jewelry, ceramic vessels, sculpture, and architecture." Students can study more about Peruvian art and compare Ehlert's illustrations to photographs of authentic art objects.

144. Eliot, T. S. **Growltiger's Last Stand: And Other Poems**. Ill. by Errol LeCain (Harcourt Brace Jovanovich, 1987).

145. Eliot, T. S. **Mistoffelees with Mungojerrie and Rumpelteazer**. Ill. by Errol LeCain (Harcourt Brace Jovanovich, 1991).

Both books feature poems from Eliot's *Old Possum's Book of Practical Cats,* made popular by the musical *Cats.*

Cats; Eliot, T. S. (1888-1965); Literature—British; Plays— Musicals; Poetry

Eliot's *Old Possum's Book of Practical Cats* (1939) was the inspiration for the musical *Cats.* Sharing both the music and these books with students is a must as many will not know these were written by a Nobel laureate who generally wrote with a more somber tone.

146. Elwell, Peter. **The King of the Pipers** (Macmillan, 1984).

Devils; Fairy Tales; Irony; Literary Devices; Music; Royalty; Trickery

Jack is known throughout the kingdom for his lack of talent at playing the bagpipes. Through a series of humorous events Jack eventually becomes king and ultimately defeats the Devil with his terrible playing.

This ironic tale will appeal to all students and serve as a concrete example of this literary device. For further reading in a similar vein, provide the short and humorous fable *The Silent Gondolier* by S. Morgenstern (Ballantine Books, 1983).

147. Emberley, Barbara, adapted by. **Drummer Hoff**. Ill. by Ed Emberley (Prentice-Hall, 1967).

Art—Woodcuts; Cannons; Rhymes; Soldiers; Symbolism; War; Weapons; Woodcuts

This cumulative rhyme marches along with the soldiers as they bring the parts for building and firing a cannon. Caldecott Medal, 1968.

The last double page shows the cannon as a home for nesting birds, plants, and insects. Discuss the possible symbolism, especially considering the political climate of the time when the book was written and illustrated. Some students might like to investigate further to discover the real story behind the Emberleys' book.

Most of the woodcuts in the Emberley books were produced on Ed Emberley's own printing press. Notice that only three colors were used to produce the illustrations, which seem to almost explode. Compare and contrast the numerous examples of woodcuts by other picture book artists and experiment with various techniques students find appealing.

148. Ende, Michael. **Ophelia's Shadow Theatre**. Ill. by Friedrich Hechelmann (Overlook Press, 1989).

Death; Heaven; Homelessness; Imagination; Magic; Read-Aloud; Shadow Theaters; Theaters

Having spent her life prompting actors but now unemployed, Miss Ophelia befriends shadows who belong to no one. After teaching them the great comedies and tragedies of the world, they travel from town to town, giving a final performance to Death.

Read this picture book aloud as an introduction to Ende's popular *The Neverending Story* (Puffin Books, 1993) or as a treat!

149. Everett, Gwen. **John Brown: One Man Against Slavery**. Paintings by Jacob Lawrence (Rizzoli International Publications, 1993).

Abolitionists; African Americans; Brown, John (1800-1859); Civil War; Douglass, Frederick (1817?-1895); Freedom; History—African Americans; Read-Aloud; Slavery; Treason

Brown's 16-year-old daughter Annie narrates this chronicle of his efforts to galvanize a regiment of 19 men to raid a U.S. arsenal in order to arm an army against slavery. Afterword. Notes.

Use this book in conjunction with the short autobiography of Frederick Douglass titled *Escape from Slavery: The Boyhood of Frederick Douglass in His Own Words,* edited and illustrated by Michael McCurdy (Alfred A. Knopf, 1994); "Frederick Douglass Always Knew He Was Meant to be Free" by Richard Conniff ([*Smithsonian* 25(11):115-27, February 1995]); and the video *Frederick Douglass: When the Lion Wrote History* (PBS, 1994). Like John Brown, Douglass was a famous abolitionist. Students can examine the effect these men had on the issues and people of their time.

Gwen Everett was inspired to write this story after viewing the paintings created in 1941 by renowned African American artist Jacob Lawrence. This book personalizes a historic event that precipitated the Civil War. Use this powerful account in any study of that time period, taking a close look at John Brown and his activities.

 = Extraordinary! 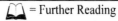 = Idea   = Further Reading   = Writing $\frac{2}{4}$ = Math   = Science   = History

150. Everett, Gwen. **Li'l Sis and Uncle Willie: A Story Based on the Life and Paintings of William H. Johnson**. Paintings by William H. Johnson (Hyperion, 1994).

African Americans; Art History; Artists; Biographies; Johnson, William H. (1901-1970)

This fictional biography uses Johnson's own paintings to depict events in his life. Note.

More than 1,000 of Johnson's paintings are preserved at the National Museum of American Art in Washington, D.C. Students who want to learn more about Johnson and his colorful style should read *Homecoming: The Art and Life of William H. Johnson* by Richard J. Powell (National Museum of American Art, Smithsonian Institution, 1991) or view the video *The Life and Art of William H. Johnson* (The Company, 1991).

F

151. Fair, Sylvia. **The Bedspread** (William Morrow, 1982).

Aging; Art—Needlework; Elderly; Individuality; Memories—Individual Perception; Needlework; Sisters

Two elderly sisters reveal their own personalities and unique memories of the house they lived in all their lives by embroidering half of a large communal bedspread.

Individual perceptions and memories of the same event are a central focus of this book. Can students think of specific instances where individuals involved have different recollections of the same event? What is the effect? How can differing perceptions and memories affect the outcome of court cases?

Provide high school students with *Having Our Say: The Delany Sisters' First 100 Years* by Sarah Louis Delany and Annie Elizabeth Delany (Kodansha International, 1993) for a look at two other elderly sisters and their personal stories.

As a true art form needlework includes a variety of techniques and styles—as can readily be seen by Maud and Amelia's work. Highlight unusual needlework such as that found in the medieval tapestries, historic quilts, beadwork, etc. Invite an expert to share examples of different types of needlework. Some students might like to undertake a simple project.

152. Faulkner, Matt. **The Amazing Voyage of Jackie Grace** (Scholastic, 1987).

Adventures; Art— Comic; Baths; Comics; Fantasy; Heroes; Hijacking; Imaginary Journeys; Imagination; Pirates

Jackie Grace's amazing voyage begins when his imagination runs away and a crew of sailors hijack his claw-footed bathtub. Jackie survives a wild storm, defeats the pirates, and becomes a hero before reality sets in.

Picture book accounts of imaginary journeys, like this story, *Free Fall* by David Wiesner (Lothrop, Lee & Shepard, 1988), and *Ben's Dream* by Chris Van Allsburg (Houghton Mifflin, 1982), can be used to introduce students to more complex novels with a similar storyline. Provide students with other pirate adventures such as Chris Van Allsburg's *The Wretched Stone* (Houghton Mifflin, 1991) or Avi's *The True Confessions of Charollette Doyle* (Orchard, 1990).

The comic style used by Matt Faulkner in this book has also been used by Maurice Sendak. How have both artists effectively used this technique? Learn more about the power of comic illustrations from Scott McCloud's *Understanding Comics* (Kitchen Sink Press, 1993).

 = Geography   = Art   = Music   = Drama   = Speech   = Research   = Read-Aloud

153. Feelings, Muriel. **Jambo Means Hello: Swahili Alphabet Book**. Ill. by Tom Feelings (Dial Press, 1974).

154. Feelings, Muriel. **Moja Means One: Swahili Counting Book**. Ill. by Tom Feelings (Dial Press, 1971).

Africa; Alphabet Books; Bilingual Books; Counting; East Africa; Geography; Languages— Swahili; Social Life and Customs—East Africa; Swahili

These companion volumes present traditional East African life by focusing on 24 letters (there are no *Q* or *X* sounds in Swahili) and 10 numbers in the Swahili language. *Jambo Means Hello: Swahili Alphabet Book* was a Caldecott Honor in 1975; *Moja Means One: Swahili Counting Book* was a Caldecott Honor in 1972.

 These anthropological books complement multicultural studies featuring East Africa (or the heritage of African Americans) and focus on the traditional life and language of the region. Though more than 800 languages are spoken throughout Africa, Swahili is the most common language used south of the Sahara Desert. Other books of interest include Jim Haskins' *Count Your Way Through Africa* (Carolrhoda Books, 1989), Verna Aardema's *Rabbit Makes a Monkey Out of Lion: A Swahili Tale* (Dial Books for Young Readers, 1989), and Barbara Knutson's retelling of *How the Guinea Fowl Got Her Spots: A Swahili Tale of Friendship* (Carolrhoda Books, 1990). Note: Use current maps to reflect contemporary country names.

155. Feelings, Tom. **Soul Looks Back in Wonder** (Dial Books for Young Readers, 1993).

African Americans; Freedom; Heritage; Oppression; Poetry; Speech

African American artists and poets portray the creativity, beauty, and strength of their heritage in this collection. Included are Maya Angelou, Lucille Clifton, Alexis DeVeaux, Mari Evans, Darryl Holmes, Langston Hughes, Rashidah Ismaili, Haki R. Madhubuti, Walter Dean Myers, Mwatabu Okantah, Eugene B. Redmond, Askia M. Touré, and Margaret Walker.

Present a celebration, perhaps during February (Black History Month), of African American poets by staging a poetry reading of the poems in this book as well as poetry from other collections featuring African American poets.

156. Fisher, Leonard Everett. **Cyclops** (Holiday House, 1991).

157. Fisher, Leonard Everett. **Jason and the Golden Fleece** (Holiday House, 1990).

158. Fisher, Leonard Everett. **The Olympians: Great Gods and Goddesses of Ancient Greece** (Holiday House, 1984).

159. Fisher, Leonard Everett. **Theseus and the Minotaur** (Holiday House, 1988).

Argonauts; Cyclops; Folklore—Greek; Gods and Goddesses; Mazes; Minotaur; Mythology— Greek; Read-Aloud; Theseus

These classic Greek myths are retold with limited text and powerful illustrations.

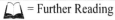 Build and expand the theme of mazes in Fisher's *Theseus and the Minotaur* using Zilpha Keatley Snyder's *The Changing Maze* (Macmillan, 1985), Chris Van Allsburg's *The Gardens of Abdul Gasazi* (Houghton Mifflin, 1979), and the section on mazes in *Anno's Math Games III* by Mitsumasa Anno (Philomel, 1991). Students can create their own mazes as a final project.

 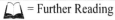

These books can provide a nonthreatening introduction to Greek mythology. After reading aloud some single story picture books, supply your students with more in-depth stories from classic collections such as *D'Aulaire's Book of Greek Myths* by Ingri D'Aulaire and Edgar Parin D'Aulaire (Doubleday, 1980), *Bulfinch's Mythology: The Greek and Roman Fables* by Thomas Bulfinch (Viking, 1979), and Edith Hamilton's *Mythology* (Little, Brown, 1942).

160. Fisher, Leonard Everett. **Galileo** (Macmillan, 1992).

Astronomy; Biographies; Galileo (1564-1642); Instruments; Inventors; Renaissance; Scientific Discoveries; Scientists; Telescopes

Fisher examines the life and discoveries of Galileo, a noted mathematician, physicist, and astronomer whose work changed the course of science. Chronology. Map. Note.

Use this book, along with Catherine Brighton's *Five Secrets in a Box* (E. P. Dutton, 1987) and Gillian Clements' *The Picture History of Great Inventors* (Alfred A. Knopf, 1994), to introduce a study of Galileo and his discoveries.

Galileo was denounced and persecuted by the Roman Catholic Church for his discoveries. In fact, he was not cleared of guilt until 1822, more than 300 years after his death. What other discoveries have flown in the face of tradition, religion, or commonly held beliefs. Can students think of current analogies?

161. Fisher, Leonard Everett. **The Great Wall of China** (Macmillan, 1986).

Art—Calligraphy; Calligraphy; China—History—221-210 B.C.; Chinese; Chinese Calligraphy; Chops; Construction; Great Wall of China; Walls

This is a brief history about the construction of the Great Wall of China, built to keep out the fierce Mongol invaders from the north.

The red block prints on each page are made from "chops." Students can find out more about chops, beginning with the explanation on the verso page. Try to assemble a collection of chops to share with students.

Each of the illustrations is titled (see the last page of the book), translated into Chinese, and written in calligraphy. Students can learn about Chinese characters by using Leonard Everett Fisher's *Alphabet Art* (Four Winds Press, 1978) and Peggy Goldstein's very informative *Long Is a Dragon: Chinese Writing for Children* (China Books & Periodicals, 1991).

162. Fisher, Leonard Everett. **Gutenberg** (Macmillan, 1993).

Art; Bible—Gutenburg; Biographies; Business; Finances; Gutenburg, Johannes (c1400-c1468); Inventions; Printing

Gutenberg is a biography of the 15th-century German printer who invented movable metal type and revolutionized printing.

Gutenberg was not much of a businessperson; many of his partnerships failed. Have students research the various financial traps into which unsavvy businesspersons can fall—defaulting on loans, equipment seizure, and bankruptcy.

Further study about the history of the *Gutenberg Bible* can be pursued by interested students.

163. Fisher, Leonard Everett. **Prince Henry the Navigator** (Macmillan, 1990).

Biographies; Explorers; Geography; Henry the Navigator; History—Explorers; Infante of Portugal (1394-1460); Portugal; Prester John; Religions—Islam; Shipbuilding; Ship's Logs

Henry was a Portuguese prince whose vision and courage altered the world of navigation. His voyages and experiments paved the way for subsequent explorations. Chronology. Map.

 = Geography   = Art   = Music   = Drama   = Speech   = Research   = Read-Aloud

Henry was responsible for the development of a new type of ship, the caravel. See *Stephen Biesty's Incredible Cross-Sections* (Alfred A. Knopf, 1992) for an "inside" look at this type of ship.

 Henry began the practice of keeping a ship's log, a detailed written account of shipboard events. This standardized practice of maintaining a ship's log has provided valuable historical information and continues to provide information today. Students can look at past ship's logs, such as those of Christopher Columbus, and compare them with today's logs. *The Log of Christopher Columbus* by Steve Lowe (Philomel, 1992) will be useful for this activity.

One of Henry's goals was to find Prester John, a Christian king who was thought to rule a huge empire. Interested students can find out more about this elusive figure.

164. Fisher, Leonard Everett. **Sailboat Lost** (Holiday House, 1991).

Adventures; Boats and Boating; Creative Writing; Fantasy; Languages— Study of; Poetry

When their boat drifts away from the island shore, two boys are stranded by high tide.

This almost wordless book has a poem on the first page. Have students study the paintings without reading the poem, then write their own prose or poem about this adventurous fantasy. They can write in either their native language or one they are studying. After they have completed and shared their writings, read aloud the poem in the book.

165. Fisher, Leonard Everett. **Stars & Stripes: Our National Flag** (Holiday House, 1993).

Flags; History—United States—Flags; Pledge of Allegiance; United States— History—Flags

Stars & Stripes features the text of the "Pledge of Allegiance" and information related to the 13 historical flags. Notes.

 Other books for middle-school students concerning the American flag and its history include *Betsy Ross* by Alexandra Wallner, (Holiday House, 1994), *The American Flag* by Ann Armbruster (Franklin Watts, 1991), *Honor the Flag: A Guide to Its Care and Display* by Ruth Radlauer (Forest, 1992), and *What You Should Know About the American Flag* by Earl P. Williams (Maryland Historical Press, 1989).

166. Fisher, Leonard Everett. **Symbol Art: Thirteen Squares, Circles, Triangles from Around the World** (Four Winds Press, 1985).

Advertising; Art—Logos; Communication; Geometry; Logos; Signs; Symbols

Fisher explores the historic use of symbols, in 13 different disciplines, for communication throughout the world.

To enhance a study of sign and symbol communication use books like Fisher's companion title *Art: Thirteen ABCs from Around the World* (Macmillan, 1984), as well as *The Book of Signs* by Rudolf Koch (Dover, 1955), which identifies symbols used up through the Middle Ages. Students can investigate other signs used in the 13 disciplines (astrology, astronomy, biology, botany, chemistry, engineering, language, mapmaking, mathematics, medicine, printing, religion, and weather) featured by Fisher.

 Logos are symbols representing business or activities. Invite a graphic artist who designs logos to discuss their development and uses. After collecting and studying famous logos, students can develop a logo of their own as a final project.

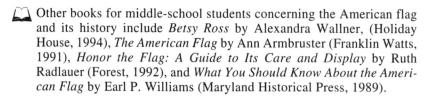

❗ = Extraordinary!   💡 = Idea   📖 = Further Reading   ✍ = Writing   ²⁄₄ = Math   🔬 = Science   📖 = History

167. Fisher, Leonard Everett. **The Tower of London** (Macmillan, 1987).

Architecture; Biographies; Buildings and Structures; History—Great Britain; London; Tower of London

The bloody history of the Tower of London from 1078 to 1666 is presented through the lives of 13 people.

Q To present history from a biographical perspective, have students research the lives of the people featured in this book.

168. Fisher, Leonard Everett. **The Wailing Wall** (Macmillan, 1989).

Biblical Events—History; History—Biblical Events; History—Judaism; Judaism— History; Middle East— Palestine; Palestine; Structures; Walls

Emphasizing events before 70 A.D., Fisher surveys the history of the Jewish people in Palestine and their activities around the First and Second Temples, the site of which is now marked by the Western or Wailing Wall. Chronology. Note.

Walls, both natural and human made, are significant in many cultures and countries. Are there important walls in your community or state? What purpose do they serve? See other books on walls such as Leonard Everett Fisher's *The Great Wall of China* (Macmillan, 1986), Margy Burns Knight's *Talking Walls* (Tilbury House, 1992), Frances Ward Weller's *Matthew Wheelock's Wall* (Macmillan, 1992), and Eve Bunting's *The Wall* (Clarion Books, 1990).

169. Fleischman, Paul. **Rondo in C**. Ill. by Janet Wentworth (Harper & Row, 1988).

Beethoven, Ludwig van (1770-1827); Memories; Music—Classical; Music Appreciation; Performances; Piano; Recitals

Each member of the audience recalls different memories as a piano student plays Beethoven's "Rondo in C" at a recital.

♪ Let the music begin! Play a recording of Beethoven's "Rondo in C" when sharing this book, or as part of an introduction to Beethoven, classical music or composers, or general music appreciation.

170. Fleischman, Paul. **Shadow Play**. Ill. by Eric Beddows (Harper & Row, 1990).

Beauty and the Beast; Drama; Fairy Tales; Morals; Pantomimes; Puppet Shows; Shadow Puppets

Two siblings are enchanted by a shadow puppet show of "Beauty and the Beast" at a country fair. When invited backstage they discover the puppets are manipulated by one person.

Fleischman's version of "Beauty and the Beast" is a fine introduction to investigating other versions such as those illustrated by Jan Brett (Clarion Books, 1989), Mercer Mayer (Four Winds Press, 1978), Warwick Hutton (Atheneum, 1985), and Hilary Knight (Simon & Schuster, 1990). Provide these for comparison, along with Robin McKinley's *Beauty: A Retelling of the Story of Beauty and the Beast* (Harper & Row, 1978), a rich novel that keeps readers of all ages interested despite their familiarity with the tale.

The moral of the play, "appearances are as thin and deceptive as shadows," doubles the power of the book when combined with the shadow play concept. Another excellent book featuring shadow plays is Elizabeth Cleaver's *The Enchanted Caribou* (Atheneum, 1985). Cleaver's book includes instructions for making these puppets and producing this kind of play. Enjoy that experience with your students.

171. Fleischman, Sid. **The Scarebird**. Pictures by Peter Sis (Greenwillow, 1987).

Farm Life; Friendship; Harmonicas; Instruments— Musical; Loneliness; Music; Read-Aloud; Scarecrows

Lonesome John is a farmer who communicates with no one but his scarecrow until an equally lonely young man drops by to offer his help and friendship.

 = Geography   = Art   = Music   = Drama   = Speech   Q = Research   = Read-Aloud

Both John and his new helper play the harmonica. Students can learn to play this relatively inexpensive instrument. Invite a harmonica player to demonstrate and teach the art.

 172. Fonteyn, Margot, retold by. **Swan Lake**. Ill. by Trina Schart Hyman (Gulliver Books, 1989).

Ballets—Classical; Fairy Tales; Good Versus Evil; Love; Music; Tchaikovsky, Peter Ilich (1840-1893)

The classic ballet story of a prince's love for a princess who is bewitched by an evil sorcerer and turned into a swan is retold by this world-famous ballerina. Information about the ballet, the productions, and the music follows the story. Note.

 This was the first ballet Tchaikovsky wrote. Listen to the music, or better yet, attend the ballet for "Swan Lake," "The Sleeping Beauty," or "The Nutcracker." Also introduce Rachel Isadora's adaptations of the ballets *Firebird* (G. P. Putnam's Sons, 1994) and *Swan Lake* (G. P. Putnam's Sons, 1991). Of further interest is Ester Kalman's *Tchaikovsky Discovers America* (Orchard, 1995), a fictional account of the composer's 1891 trip to America that is on a cassette/compact disc by Classical Productions for Children Unlimited.

 There are few picture books that feature classic performing arts. Along with Fonteyn's book, introduce students to Leontyne Price's retelling of the opera *Aïda* (Harcourt Brace Jovanovich, 1990); Mark Helprin's *Swan Lake* (Ariel Books/Houghton Mifflin, 1989), a literary retelling; and E. T. A. Hoffmann's *Nutcracker* (Crown, 1984), illustrated by Maurice Sendak and somewhat similar to the sets he designed for the Pacific Northwest Ballet's Christmas production. Geraldine McCaughrean's *Random House Book of Stories from the Ballet* (Random House, 1994) is also a good companion.

 173. Foreman, Michael. **War Boy: A Country Childhood** (Arcade, 1989).
174. Foreman, Michael. **War Game** (Arcade, 1994).

Autobiographies; Children and War; England; Friendship; Graphic Novels; History—World War I; History—World War II; Memoirs; Soldiers; War—Nature of; World War I; World War II;

In *War Boy*, Foreman recalls his boyhood during World War II, living on the Suffolk coast, the closest point to Germany. Foreman's companion book, *War Game*, written about World War I and in memory of his four uncles who died in that war, addresses the nature of war generally.

 Depending on the age of the students, the following books are fine companion titles to include. James Stevenson's autobiographical *Don't You Know There's a War Going On?* (Greenwillow Books, 1992) is especially appropriate for preteens, while the dynamic and disturbing graphic novel about the horror of war, *Enemy Ace: War Idyll* by George Pratt (Warner Books, 1990), will be of interest to more sophisticated teen readers.

These books are excellent for reading lists and book collections about World War I and II. They read like novels, transcend age barriers, and will intrigue reluctant readers.

Provide students with "Christmas in the Trenches" by John McCutcheon (Rounder Records, 1995), a story song about a game of soccer played during a temporary peace on a Christmas Eve in World War I.

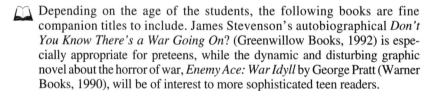

175. Forest, Heather. **The Woman Who Flummoxed the Fairies**. Ill. by Susan Gaber (Harcourt Brace Jovanovich, 1990).

Baking; Courage; Drama; Folktales—Scottish; Food; Scotland; Tricks

Based on a seanchie household tale from the Scottish Highlands, this rendition concerns a clever bakerwoman who must figure out a way to prevent the fairies from keeping her hostage to bake for them.

 Discuss this final quote from the book: "For fairies' gold, they say, is like love or knowledge—or a good story. It's most valuable when it's shared."

 Students can script and dramatize this fun tale and present it to younger elementary students or preschoolers.

 176. Fox, Mem. **Wilfrid Gordon McDonald Partridge**. Ill. by Julie Vivas (Kane/Miller, 1989).

Aging; Friendship; Intergenerational Relationships; Memorabilia; Memories; Nursing Homes; Old Age; Read-Aloud; Social Issues— Aging

Wilfrid (with his four names) lives next door to a nursing home where his favorite person is Miss Nancy, who also has four names. When Wilfrid hears she is losing her memory he begins collecting memories for her.

This heartwarming story appeals to listeners of all ages. Use it to introduce a study about intergenerational relationships. Consult the citations focusing on intergenerational relationships in *Book Links* 4(4), March 1995.

Other picture books that give an honest look at aging include: Cynthia Rylant's *Miss Maggie* (E. P. Dutton, 1983), Mary Bahr's *The Memory Box* (Whitman, 1992), Barbara Dugan's *Loop the Loop* (Greenwillow Books, 1992), Helen V. Griffith's *Georgia Music* (Greenwillow Books, 1986), Tony Johnston's *Grandpa's Song* (Dial Books for Young Readers, 1991), Eve Bunting's *Sunshine Home* (Clarion Books, 1994), and Norma Farber's *How Does It Feel to Be Old?* (Dutton Children' Books, 1988). Use these thought-provoking books to develop student awareness of old age and the special relationships that can develop among people of all ages.

177. Fraser, Mary Ann. **On Top of the World: The Conquest of Mount Everest** (Henry Holt, 1991).

Courage; Hillary, Sir Edmund (1914-); Mountain Climbing; Mountaineers; Mountains; Norgay, Tenzing (1914-); Records; Sports—Mountain Climbing; Survival

On May 29, 1953, Sir Edmund Hillary and Tenzing Norgay became the first men to climb the highest mountain in the world when they reached the summit of Mount Everest. Note. Glossary.

Budding mountain climbers or explorers will find this short account of Hillary and Norgay's adventure very exciting. Provide other books about Mount Everest such as *Beyond the Limits: A Woman's Triumph on Everest* by Stacy Allison (Little, Brown, 1993), *The Everest Years: A Climber's Life* by Chris Bonington (Viking, 1987), and *First on Everest: The Mystery of Mallory and Irvine* by Tom Holzel (Henry Holt, 1986).

Humankind seems driven to constantly break new ground and set new records. Use this book along with *The Guinness Book of Records* (Facts on File, 1995) and *The World Sports Record Atlas* by David Emery (Facts on File, 1986) to take a look at other famous feats.

178. Fraser, Mary Ann. **Sanctuary: The Story of Three Arch Rocks** (Henry Holt, 1994).

Art—Photography; Endangered Species; Environmentalists; History—Wildlife Conservation; Lobbying; Naturalists; Photography; Wildlife Conservation— History; Wildlife Refuges

Fraser recounts the difficulties encountered by two young naturalists who collected data on the marine birds and mammals off the coast of Oregon in 1903 and then lobbied President Theodore Roosevelt to establish a national refuge to protect that wildlife habitat. Maps. Environmental organizations list. Glossary.

This story can be used to launch, or supplement, a study on the history of environmental action. Historic references cited by the author can be used in conjunction with a study of the impact of other early environmentalists such as John Muir (founder of the Sierra Club), Theodore Roosevelt, and Gifford Pinchot (director of the U.S. Forest Service under Theodore Roosevelt).

Photography has always been a popular way to record the beauty and plight of the natural wonders of our country. Provide a collection of books featuring nature photography for your students to view. Invite a nature photographer to your class.

179. French, Fiona. **Snow White in New York** (Oxford University Press, 1986).

City Life; Drama; Fairy Tales—Modern Retelling; Good Versus Evil; Jazz; Mafia; New York Mafia

This modern Snow White lives in the skyscraper world of New York with a stepmother who is Queen of the Underworld and likes to see herself featured in the local paper, the *New York Mirror*.

Adolescents will be attracted to this sophisticated version of a classic fairy tale. Following the style of French's illustrations students can create costuming and staging for a dramatic production of this retelling. Other students might wish to rewrite and produce another folktale in French's style.

180. Frost, Robert. **Birches**. Ill. by Ed Young (Henry Holt, 1988).

Choices; Frost, Robert (1874-1963); Imagination; Observation; Poetry; Read-Aloud

This is an illustrated presentation of Frost's 1916 poem "Birches."

The combination of Frost's prose and Young's power of observation and imagination combine to create this noteworthy picture book. First read the poem in its entirety (found on the final two pages of the book) and then read it again, this time showing Young's paintings. Discuss the poem's power after each reading. Do students prefer to hear the poem with or without seeing the accompanying illustrations? Do the illustrations change the meaning of the poem for the students? Discuss individual preferences.

181. Frost, Robert. **Stopping by Woods on a Snowy Evening**. Ill. by Susan Jeffers (E. P. Dutton, 1978).

Frost, Robert (1874-1963); New England; Poetry; Read-Aloud; Winter

The wintry magic of New England is felt through this picture book presentation of one of Frost's most famous poems.

This book is a perfect introduction to poetry for children and adults. Feel free to use it with multigenerational groups.

Collect other books of individually illustrated poems to study the impact of the illustrations. Be sure to read and discuss the poems first without showing the illustrations. Then read them showing the pictures. Consider using William Blake's *The Tyger* (Harcourt Brace Jovanovich, 1993), Maya Angelou's *Life Doesn't Frighten Me* (Stewart, Tabori & Chang, 1993), and others listed in the subject index of this book.

G

182. Galdone, Joanna. **The Tailypo: A Ghost Story**. Ill. by Paul Galdone (Seabury Press, 1977).

Fear; Folktales—United States; Scary Stories; Storytelling; Urban Legends

A woodsman cuts off the tail of a strange creature and never rests again.

Students love to be scared, and this classic tale serves that purpose. Compare and contrast it with other versions of the tailypo such as "The Peculiar Such Thing" in Virginia Hamilton's *The People Could Fly: American Black Folktales* (Alfred A. Knopf, 1985) or Jan Wahl's *Tailypo!* (Henry Holt, 1991).

The spread of scary urban legends is an integral part of American culture. Provide titles such as Jan Harold Brunvand's *The Choking Doberman and Other "New" Urban Legends* (W. W. Norton, 1984), *Curses, Broiled Again: The Hottest Urban Legends Going* (W. W. Norton, 1980), and *The Mexican Pet: More "New" Urban Legends and Some Old Favorites* (W. W. Norton, 1986) for students to read and share. Paul Dickson and Joseph C. Goulden's *There Are Alligators in Our Sewers and Other American Credos* (Delacorte Press, 1983) is another good title. Many of the tales will be familiar and can be used for student storytelling contests.

183. Gallico, Paul. **The Snow Goose**. Ill. by Beth Peck (Alfred A. Knopf, 1992).

Artists; Birds; Death; Disabilities—Hunchbacked; Friendship; Geese; Heroism; Read-Aloud; Science— Wildlife; World War II

The developing friendship between the lonely hunchbacked painter and a village girl is seen against the backdrop of World War II as the two care for an injured snow goose.

The hunchback, Rhayader, created a marshland bird sanctuary at his home on the Essex coast. Interested students can learn about migration flyways and scientific efforts to help birds alter these age-old routes when urban development threatens them. Use both current books and periodical articles.

184. Gantschev, Ivan. **Two Islands** (Picture Book Studio USA, 1985).

Cautionary Tales; Conflict; Conservation; Ecology; Environment; Greed; Industrialism

Two islands develop differently; Graynel becomes an industrial mess while Greenel remains peaceful and simple. Trouble erupts when the Boss of Graynel wants to build a bridge to Greenel so his citizens can enjoy the countryside.

Political and environmental cautionary tales warn of impending disaster if humankind does not mend its ways. Provide students with similar picture book cautionary tales such as Brian Wildsmith's *Professor Noah's Spaceship* (Oxford University Press, 1980), Raymond Briggs' *When the Wind Blows: The Story of the Bloggs and the Bomb* (Schocken Books, 1982), and *The Tin-Pot Foreign General and the Old Iron Woman* (Little, Brown, 1984), as well as Graham Oakley's *Henry's Quest* (Atheneum, 1986).

185. Garfield, Leon. **The Wedding Ghost**. Ill. by Charles Keeping (Oxford University Press, 1985, 1992).

Art—Styles; Ghosts; Horror Stories; Love; Maps; Romance; Secrets; Sleeping Beauty; Weddings

Jack receives a strange map as a wedding present and is compelled to see where it leads. He discovers Sleeping Beauty and knows he must awaken her.

This classic ghost story will appeal to readers who devour books by R. L. Stine and Christopher Pike. Students can note how the evocative illustrations enhance the spine-tingling tale. Budding illustrators can select a classic scary tale, such as those by Edgar Allan Poe, and draw accompanying art in Keeping's style.

 = Geography   = Art   = Music   = Drama   = Speech   Q = Research   = Read-Aloud

186. Garfield, Leon and Michael Bragg. **King Nimrod's Tower** (Lothrop, Lee & Shepard, 1982).

Babylon; Bible Stories; Construction; God; Languages—Origins and Changes; Nimrod; Parody; Tower of Babel; Vanity

The greedy and vain King Nimrod will stop at nothing to own a tower "as high as heaven," which will put him on the same level as God. But God causes each workman to speak a different language, which creates such confusion that the tower is never completed.

 Students can study the origins of various languages, noting similarities and differences. In 1994, the French proposed a law to prevent widespread use of English words by French citizens and attempted to levy fines against those who persisted in using American or English words or phrases. What was the outcome of this action? What French words are part of our English language? Consult Kay Cooper's *Why Do You Speak as You Do? A Guide to World Languages* (Children's Press, 1992).

 This is a parody of the Bible story about the Tower of Babel from the book of Genesis. The authors use the characters of a boy and his dog to attract God's interest. He mixes languages instead of destroying the tower in order to avoid harming the boy and his pet. Students can read the biblical version of the story and compare. Look at other picture version of Bible stories such as the Warwick Hutton retellings.

 187. Garland, Sherry. **I Never Knew Your Name**. Ill. by Sheldon Greenberg (Ticknor & Fields, 1994).

Friendship; Loneliness; Social Issues—Teen Suicide; Suicide—Teens; Suicide Prevention; Teen Suicide

A boy laments the fact that he didn't reach out to a lonely teenager he had admired and watched from a distance. Now it's too late; the lonely boy has committed suicide.

 This poignant and somber book is ideal for adults to use in initiating discussions on teen suicide and the sense of isolation felt by many adolescents. What are the statistics for teen suicide in your state or city? What services are available for prevention? Hot lines? Crisis prevention centers? Emergency counseling? Self-help groups? Provide books, pamphlets, videos, and other materials that give information about this issue. Helpful books include *Silent Grief: Living in the Wake of Suicide* by Christopher Lukas and Henry M. Seiden (Macmillan, 1988), *The Power to Prevent Suicide: A Guide for Teens Helping Teens* by Richard E. Nelson and Judith C. Galas (Free Spirit, 1994), *Coping with Suicide: A Resource Book for Teenagers and Young Adults* by Judie Smith (Rosen, 1986), *Teenage Wasteland: Suburbia's Dead End Kids* by Donna Gaines (Pantheon Books, 1991), *After Suicide: Young People Speak Up* by Susan Kuklin (Putnam, 1994), *When a Friend Dies: A Book for Teens About Grieving* by Marilyn E. Gootman (Free Spirit, 1994), and *Suicide* by Margaret O. Hyde and Elizabeth Held Forsyth (Franklin Watts, 1991).

 188. Garland, Sherry. **The Lotus Seed**. Ill. by Tatsuro Kiuchi (Harcourt Brace Jovavovich, 1993).

Boat People; Children and War; Civil War; Cultural Heritage; Families; History—Vietnam; Refugees; Vietnam History (1945-Late 1970s); Vietnam War

This deceptively simple story tells of a Vietnamese family's flight from their homeland to escape the civil war. The lotus seed serves as a tangible example of how a family's heritage is passed down through the generations.

 Garland's interest in Vietnam comes from her association with Vietnamese refugee families. If possible, invite some resettled Laotian, Hmong, or Vietnamese individuals or families in your area to your class to share their resettlement and refugee experiences.

Related books include *Bôàt People*, a novel for young adults, by Mary Gardner (Norton, 1995), *The Whispering Cloth: A Refugee's Story about the Hmong* by Pegi Deitz Shea (Boyds Mills Press, 1995), and Brent Ashabranner and Melissa Ashabranner's *Into a Strange Land* (Dodd, Mead, 1987).

 This book introduces students to a historical period in Vietnam beginning with the last emperor, Bao Dai, who abdicated his throne in 1945, to the late 1960s, when the United States became heavily involved in its civil war. Use this book to launch a more in-depth study of this time period.

 189. Gauch, Patricia Lee. **Thunder at Gettysburg**. Ill. by Stephen Gammell (G. P. Putnam's Sons, 1975).

Battle of Gettysburg; Bravery; Civil War (1861-1865); Gettysburg— Battle; Historical Fiction; History—United States— Civil War (1861-1865); Read-Aloud; Tragedy; United States—History— Civil War; War

Based on a book by Tillie Pierce Alleman, Gauch tells of 14-year-old Alleman's involvement in the Battle of Gettysburg.

 Use this book, with its haunting illustrations, along with Gary Wills' *Lincoln at Gettysburg* (Simon & Schuster, 1992), Neil Johnson's *The Battle of Gettysburg* (Four Winds Press, 1990), Mackinley Kantor's *Gettysburg* (Random House, 1987), Susan Provost Beller's *To Hold This Ground: A Desperate Battle at Gettysburg* (Margaret K. McElderry, 1995), Jim Murphy's *The Long Road to Gettysburg* (Clarion Books, 1992), and Michael McCurdy's illustrated version of *The Gettysburg Address* by Abraham Lincoln (Houghton Mifflin, 1995).

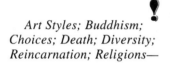 **190.** Gerstein, Mordicai. **The Mountains of Tibet** (Harper & Row, 1987).

Art Styles; Buddhism; Choices; Death; Diversity; Reincarnation; Religions— Buddhism; Styles—Art; Tibet

After his death, a Tibetan woodcutter chooses reincarnation over heaven and is faced with the difficult choice of what life to live.

Mordicai Gerstein has no one style of art that is easily identifiable. For comparison purposes, look at the watercolors in *The Seal Mother* (Dial Books for Young Readers, 1986), the cartoon style of *Arnold of the Ducks* (Harper & Row, 1983), and the opaque gouaches in *The Mountains of Tibet*. Students might be interested in finding out more about Gerstein's art background and career, which includes working in animation.

Gerstein was inspired to write this book after reading *The Tibetan Book of the Dead*. Students can learn more about Tibet, Buddhism, and reincarnation through research.

191. Giblin, James Cross. **George Washington: A Picture Book Biography**. Ill. by Michael Dooling (Scholastic, 1992).

 192. Giblin, James Cross. **Thomas Jefferson: A Picture Book Biography**. Ill. by Michael Dooling (Scholastic, 1994).

Biographies; Declaration of Independence; Jefferson, Thomas (1743-1826); History—United States; Monticello; Monuments— National; Presidents; Slavery; Washington, George (1732-1799)

Full-color oil paintings plus text relate the details of George Washington and Thomas Jefferson's lives. Chronology. Notes. Index.

 Notes about the numerous monuments throughout our country in honor of Washington can help focus attention on national monuments.

 An extensive note entitled "A Visit to Monticello" gives details about Jefferson's famous home. Students who want to know more can write to the Virginia Division of Tourism, 1021 E. Cary Street, Richmond, VA 23219 for a free brochure. For a newsletter on historic plants grown at Monticello and how to buy seeds for some 50 varieties, write to The Center for Historic Plants, Dept. P, Monticello, P.O. Box 316, Charlottesville, VA 22902.

These beautiful biographies present a clear and easy-to-understand picture of Washington and Jefferson, two of our country's most influential leaders. Use these books as a springboard to further study these presidents and their impact on life in the United States today. Milton Meltzer's *Thomas Jefferson: The Revolutionary Aristocrat* (Viking, 1991) will be of particular interest.

193. Giono, Jean. **The Man Who Planted Trees**. Wood engravings by Michael McCurdy (Chelsea Green, 1985).

Conservation; Earth Day; Environmental Action—Forestation; Forestry; Love; Nature; Trees; Woodcuts

McCurdy's woodcuts enhance this story of a Frenchman, Elzéard Bouffier, who planted 100 acorns every day in an attempt to reforest a desolated area of Provence, in the south of France. Afterword.

Global ReLeaf, an American Forestry Association program, and this book's publisher are working on a joint project to get individuals to plant millions of trees to help enrich the earth for all of humankind. Students can learn how to get involved, as individuals or as a group, by contacting these organizations or others with a similar purpose.

Both *The Man Who Planted Trees* (Direct Cinema, 1990) and *The Lorax* by Dr. Seuss (Random House, 1971), a cautionary tale about deforestation and pollution, are available on video. Provide these for student viewing and discussion.

Compare and contrast the story of Elzéard Bouffier with versions of *Johnny Appleseed* by authors such as Reeve Lindbergh (Little, Brown, 1990) and Steven Kellogg (William Morrow Junior Books, 1988) or Aliki's *The Story of Johnny Appleseed* (Prentice-Hall, 1987).

194. Goble, Paul. **Adopted by Eagles** (Bradbury Press, 1994).

195. Goble, Paul. **Buffalo Woman** (Bradbury Press, 1984).

196. Goble, Paul. **Crow Chief** (Bradbury Press, 1992).

197. Goble, Paul. **Dream Wolf** (Bradbury Press, 1990).

198. Goble, Paul. **The Gift of the Sacred Dog** (Bradbury Press, 1980).

199. Goble, Paul. **The Girl Who Loved Wild Horses** (Bradbury Press, 1978).

200. Goble, Paul. **The Great Race of the Birds and Animals** (Bradbury Press, 1985).

201. Goble, Paul. **Love Flute** (Bradbury Press, 1992).

Buffaloes; Creation; Endangered Animals; Horses; Indians of North America; Legends—Plains Indians; Love; Music; Plains Indians; Pourquoi Tales; Wolves

These Plains Indian legends focus on the idea of humans living in harmony with nature and emphasize the kinship between man and animal. Included in these stories are tales of a buffalo that turns into a beautiful girl, a wolf that guides two children home, a girl who lives with wild horses, and a young man who learns how to tell a girl of his love. Readers also discover why crows have black feathers, how Indians came to have horses, and why humans became the "Guardians of Creation" in three pourquoi tales—"why" tales that answer a question or explain such things as human and animal characteristics. The 1979 Caldecott Medal was awarded to Goble for *The Girl Who Loved Wild Horses*.

For an audio experience to accompany Goble's *Love Flute,* provide traditional Lakota flute music such as that found on cassette tapes recorded by Kevin Locke.

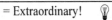 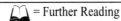

Though these legends promote the idea of humans living in harmony with nature, none of the animals (except the crow) featured in these legends have fared well since the end of the 19th century. Students can study the plight of the buffaloes, wolves, and wild horses since that time.

202. Goble, Paul. **Death of the Iron Horse** (Bradbury Press, 1987).

In 1867 a band of young Cheyenne braves derailed and raided a freight train. This act of defiance and bravery was a chance for them to act out against the encroachment of the White man.

Cheyenne Indians; Courage; Creative Writing; Ecology; Environmental Action; Indians of North America—History—1867; Personification; Railroads—History; Trains

Compare the last picture in the book, featuring the litter, with the ones before the derailment. What has happened to the land? Do students see a similar disrespect for the environment in your geographic area? If so, what can students do to create change? Use *The Kids Guide to Social Action: How to Solve the Social Problems You Choose—and Turn Creative Thinking into Positive Action* by Barbara A. Lewis (Free Spirit, 1991) as a source of ideas.

The train seems alive to the Cheyenne braves. They ascribe living traits to it—hisses, pants, and screams. They shoot arrows at it and attempt to lasso it. This is a great example of the literary device personification—assigning human qualities, actions, or characteristics to an animal, object, idea, or natural force. Students can write their own stories using this or other literary devices.

Study the geography of the United States, noting its effect on the placement of the tracks and the development of cities as the intercontinental railway system grew. Students can do an in-depth study of rail development by using references such as *The Iron Dragon Never Sleeps* by Stephen Krensky (Delacorte Press, 1994) and John Hoyt Williams' *A Great & Shining Road: The Epic Story of the Transcontinental Railroad* (Times Books, 1988).

203. Goble, Paul. **Her Seven Brothers** (Bradbury Press, 1988).

204. Goble, Paul. **The Lost Children: The Boys Who Were Neglected** (Bradbury Press, 1993).

205. Goble, Paul. **Star Boy** (Bradbury Press, 1983).

These three legends from tribes of the Great Plains explain the origins of some stars—a girl and her brothers become the Big Dipper, six neglected orphaned brothers choose to become the Pleiades (the Bunched Stars or the "Lost Children")—and the sacred meaning of the Sun Dance is explained. Notes.

Astronomy; Blackfeet Indians—Legends; Cheyenne Indians—Legends; Child Neglect; Designs—Art; Indians of North America; Legends—Indians of North America; Science—Astronomy; Stars—Folklore

Have students share these and other legends about the stars with others. Books of similar interest include *The Heavenly Zoo: Legends and Tales of the Stars* by Alison Lurie and Monika Beisner (Farrar, Straus & Giroux, 1979) and *They Dance in the Sky: Native American Star Myths* by Jean Guard Monroe and Ray A. Williamson (Houghton Mifflin, 1987). Goble expands on each legend in the Note section.

Provide Goble's books to students who are studying the stars. Find Pleiades, the Big Dipper, and the Evening Star or Morning Star during a stargazing celebration with an astronomer. Among astronomy books, consider using *3-D Galaxy: See the Hidden Pictures in the Stars* (William Morrow, 1994). It makes the constellations such as Orion, Ursa Major, Pisces, and the stars of a seasonal night sky look like they are literally floating in front of the viewer's eyes.

 = Geography   = Art   = Music   = Drama   = Speech   = Research   = Read-Aloud

The illustrations in these books represent designs from the Cheyenne and Lakota tribes. The Note section has more detail about the designs on the clothes and tipi art. Students can look at other books by Goble to see additional designs. Use books such as Andrew Hunter Whiteford's *North American Indian Arts* (Western, 1990) to further teach students about Indian art.

206. Goble, Paul. **Iktomi and the Berries** (Orchard, 1989).

207. Goble, Paul. **Iktomi and the Boulder: A Plains Indian Story** (Orchard, 1988).

208. Goble, Paul. **Iktomi and the Buffalo Skull** (Orchard, 1991).

209. Goble, Paul. **Iktomi and the Ducks** (Orchard, 1990).

Humor; Indians of North America; Legends; Plains Indians; Reader's Theater; Read-Aloud; Sioux; Storytelling; Trickster Tales

This series of trickster tales features the charming, curious Iktomi, who attempts to trick others but and always ends up fooling himself. Each book includes notes about the references Goble used, information about Iktomi, and read-aloud information.

 Chart the characteristics of a variety of tricksters in folklore. Characters might include these from North American Indian stories: "Spider" from the Cheyenne, "Coyote" from the Crow, and "Iktomi" from the Sioux; "Anansi the Spider" from Africa; and "Brer Rabbit" from African American traditional literature.

The use of three types of printed text on each page results in books that can be shared several ways:

1. Various illustrated items are identified and Iktomi's thoughts are revealed in the small type. These comments are not meant to be read aloud as part of the story but can be mentioned when showing the pictures.

2. The passages in gray italics are asides intended to encourage audience participation.

3. The larger black type is the storyline.

These visual guides make these books ideal for students to practice reading interactive stories aloud or for reader's theater productions. The format of the books make sharing possibilities limitless.

210. Goffstein, M. B. **An Actor** (Harper & Row, 1987).

211. Goffstein, M. B. **An Artist** (Harper & Row, 1980).

212. Goffstein, M. B. **School of Names** (Harper & Row, 1986).

213. Goffstein, M. B. **A Writer** (Harper & Row, 1984).

Actors; Analogy; Artists; Authors; Literary Devices; Metaphor; Nature; Painting; Plays; Writing

Goffstein's deceptively simple books are remarkably sophisticated, all illustrated and written in a minimalist style. In *School of Names* she describes the interconnectedness among places and species all over the world. In *A Writer*, Goffstein explains succinctly what writing entails. *An Actor* and *An Artist* describe the emotion and creativity of those careers.

 Goffstein is a master at using metaphors, analogies, and concise language. Students can follow her example and refine their writing skills.

214. Gogol, Nikolai. **The Nose**. Ill. by Gennady Spirin (Godine, 1993).

Bureaucrats;
Gogol, Nikolai (1809-1852);
Noses; Read-Aloud;
Russia—19th Century;
Russian Literature; Satire;
Short Stories; Surrealism

While breakfasting, a barber discovers the nose of a civil servant in his wife's bread. The nose, assuming a life as an officer, is finally reunited with its frustrated owner.

The Nose is an excellent title to include in a literature study of satire or as an example to help students write their own satirical stories.

Include this book, with its detailed and informative illustrations, in a study of either Russian literature or the short story. Other examples of Russian literature in picture book format include Gogol's *Sorotchintzy Fair* (Godine, 1991), also illustrated by Gennady Spirin, and Samuel Marshak's absurd poem about bureaucracy, *The Pup Grew Up!* (Henry Holt, 1989), first published in 1926.

215. Goldin, Barbara Diamond. **The Passover Journey: A Seder Companion**. Ill. by Neil Waldman (Viking, 1994).

Bible Stories;
Celebrations; Holidays;
Jews—History; Judaism;
Moses; Passover; Religions—
Judaism; Seder

Goldin retells the story of the Israelite's fight for liberation from slavery in Egypt and explains the traditions of the Passover Seder. Glossary.

This book describes 14 steps of Seder in detail. In the spirit of multiculturalism, invite a rabbi or Jewish community member to demonstrate and explain this important Jewish celebration. Another picture book focusing on Jewish tradition is *The Always Prayer Shawl* by Sheldon Oberman (Boyds Mills Press, 1994).

216. Golenbock, Peter. **Teammates**. Ill. by Paul Bacon (Gulliver Books/ Harcourt Brace Jovanovich, 1990).

African Americans;
Baseball—Major League;
Baseball—Negro League;
Biographies; Reese, Pee Wee
(1919-); Prejudice—Racial;
Robinson, Jackie (1919-1972);
Racial Prejudice; Sports—
Baseball

Using watercolors and depictions of an assortment of baseball memorabilia, *Teammates* tells about the racial prejudice Jackie Robinson experienced when he became the first Black Major League baseball player and the support he received from his White teammate Pee Wee Reese.

Dan Gutman presents 14 suggestions for getting students excited about school subjects through baseball in "Reading, Writing, and Baseball" [*Book Links* 4(5):48, May 1995].

Students interested in learning more about the Negro Leagues should consult books such as *Leagues Apart: The Men and Times of the Negro Baseball Leagues* by Lawrence S. Ritter (Morrow Junior Books, 1995), *The Forgotten Players: The Story of Black Baseball in America* by Robert Gardner and Dennis Shortelle (Walker, 1993), *Professional Baseball Franchises: From the Abbeville Athletics to the Zanesville Indians* by Peter Filichia (Facts on File, 1993), and *Baseball: An Illustrated History* by Geoffrey C. Ward and Ken Burns (Alfred A. Knopf, 1994).

217. Goodall, John S. **An Edwardian Christmas** (Atheneum, 1978).
218. Goodall, John S. **Edwardian Entertainments** (Atheneum, 1982).
219. Goodall, John S. **An Edwardian Holiday** (Atheneum, 1979).
220. Goodall, John S. **An Edwardian Season** (Atheneum, 1980).

*Edwardian Period
(1901-1910); England;
History—England—
1901-1910; Social Life
and Customs—England—
1901-1910; Wordless Books*

221. Goodall, John S. **An Edwardian Summer** (Atheneum, 1976).

The social history of the brief Edwardian era (1901-1910) in England is authentically chronicled in this series of wordless books. The books include detailed watercolor portraits of some of the main performers of the era and the joys and delights of holidays and seasons.

Include this series of books in a world history class on European life just prior to World War I. Why was the Edwardian era (1901-1910) such a peaceful time in England?

Go beyond the pictures of the upper class shown in these books. Have students research what life was like for the working class and the lower class.

222. Goodall, John S. **The Story of a Castle** (Atheneum, 1986).
223. Goodall, John S. **The Story of a Farm** (Atheneum, 1989).
224. Goodall, John S. **The Story of a Main Street** (Atheneum, 1987).
225. Goodall, John S. **The Story of an English Village** (Atheneum, 1978).
226. Goodall, John S. **The Story of the Seashore** (Margaret K. McElderry, 1990).

*Architecture; Beaches;
Book Design; Clothing;
England; Historical
Fiction; Seashore—
England; Social Life and
Customs—England;
Wordless Books*

The evolution and transformation of an English seashore, village, main street, farm, and castle is traced from medieval times to the present through detailed impressionistic watercolors. Changes in the land, architecture, artifacts, clothing, and customs are featured.

The Story of an English Village and *The Story of a Main Street* are good companion books to use with *New Providence: A Changing Cityscape* by Renata Von Tscharner and Ronald Lee Fleming (Harcourt Brace Jovanovich, 1987). Meanwhile, *The Story of a Castle* can be used with *Stephen Biesty's Incredible Cross-Sections* (Alfred A. Knopf, 1992) and David Macaulay's *Castle* (Houghton Mifflin, 1977).

Sections of these books can be used as support for other projects. For example, the section on World War II (pages 44-47) in *The Story of the Seashore* ties in perfectly with Michael Foreman's *War Boy: A Country Childhood* (Arcade, 1989) to set the scene for the action in this memoir.

Goodall incorporates the use of alternating full and half pages in these books. Turning the half page changes the action while the background remains the same. Bring samples of "lift-the-flap" and "pop-up" books, along with these books, to class for students to investigate the different book designs and their effects. Following a discussion of the designs, students could produce samples of their own.

227. Graham, Alastair. **Full Moon Soup; Or, the Fall of the Hotel Splendide** (Dial Books for Young Readers, 1991).

*Drama; Hotels; Humor;
Monsters; Nonlinear
Narratives; Soup;
Wordless Books*

When the chef takes his first sip of soup under the full moon, strange and unusual things happen simultaneously in the many rooms and surrounding areas of the hotel.

David Macaulay's *Black and White* (Houghton Mifflin, 1990) and *Shortcut* (Houghton Mifflin, 1995) are very similar to *Full Moon Soup* with their nonlinear narratives. All three books will appeal to sophisticated students who appreciate unusual art and story.

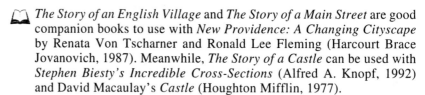

Using the idea of cross sections of a building with actions occurring simultaneously within them, students can produce a play with stop-and-go scenarios moving randomly. The finale doesn't have to pull everything together, though it might. *Noises Off* by Michael Frayn is a popular play (S. French, 1982) and subsequent film (Touchstone Home Video, 1992) with a similar format. Provide the video or read through the play so students get an idea of the simultaneous happenings occurring backstage and in front of the audience.

228. Gray, Libba Moore. **Dear Willie Rudd**. Ill. by Peter M. Fiore (Simon & Schuster, 1993).

African Americans; History—Race Relations; Letters; Memories; Prejudice; Race Relations— History; Racism

Recalling her childhood of 50 years ago, a White woman remembers how badly her family treated their Black housekeeper, Willie Rudd. To belatedly thank Willie and to apologize for her racist actions, the woman writes Willie a letter and sends it heavenward attached to a kite.

 A novel dealing with the theme of racial interaction during the Civil War is *Steal Away* by Jennifer Armstrong (Orchard, 1992).

 This bittersweet story is most appropriate for use with students studying race relations in the United States from the days of slavery to the present. After learning about our history of racism, solicit student suggestions for ways in which racism might be ameliorated. What are their reactions to this story?

229. Greene, Ellin. **The Legend of the Cranberry: A Paleo-Indian Tale**. Ill. by Brad Sneed (Simon & Schuster, 1993).

Delaware Indians; Extinct Animals; Folktales; Food—Legends; Indians of North America; Legends; Prehistoric Animals; Science— Extinct Species

This retelling of a Delaware Indian legend relates the story of the Great Spirit who gave the People the cranberry to remind them of their great battle with the mastodons and woolly mammoths.

 Scientific discoveries about extinct animals continue to be publicized. Students can select an extinct animal for further research.

 The Paleo-Indians were those who journeyed from Asia across a land bridge over the Bering Strait to the Atlantic seaboard. They were probably the first people in America and the prehistoric ancestors of Native Americans. Students can research this time period to discover more about what is known of these people, their customs, and their habitat.

 230. Greenfield, Eloise. **Nathaniel Talking**. Ill. by Jan Spivey Gilchrist (Black Butterfly Children's Books, 1988).

African American Poetry; Children—Poetry; Music—Rap; Poetry; Rap Poetry

Nine-year-old Nathaniel thinks about his world and his place in it—his family, his day-to-day experiences, and his future. Note.

Nathaniel's "voice" will appeal to any student of poetry. Using this book as a guide, have the students write their own poems about their daily lives. Also, refer to Greenfield's note, which explains how to create a 12-bar blues poem. For a similar book of African American poetry told through a child's point of view, consult *Brown Honey in Broomwheat Tea* by Joyce Carol Thomas (HarperCollins, 1992).

Rap music has "rhythmic rhyming lines set to an insistent beat." Greenfield was the first to use the rap rhyme scheme and verse form in children's literature. "Nathaniel's Rap" is the only rap poem in this collection. However, five poems with a rap beat are found in Greenfield's *Night on Neighborhood Street* (Dial Books for Young Readers, 1991): "Little Boy Blues," "Fambly Time," "When Tonya's Friends Come to Spend the Night," "Buddy's Dream," and "Lawanda's Walk."

 = Geography   = Art   = Music   = Drama   = Speech   = Research   = Read-Aloud

David Vozar adapted three familiar stories ("The Three Little Pigs," "Little Red Riding Hood," and "The Boy Who Cried Wolf") with a rap beat and a clever twist to the story in his picture book *Yo, Hungry Wolf! A Nursery Rap* (Delacorte Press, 1993). These poems and stories are full of energy for kids and are great fun to perform with or without music.

231. Gregory, Valiska. **Through the Mickle Woods**. Ill. by Barry Moser (Little, Brown, 1992).

Death; Fairy Tales; Grief; Hope; Kings; Love; Mourning; Parables

Following his dead wife's wishes, a grieving king, accompanied by a young boy, travels to a bear's cave in the mickle woods. There he hears three tales that help him go on living.

The parables told to the king by the bear prompt the king to begin to work through the stages of grieving. Read and discuss the parables, looking for further interpretation. Use this book as a springboard for a discussion of death and the grieving process.

232. Griffith, Helen V. **Plunk's Dream** (Greenwillow, 1990).

Creative Writing; Dogs; Families; Writing

A family imagines what their dog is dreaming about—chasing rabbits, scaring aliens away, running for dinner, etc.

Plunk's Dream and Susan Meddaugh's whimsical talking dog story, *Martha Speaks* (Houghton Mifflin, 1992), are great companion books for this creative writing assignment: Using photographs and illustrations have students write about the conversation other animals (or even inanimate objects) are having.

233. Grossman, Bill. **The Guy Who Was Five Minutes Late**. Ill. by Judy Glasser (Harper & Row, 1990).

Fairy Tales—Modern; Humor; Read-Aloud; Tardiness; Time

Born five minutes late and never able to catch up, the hero misses trains, planes, and even his own wedding. That is, until he meets Princess Carrie!

This modern fairy tale is for anyone, especially adolescents and adults who are perpetually late. Read it to "audiences" in college classes, faculty meetings, business meetings, etc.

234. Gwynne, Fred. **A Chocolate Moose for Dinner** (Prentice-Hall, 1976).
235. Gwynne, Fred. **The King Who Rained** (Prentice-Hall, 1970).
236. Gwynne, Fred. **A Little Pigeon Toad** (Simon & Schuster, 1988).
237. Gwynne, Fred. **The Sixteen Hand Horse** (Prentice-Hall, 1980).

Creative Writing; English Language; Figures of Speech; Homonyms; Humor; Idioms; Parts of Speech; Terms and Phrases

These are Gwynne's humorously illustrated collections of homonyms and figures of speech as visualized by a girl listening to her parents speak.

These books are not only excellent to use as examples of parts of speech but also can provide models for students who wish to select other homonyms and illustrate them accordingly.

238. Gwynne, Fred. **Easy to See Why** (Simon & Schuster, 1993).

Animals; Art Shows; Competitions; Dogs; Humor; Pets; Photography; Portraits; Stories in Rhyme

A young girl and her dog have high hopes of winning the dog show. She meets other competitors and surprisingly enough the pets all bear a remarkable resemblance to their owners. But her pet looks exactly like the judge. It's "easy to see why" her dog is the winner!

Students can draw or paint a gallery of portraits featuring pets and their owners in the style of Gwynne. If there are resemblances, so much the better. Other students may choose to photograph pets and their owners.

! = Extraordinary!   💡 = Idea   📖 = Further Reading   ✍ = Writing   2/4 = Math   ⚛ = Science   📖 = History

H

 239. Hall, Donald. **The Farm Summer 1942**. Pictures by Barry Moser (Dial Books for Young Readers, 1994).

A boy spends the summer of 1942 on his grandparents' New Hampshire farm while his father serves on a destroyer in the Pacific and his mother works on a secret project.

Farm Life; Grandparents; Historical Fiction; History—United States—World War II; Read-Aloud; Social Life and Customs—United States—1942; United States—History—World War II

Several companion books that help paint a picture of what life was like in the United States during World War II include James Stevenson's autobiographical *Don't You Know There's a War Going On?* (Greenwillow Books, 1992), Deborah Kogan Ray's *My Daddy Was a Soldier: A World War II Story* (Holiday House, 1990), *This Fabulous Century 1940-1950* by the editors of Time-Life Books (Time-Life, 1969), Sylvia Whitman's *V Is for Victory: The American Home Front During World War II* (Lerner, 1993), *Rosie the Riveter: Women Working on the Home Front in World War II* by Penny Colman (Crown, 1995), and Kathleen Krull's *V Is for Victory: America Remembers World War II* (Alfred A. Knopf, 1995).

240. Hall, Donald. **Ox-Cart Man**. Ill. by Barbara Cooney (Viking, 1979).

Life on this 19th-century New England farm centers on the dependence of people on the land, hard work, and the goods produced. Caldecott Medal, 1980.

Art—Primitive; Farm Life—19th Century; Historical Fiction; History—United States—19th Century; New England—19th Century; Primitive Art; Social Life and Customs—United States—19th Century

Tony Johnston's *Yonder* (Dial Books for Young Readers, 1988) and Geoffrey Patterson's *Chestnut Farm 1860* (Andre Deutsch, 1980) are good companion books, focusing on family and the seasonal cycle of farm life prior to the Industrial Revolution, while Patricia MacLachland's *All the Places to Love* (HarperCollins, 1994) is a more modern celebration of the American family farm. Thomas Locker's *Family Farm* (Dial Books for Young Readers, 1988) presents a more somber portrait of the struggling family farm.

Barbara Cooney used a "primitive art" style in several books, including the *Ox-Cart Man*. Primitive art is the term used to describe the style of early American painters such as *The Peaceable Kingdom* artist Edward Hicks (1780-1849) and later Grandma Moses (1860-1961). Students can learn more about primitive art through research and by visiting an art museum.

241. Hamanaka, Sheila. **The Journey: Japanese Americans, Racism, and Renewal** (Orchard, 1990).

In this book, featuring portions of her mural, which melds the artist's family history with the 20th-century Japanese American experience, Hamanaka focuses on the injustices endured by Japanese Americans during World War II when United States government policy became blatantly racist. Index.

Art—Murals; Autobiographies; Children and War; Internment Camps; Japanese Americans; Murals; Prejudice; Racism; World War II

Hamanaka mentions the issue of redress for the injustice suffered by those interned. Have students do research to answer this question: What has the United States government done since the publication of this book?

This story can serve as an introduction to the U.S. policy of interning Japanese Americans during World War II. Hamanaka's goal is to "open the past, hoping to help chase away the demons of prejudice and injustice." For additional information and reading, provide students with Jerry Stanley's *I Am an American: A True Story of Japanese Internment* (Crown, 1994), Ken Mochizuki's *Baseball Saved Us* (Lee & Low Books, 1993) and *Heroes* (Lee & Low Books, 1995), Ellen Levine's *A Fence away from Freedom: Japanese Americans and World*

War II (G. P. Putnam's Sons, 1995), and photographer Ansel Adams' sobering chronicle of the relocation camp at Manzanar, California— *Manzanar* by John Armor and Peter Wright with commentary by John Hersey (Times Books, 1988).

242. Hammond, Anna and Joe Matunis. **This Home We Have Made, Esta Casa Que Hemos Hecho** (Crown, 1993).

Art—Murals; Bilingual Books; Homeless; Languages— Spanish; Murals; New York; Social Issues—Homeless

A homeless child joins a magical nighttime parade in hopes of finding a home of her own in this bilingual story. A foldout reproduction of the mural that inspired this story is included.

An interesting companion book for discussion purposes is *We Are All in the Dumps with Jack and Guy: Two Nursery Rhymes with Pictures* by Maurice Sendak (HarperCollins, 1993).

A mural, designed and painted by former homeless children in the Bronx (New York City), inspired this story. The book also includes information about the mural and its history. Use this as a beginning point for learning about the increasing popularity of wall art in communities trying to reclaim their streets. Consult *Wall Art: Megamurals & Supergraphics* by Stefan Merken (Running Press, 1987), *SoHo Walls: Beyond Graffiti* by David Robinson (Thames and Hudson, 1990), and articles found in the *Readers' Guide to Periodical Literature,* including "On Streets of New York, Grief Makes Room for Art" (*USA Today,* January 3, 1995, page 2A).

243. Handel, George Frideric. **Messiah: The Wordbook for the Oratorio**. Ill. by Barry Moser (Willa Perlman Books/HarperCollins, 1992).

Baroque Music; Bible; Biographies; Choral Groups; Classical Music; Handel, George Frideric (1685-1759); Music—Classical

This celebration of Handel's *Messiah* is a unique combination of Biblical quotations, the words to the songs and choral sections, and paintings. Introduction. Afterword.

This book is perfect for student choral groups who participate in productions of the *Messiah*. Christopher Hogwood's scholarly introduction provides great insight into this libretto. When you share this book be sure to play a recording of this piece.

244. Harper, Isabella. **My Dog Rosie**. Ill. by Barry Moser (Blue Sky/Scholastic, 1994).

Artists; Author Studies; Autobiographies; Dogs; Grandfathers; Pets

While Moser works at his studio drawing board his three-year-old granddaughter cares for (and is tolerated by) his Rottweiler Rosie.

Although this is an autobiographical picture book intended for preschoolers, it gives a glimpse into Moser's life and can be used to introduce the vast contribution he has made to the picture book field as both an author and illustrator. Some of Moser's books include *Ariadne, Awake!* by Doris Orgel (Viking, 1994); a retelling of *John Bunyan's Pilgrim's Progress* by Gary D. Schmidt (W. B. Eerdmans, 1994); *Grass Songs* by Ann Warren Turner (Harcourt Brace Jovanovich, 1993); and *The Magic Hare* by Lynne Reid Banks (Morrow Junior Books, 1993). Have students compare, contrast, and evaluate his works.

245. Harris, Joel Chandler. **Jump: The Adventures of Brer Rabbit**. Adapted by Van Dyke Parks and ill. by Barry Moser (Harcourt Brace Jovanovich, 1986).

246. Harris, Joel Chandler. **Jump Again! More Adventures of Brer Rabbit**. Adapted by Van Dyke Parks and ill. by Barry Moser (Harcourt Brace Jovanovich, 1987).

247. Harris, Joel Chandler. **Jump on Over! The Adventures of Brer Rabbit and His Family**. Adapted by Van Dyke Parks and ill. by Barry Moser (Harcourt Brace Jovanovich, 1989).

African Americans; Folklore—African American; Read-Aloud; South; Storytelling; Trickery; Uncle Remus Tales

These companion volumes feature the classic tales of Brer Rabbit outwitting Brer Fox, Brer Wolf, and Brer Bear. Harris originally collected these "Uncle Remus Tales" and published them in the dialects used in the late 19th century in the South.

 These picture book retellings are a good introduction to these important stories in American folklore. Depending on the age of your students, share the original "Uncle Remus Tales" and/or the four-book collection retold by Julius Lester and illustrated by Jerry Pinkney: *Tales of Uncle Remus* (Dial Press, 1987), *More Tales of Uncle Remus* (Dial Press, 1988), *Further Tales of Uncle Remus* (Dial Press, 1990), and *Last Tales of Uncle Remus* (Dial Press, 1994). Also of interest will be *Bo Rabbit Smart for True: Folktales from the Gullah* (Philomel, 1981) retold by Priscilla Jaquith with a nontraditional picture format by Ed Young. Students can select a story to compare and contrast.

 Van Dyke Parks is a southern composer who recorded some of these stories on the album *Jump!* in 1984. Use this recording in conjunction with these books and stories.

248. Harvey, Brett. **Cassie's Journey: Going West in the 1860s**. Ill. by Deborah Kogan Ray (Holiday House, 1988).

Covered Wagons; Diaries; Frontier and Pioneer Life; Geography; Historical Fiction; History—United States—1840-1870; Pioneer Life; Wagon Trains; Westward Expansion (1840-1870); Women Pioneers

Cassie's Journey portrays the hardships of migrating to California in a covered wagon during the 1860s. Historical note. Map.

The information in this book is based on real accounts, many from *Women's Diaries of the Westward Journey* by Lillian Schliffel (Schocken Books, 1982). Another picture book, *Along the Santa Fe Trail: Marion Russell's Own Story* (Whitman, 1993) by Marion Russell was adapted from her memoirs; *Araminta's Paint Box* by Karen Ackerman (Atheneum, 1990) is a picture book story about a paint box that travels West. Consult the entry for Ann Turner's *Dakota Dugout* (entry 574) for a list of diaries kept by women pioneers. Another great source of information is *Atlas of Western Expansion* by Alan Wexler (Facts on File, 1995).

 This book is a fine companion to computer software programs reenacting wagon train life as pioneers moved west across the United States in the mid-19th century. Consider using The Oregon Trail (MECC), Wagons West (Focus Media), and Santa Fe Trail (Educational Activities). *Daily Life in a Covered Wagon* by Paul Erickson (Preservation Press, 1994), with double-page spreads featuring period photographs, artifacts, and sketches, will enhance student understanding of this period in history.

249. Harvey, Brett. **My Prairie Christmas**. Ill. by Deborah Kogan Ray (Holiday House, 1990).

250. Harvey, Brett. **My Prairie Year: Based on the Diary of Elenore Plaisted**. Ill. by Deborah Kogan Ray (Holiday House, 1986).

Christmas; Dakota Territory; Farm Life; Frontier Life; Historical Fiction; History—United States—19th Century; Homesteading; United States—History—19th Century

These books describe a year and a holiday that take place in the Dakota Territory in the late 19th century. These fictional accounts described by nine-year-old Elenore are based on the diaries of the author's grandmother.

Use these books in a study of American history to introduce students to prairie life for homesteaders. For further reading provide the books in the "Little House" series by Laura Ingalls Wilder (Harper & Row), *Dandelions* by Eve Bunting (Harcourt Brace, 1995), *If You're Not From the Prairie . . .* by David Bouchard (Raincoast Books, 1993), *Grasshopper Summer* by Ann Warren Turner (Macmillan, 1989), as well as Pam Conrad's novel *Prairie Songs* (Harper & Row, 1985) and biography *Prairie Visions: The Life and Times of Solomon Butcher* (HarperCollins, 1991).

251. Haseley, Dennis. **Horses with Wings**. Paintings by Lynn Curlee (Laura Geringer Book/HarperCollins, 1993).

Balloons—Hot Air;
Clouds; France—History;
Franco-Prussian War
(1870-1871); Gargoyles;
Hot Air Balloons; Patriotism;
War—Franco-Prussian
(1870-1871);
War—Strategies

When Paris was surrounded by the Prussian army, Léon Gambetta devised a plan to fly over the troops in a hot air balloon, raise an army, and attack from behind.

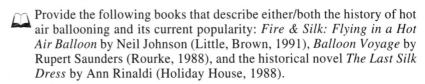 Provide the following books that describe either/both the history of hot air ballooning and its current popularity: *Fire & Silk: Flying in a Hot Air Balloon* by Neil Johnson (Little, Brown, 1991), *Balloon Voyage* by Rupert Saunders (Rourke, 1988), and the historical novel *The Last Silk Dress* by Ann Rinaldi (Holiday House, 1988).

 This episode from the Franco-Prussian War (1870-1871) can be incorporated into any study of that period.

252. Haseley, Dennis. **The Old Banjo**. Drawings by Stephen Gammell (Macmillan, 1983).

Banjos; Enchantment;
Farm Life; Historical
Fiction; Literary Devices;
Musical Instruments;
Poetry; Simile

A hardworking farmer and son don't have time to play the instruments on their Depression-era homestead. But, mysteriously, music returns to the farm as the instruments begin to play on their own.

 The Old Banjo is a perfect book to read aloud for examples of the simile *like*. The language is poetic, and the similes reflect numerous images that spark imagination.

A school orchestra and/or band can adapt this story to a short musical drama. A narrator, two actors (the farmer and son), and six musicians (banjo, trombone, piano, violin, trumpet, and clarinet) will be needed. Use various musical selections featuring the individual instruments and maybe an original composition for the grand finale.

253. Hastings, Selina. **Sir Gawain and the Loathly Lady**. Ill. by Juan Wijngaard (Lothrop, Lee & Shepard, 1985).

Arthurian Legends;
Beauty; Chivalry; Courage;
Enchantments; Knights;
Riddles; Romance

A black knight challenges King Arthur to answer a riddle, and a horrible hag saves his life by providing him with the answer to the question "What is it that women most desire?" Arthur's loyal knight Sir Gawain agrees to marry the hag and releases her from an evil enchantment.

For a version of this tale told in historical context refer students to *The Ramsay Scallop* by Frances Temple (Orchard, 1994). The story of Sir Gawain and the Loathly Lady is one told on a pilgrimage by the characters in this medieval novel.

Students who wish to read more about these times in longer books have many options. They can read the original stories in Edmund Spenser's *Faerie Queene* (Penguin Books, 1979) and Sir Thomas Malory's *Le Morte d'Arthur* (Potter, 1962) or in other retellings like T. H. White's *The Once and Future King* (Putnam, 1958), Howard Pyle's *The Story of King Arthur and His Knights* (Macmillan, 1984), Robert Sabuda's

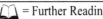

Arthur and the Sword (Simon & Schuster/Atheneum, 1995), Jane Yolen's *Merlin and the Dragons* (Cobblehill Books, 1995), and Rosemary Sutcliff's Arthurian trilogy *The Sword and the Circle* (E. P. Dutton, 1981), *The Light Beyond the Forest* (E. P. Dutton, 1980), and *The Road to Camlann* (E. P. Dutton, 1982). Barbara Cohen's adaptation of Geoffrey Chaucer's *Canterbury Tales* (Lothrop, Lee & Shepard, 1988) is another fine choice.

Students interested in trying to separate the myth of King Arthur from the reality will enjoy Catherine M. Andronik's *Quest for a King: Searching for the Real King Arthur* (Atheneum, 1989).

Cats; Children—Homeless; City Life; Companionship; Friendship; Homeless—Children; Read-Aloud; Social Issues—Homeless

254. Hathorn, Libby. **Way Home**. Ill. by Gregory Rogers (Crown, 1994).
This is a provocative look at city life where homeless young Shane finds a wild "no-name cat" and takes it home to his alley corner.

The perfect companion book to *Way Home* is *We Are All in the Dumps with Jack and Guy: Two Nursery Rhymes with Pictures* (HarperCollins, 1993) illustrated by Maurice Sendak. These books are ideal for launching discussions about the homeless, especially as the protagonists are children, with whom students can identify more easily. Colin Thompson's *Pictures of Home* (Green Tiger Press, 1993) can also work well with these books.

Black Market; Elephants; Endangered Species—African Elephants; Ivory Trade; Poachers; Trade Sanctions

255. Havill, Juanita. **Sato and the Elephants**. Ill. by Jean Tseng and Mou-Sien Tseng (Lothrop, Lee & Shepard, 1993).
Sato, a Japanese carver, discovers the plight of the endangered elephants while carving a piece of ivory. Note.

Although ivory sales are banned throughout the world elephants are still being killed for their tusks, and the illegal ivory trade continues on the black market. Using periodicals, students can learn more about the illegal trade of elephant tusks and other body parts from endangered and/or protected species.

Children and War; Civil War—Lebanon (1975-); Current Events; Family Life; Geography; Lebanon; Middle East; United Nations; War

256. Heide, Florence Parry and Judith Heide Gilliland. **Sami and the Times of the Troubles**. Ill. by Ted Lewin (Clarion Books, 1992).
On quiet days Sami attends school, goes on picnics, and plays with his friends. On bad days, when there is gunfire in the streets and bombs exploding, he and his family hide in an uncle's basement.

Most middle school students cannot imagine what war is like. This book presents a powerful and poignant look at a war-torn country from a child's perspective. Books about children and war, the United Nations' "Declaration of the Rights of the Child," and prospects for peace provide students with a greater understanding of humankind's continuous struggle to get along with one another. (See the subject index to this book for useful titles.) Students especially interested in the civil war in Beirut can refer to magazines and newspapers to collect pictures of the area prior to and since 1975 for comparison.

Other picture books can help students better grasp current events and the social life and customs of countries in the Middle East. Consult *The Day of Ahmed's Secret* (Lothrop, Lee & Shepard, 1990) by Florence Parry Heide and Judith Heide Gilliland, set in modern-day Cairo; *Sitti's Secrets* (Four Winds Press, 1994) by Naomi Shihab Nye, about a grandmother living in a Palestinian village on the West Bank; and *Jerusalem, Shining Still* by Karla Kuskin (Harper & Row, 1987), which portrays 3,000 years of Jerusalem's history.

257. Heller, Ruth. **A Cache of Jewels and Other Collective Nouns** (Grosset & Dunlap, 1987).

258. Heller, Ruth. **Kites Sail High: A Book About Verbs** (Grosset & Dunlap, 1988).

259. Heller, Ruth. **Many Luscious Lollipops: A Book About Adjectives** (Grosset & Dunlap, 1990).

260. Heller, Ruth. **Merry-Go-Round: A Book About Nouns** (Grosset & Dunlap, 1990).

261. Heller, Ruth. **Up, Up, and Away: A Book About Adverbs** (Grosset & Dunlap, 1991).

Adjectives; Adverbs; Language; Nouns; Nouns— Collective; Verbs; Writing

Heller uses vivid paintings and sometimes rhyme to illustrate language and various parts of speech.

For students who need concrete examples illustrating various parts of speech, the Heller books are perfect. Her sophisticated illustrations and unusual selections will easily anchor understanding.

262. Hendershot, Judith. **In Coal Country**. Ill. by Thomas B. Allen (Alfred A. Knopf, 1987).

Appalachia; Coal Mining; Family Life; Historical Fiction; Industrial Development; Memories; Mining—Coal;

The author reminisces about growing up and living in a coal mining town. Interspersing her memories with those of her parents, Hendershot shares their experiences of growing up in a mining town in the 1930s.

Students can investigate which local industries in your region are interrelated like coal mining and the steel mills in Hendershot's book. (Examples include the timber industry with log home manufacturers and pulp mills or fruit or vegetable farming and canning factories.) How have recent economic, political, and/or environmental issues affected these industries?

Judith Hendershot's sequel, *Up the Tracks to Grandma's* (Alfred A. Knopf, 1993), contains additional childhood memories. Other companion books include Lauren Mills' *The Rag Coat* (Little, Brown, 1991), Anna Egan Smucker's *No Star Night* (Alfred A. Knopf, 1989), and Cynthia Rylant's *When I Was Young in the Mountains* (Dutton Children's Books, 1985).

263. Henry, O. **The Gift of the Magi**. Ill. by Lisbeth Zwerger (Picture Book Studio, 1982).

Christmas; Gifts; Irony; Literary Devices; Love; Read-Aloud; Sacrifice

Poverty stricken but determined to celebrate Christmas, Della and Jim sell their greatest treasures in order to buy each other a gift. Evocative illustrations assist in the telling of this classic story of love and sacrifice.

To celebrate the spirit of Christmas provide this book and other versions of the classic, such as the one illustrated by Rita Marshall (Creative Education, 1984), along with one or more of the many available film and video versions.

This timeless story is a classic example of irony, a literary device that is sometimes missed by readers. Use it, along with the illustrated version of Guy de Maupassant's *The Necklace* (Creative Education, 1993), to help explain irony.

 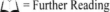

264. Hernandez, Xavier and Jordi Ballonga. **Lebek: A City of Northern Europe Through the Ages**. Ill. by Francesco Corni (Houghton Mifflin, 1991).

265. Hernandez, Xavier and Pilar Comes. **Barmi: A Mediterranean City Through the Ages**. Ill. by Jordi Ballonga (Houghton Mifflin, 1990).

Architecture; Cities and Towns—History; City Planning; History—Urban Growth and Development; Urban Growth and Development—History

Using fictional, but representative, composites, these books present the development of a northern European seaside city from the 10th century B.C. and a Mediterranean city from the 4th century B.C. to the present. Panoramic overviews, detailed drawings, and text present the history, architecture, and culture during the significant stages of development.

Invite city planners to discuss the reality of their tasks. Then have students plan changes they think should be considered for their community, or have them design an ideal future city.

For further reading provide companion books such as David Macaulay's *City: A Story of Roman Planning and Construction* (Houghton Mifflin, 1983) and *Underground* (Houghton Mifflin, 1983); Mitsumasa Anno's *Anno's Journey* (Putnam, 1977), *Anno's Britain* (Philomel, 1982), *Anno's U.S.A.* (Philomel, 1983), and *Anno's Italy* (Collins, 1978); and John Goodall's *The Story of an English Village* (Atheneum, 1978) and *The Story of a Main Street* (Atheneum, 1987).

266. Hinton, Leanne, translator. **Ishi's Tale of Lizard**. Ill. by Susan L. Roth (Farrar, Straus & Giroux, 1992).

Anthropology; Biographies; California—Indians; Folktales—Yahi Indians; Indians—Yahi; Ishi (d. 1916)

This Yani Indian folktale about a lizard who was swallowed by a bear was told to anthropologists by Ishi, the last remaining member of the Yani tribe. Ishi came out of hiding in 1911 and was befriended by a University of California anthropologist who arranged for Ishi to live in a room at the University's museum.

Use this book in conjunction with David Petersen's picture book biography *Ishi: The Last of His People* (Children's Press, 1991) and Louis V. Jeffredo-Warden's *Ishi* (Raintree/Steck-Vaughn, 1993) for further study of a fascinating individual.

Students studying folklore from various cultures will note similar motifs in Ishi's "Lizard Story." What other tales include a character swallowed whole by an animal? How are these tales similar? How are they different?

267. Hodges, Margaret. **Brother Francis and the Friendly Beasts**. Ill. by Ted Lewis (Charles Scribner's Sons, 1991).

Animals; Biographies; Christianity; Francis of Assisi, Saint (1182-1226); Kindness; Religions; Saints

Rejecting his wealthy background, a young man chooses a life of poverty and good works to humans and beasts alike.

How do individuals become saints? Interested students can choose a saint for further study. Information about saints can be found in Carole Armstrong's *Lives and Legends of the Saints: With Paintings from the Great Art Museums of the World* (Simon & Schuster, 1995), *Lives of the Saints* by Reverend Alban Butler (Christian Classics, 1981), and *One Hundred Saints: Their Lives and Likeness* (Little, Brown, 1993).

268. Hodges, Margaret retold by. **The Kitchen Knight: A Tale of King Arthur**. Ill. by Trina Schart Hyman (Holiday House, 1990).

269. Hodges, Margaret retold by. **Saint George and the Dragon**. Ill. by Trina Schart Hyman (Little, Brown, 1984).

Arthurian Legends; Dragons; Folklore— England; George, Saint (d. 303); History— Middle Ages; Knights— Legends; Medieval Tales; Middle Ages; Romance

Both English legends are retold in the spirit of the times when King Arthur's nephew becomes a knight and saves a maiden and when the Red Cross Knight slays the fearsome dragon. *Saint George and the Dragon* received the Caldecott Medal in 1985.

Students who wish to read more about these times in longer books have two options. They can read the original stories in Edmund Spenser's *Faerie Queene* (Penguin Books, 1979) and Sir Thomas Malory's *Le Morte d'Arthur* (Potter, 1962) or read other retellings like T. H. White's *The Once and Future King* (Putnam, 1958); Robert Sabuda's *Arthur and the Sword* (Simon & Schuster/Atheneum, 1995); Howard Pyle's *The Story of King Arthur and His Knights* (Macmillan, 1984); Jane Yolen's *Merlin and the Dragons* (Cobblehill Books, 1995); and Rosemary Sutcliff's Arthurian trilogy *The Sword and the Circle* (E. P. Dutton, 1981), *The Light Beyond the Forest* (E. P. Dutton, 1980), and *The Road to Camlann* (E. P. Dutton, 1982). Barbara Cohen's adaptation of Geoffrey Chaucer's *Canterbury Tales* (Lothrop, Lee & Shepard, 1988) is another fine choice.

These medieval tales can spark an investigation into medieval times. Search the subject index in this book to find many nonfiction entries that will appeal to students and expand their knowledge about this time period. Also see "The Middle Ages" by Stanley Steiner and Linda Marie Zaerr [*Book Links* 4(2):11-15, November 1994] for a variety of book recommendations for classroom use.

270. Hodges, Margaret. **St. Jerome and the Lion**. Ill. by Barry Moser (Orchard, 1991).

Calligraphy; Christianity; Faith; Jerome, Saint (d. 419 or 420); Kindness; Legends; Libraries; Lions; Miracles; Monasteries; Read-Aloud; Religions; Saints

Hodges and Moser present an illustrated retelling of the legend of St. Jerome and the lion he sheltered in his monastery.

A patron saint of libraries, Saint Jerome (also known as Hieronymus Eusbius, or Sophronius) is known mostly for translating the Holy Bible into Latin. He is considered the patron saint of translators, scholars, and editors, and by association, the patron saint of libraries and librarians. His feast day is celebrated in the Roman Catholic Church on September 30. Interested students can find out more about Saint Jerome and other saints in Carole Armstrong's *Lives and Legends of the Saints: With Paintings from the Great Art Museums of the World* (Simon & Schuster, 1995), *Lives of the Saints* by Reverend Alban Butler (Christian Classics, 1981), and *One Hundred Saints: Their Lives and Likeness* (Little, Brown, 1993).

271. Hodges, Margaret. **Saint Patrick and the Peddler**. Paintings by Paul Brett Johnson (Orchard, 1993).

Catholicism; Dreams; Folklore—Irish; Generosity; Ireland; Poverty; Saint Patrick; Treasure

A poor Irish peddler receives instructions from Saint Patrick in a dream. When he follows them, his life is changed. Includes background information about Saint Patrick and the origin of this story.

According to the notes for this book, the author was inspired to tell this story after seeing other versions by a variety of authors. Search for other variations to compare and contrast.

❗ = Extraordinary!   💡 = Idea   📖 = Further Reading   = Writing $\frac{2}{4}$ = Math   = Science   = History

272. Honda, Tetsuya. **Wild Horse Winter** (Chronicle Books, 1992).

Adaptation; Animals—Adaptation; Biology—Adaptation; Evolution; Horses; Japan; Science—Adaptation; Survival; Winter

Based on an actual event, a colt struggles to survive its first winter on a deserted Japanese island. Note.

The editor's note tells of the adaptation of Dosanko horses, descendants of the Nambu horses brought to Hokkaido Island more than 300 years ago. Over time their behavioral and physical characteristics have changed to ensure their survival. Use this book to begin a study of evolution, including specific studies of evolution theories such as the Founder's Principle or the bottleneck phenomenon.

273. Hopkinson, Deborah. **Sweet Clara and the Freedom Quilt**. Paintings by James Ransome (Alfred A. Knopf, 1993).

African Americans; Courage; Crafts—Quilting; Freedom; Historical Fiction; History—United States—Underground Railroad; Internet; Maps; Quilts; Slavery; Underground Railroad

Sweet Clara was inspired to sew a quilt that would serve as a map to help runaway slaves escape to the North. Based on a true but little-known African American story, this Underground Railroad story features a young courageous seeker of freedom.

A fine companion book is *Stitching Stars: The Story Quilts of Harriet Powers* by Mary E. Lyons (Charles Scribner's Sons, 1993). Other books that tell of slaves escaping from the South include Virginia Hamilton's *Many Thousand Gone, African Americans from Slavery to Freedom* (Random House, 1992), featuring portraits of freedom fighters; Jacob Lawrence's *Harriet and the Promised Land* (Simon & Schuster, 1993), a celebration of Harriet Tubman's 19 trips to the South to lead fellow slaves to freedom in the North; Faith Ringgold's *Aunt Harriet's Underground Railroad in the Sky* (Crown, 1992); and Jannette Winter's *Follow the Drinking Gourd* (Alfred A. Knopf, 1988), which honors the folk song, with its hidden directions to freedom. Use all of these in a study of that time period. Another aspect of the history of fugitive slaves can be found in Dolores Johnson's *Seminole Diary: Remembrances of a Slave* (Macmillan, 1994).

Author Deborah Hopkinson is willing to discuss her books with students via E-mail using the Internet. Her address is hopkinda@wpoffice.whitman.edu. There are also other "Children's Authors on the Net" willing to correspond with their audiences through E-mail and listed on the Children's Literature Gopher at New Mexico State University. Telnet to library.nmsu.edu, select "Library gopher," select "Resources by Subject," select "Education," select "Children's Literature," and then select "Children's Authors on the Net."

274. Horibuchi, Seiji, ed. **Stereogram** (Cadence Books, 1994).

275. Horibuchi, Seiji, ed. **Super Stereogram** (Cadence Books, 1994).

Art—Stereo Painting; Computer Graphics; History—Stereograms; Optical Illusions; Salitsky Dot; Science—Computer Technology; Science—Optics; Stereograms; 3-D; Visual Perception

Essays with accompanying stereographic images trace the history and development of this 3-D art form.

Reading the essays in Horibuchi's books can give students a new perspective when they examine the hidden images concealed in the seemingly random fields of art in these books and numerous others, including *3-D Galaxy: See the Hidden Pictures in the Stars* (William Morrow, 1994) and N. E. Thing Enterprises' three books, *Magic Eye: A New Way of Looking at the World* (Andrew and McMeel/Universal Press, 1993), *Magic Eye II: Now You See It . . .* (Andrew and McMeel/Universal Press, 1994), and *Magic Eye III—Visions: A New Dimension in Art* (Andrew and McMeel/Universal Press, 1994). For the inexperienced observer, the viewing techniques are explained in all of these books.

= Geography   = Art   = Music   = Drama   = Speech   = Research   = Read-Aloud

Research in visual perception led to the development of 3-D computer technology. Pique student interest in visual perception (and further research in the field) by sharing these books and an antique stereoscope with accompanying viewing cards. See "Outrageous Optics!" by Elizabeth Cronemeyer [*Book Links* 3(7):46-49, July 1994] for a plethora of books and activities about visual perception.

A study of the history and techniques of 3-D can be expanded beyond the technical information in these books. Consult *The Authorized Collection of Holusion Art: How and Why It Works* (NVision Grafix, 1994)

276. Houston, Gloria. **But No Candy**. Ill. by Lloyd Bloom (Philomel, 1992).

Candy; Food—Shortages; Historical Fiction; History—United States— World War II; Shortages— Food; Uncles; United States—History—World War II; World War II

While Lee's family awaits Uncle Ted's return from the fighting of World War II, the candy gradually disappears from the shelves of their family store.

Much World War II fiction for young people is set in Europe and Asia. Provide a collection of books set in the United States during this time period for further reading. Novels include *Stepping on the Cracks* by Mary Downing Hahn (Clarion Books, 1991), *The Cookcamp* by Gary Paulsen (Orchard, 1991), *Who Was That Masked Man, Anyway?* by Avi (Orchard, 1992), *Salted Lemons* by Doris Buchanan Smith (Four Winds Press, 1980), and *Summer of My German Soldier* by Bette Greene (Dial Press, 1973).

277. Houston, Gloria. **My Great-Aunt Arizona**. Ill. by Susan Condie Lamb (HarperCollins, 1992).

Appalachia; Biographies; Historical Fiction; Hughes, Arizona Houston (1876-1969); Memories; Read-Aloud; Reading; Social Life and Customs—Appalachia; Teachers

Houston relates the story of her great-aunt's life in the Blue Ridge Mountains as a child and later as a teacher who inspired generations of students.

Square dancing can be a lot of fun and may be a novel experience for many students. There may be square dance clubs in your community with individuals who will be delighted to demonstrate, teach, and call out the steps.

In many of the illustrations Great-Aunt Arizona is seen reading books. As part of reading celebration direct your students to create posters featuring favorite book characters, themselves, etc. Check out the American Library Association's celebrity "Read" posters for inspiration!

A tribute to reading with contributions from 28 authors and illustrators can be found in *Once Upon a Time . . . Celebrating the Magic of Children's Books in Honor of the Twentieth Anniversary of Reading Is Fundamental* (Putnam, 1986).

278. Huck, Charlotte. **Princess Furball**. Ill. by Anita Lobel (Greenwillow Books, 1989).

Architecture; Cinderella Stories; Costumes; Fairy Tales; History—Medieval Period; Love; Medieval Period; Read-Aloud

A spunky princess, determined not to marry the Ogre her father has betrothed her to, hides her identity and escapes to meet and fall in love with a young king. Notes.

In the note preceding the story, Huck shares information concerning the 500+ variations of the Cinderella story. Have students find other versions such as Ai-Ling Louie's *Yeh Shen, A Cinderella Story from China* (Putnam, 1982), Shirley Climo's *Egyptian Cinderella* (Harper & Row, 1989), Rafe Martin's *The Rough-Face Girl* (Putnam, 1992), and Ellen Jackson's *Cinder Edna* (Lothrop, Lee & Shepard, 1994) for comparison. How do these various stories represent different times and cultures?

 = Extraordinary!   = Idea 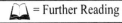 = Further Reading   = Writing $\frac{2}{4}$ = Math   = Science   = History

This story is presented on a medieval background provided by Lobel's paintings. Students can identify the medieval images Lobel included and then do more research concerning the architecture and costumes of the period.

279. Hughes, Langston. **The Sweet and Sour Animal Book**. Ill. by Students from the Harlem School of Arts (Oxford University Press, 1994).

African Americans; Alphabet Books; Animals; Art—Children's; Biographies; Children's Art; Harlem Renaissance; Hughes, Langston (1902-1967); Humor; Poetry

Written in the 1930s, these unpublished alphabet verses were rejected by publishers and only recently rediscovered among Hughes' papers in the rare book library at Yale University. Introduction. Afterword. Note.

Though known mainly as a poet, Hughes also wrote essays, plays, short stories, and novels. A study of Hughes' work should include books such as the republished *The Dream Keeper and Other Poems* (Alfred A. Knopf, 1994) illustrated by Brian Pinkney, *Black Misery* (Oxford University Press, 1994), and *The Block* (Viking, 1995), a picture book featuring 13 poems by Hughes matched with pieces of a collage by Romare Bearden that is owned by the Metropolitan Museum of Art. Other poets exploring the theme of African American identity include Joyce Carol Thomas in *Brown Honey in Broomwheat Tea* (HarperCollins, 1993), Nikki Giovanni, and Maya Angelou.

The afterword is an excellent in-depth resource for biographical information concerning Langston Hughes' literary life, his verse and poetry, and his dedication to African Americans. In addition, provide S. L. Berry's *Langston Hughes* (Creative Education, 1994) and Floyd Cooper's picture book *Coming Home: From the Life of Langston Hughes* (Philomel Books, 1994) to learn more about Langston Hughes.

280. Hunt, Jonathan. **Illuminations** (Bradbury Press, 1989).

Alphabet; Alphabet Books; Art—Calligraphy; Books; Calligraphy; Communication; Illuminations; Language—Written; Manuscripts; Medieval Period; Middle Ages; Social Life and Customs—Medieval Period

This illuminated alphabet presents 26 words (from *alchemist* to *zither*) associated with the Middle Ages. Notes. Reading list. Bibliography.

An outstanding companion book to the manuscripts from the Middle Ages is Elizabeth B. Wilson's *Bibles and Bestiaries: A Guide to Illuminated Manuscripts* (Farrar, Straus & Giroux, 1994). Students can begin a study of the written word and the ways it has been recorded throughout history with Karen Brookfield's *Book* (Alfred A. Knopf, 1993).

Hunt illuminated the letters based on a 12th-century alphabet. While beginning calligraphy students generally use an italic script, more advanced students will enjoy learning more challenging scripts such as this one. Various alphabets are presented in calligraphy books; provide a variety and allow students to select an alphabet that appeals to them.

281. Hurwitz, Johanna, selected by. **A Word to the Wise and Other Proverbs**. Ill. by Robert Rayevsky (Morrow Junior Books, 1994).

Adages; Franklin, Benjamin (1706-1790); Proverbs; Sayings; Truths; Wisdom

This is a collection of currently used proverbs. Preface. Afterword.

Cover the proverbs written in the borders around the endpaper illustrations. Identify a proverb that is illustrated. How many other proverbs can your students (working alone or in groups) find?

The most famous American who wrote proverbs was Benjamin Franklin. Use his *Poor Richard's Almanack* (University Press of Virginia, 1977) for an in-depth presentation of the simple truths Franklin collected from 1732 to 1757. Some of his proverbs include "Well done is better than well said," "Make haste slowly," and "Early to bed and early to rise, Makes a man healthy, wealthy, and wise."

 = Geography   = Art   = Music   = Drama   = Speech   = Research   = Read-Aloud

282. Hutton, Warwick. **Adam and Eve: The Bible Story** (Margaret K. McElderry, 1987).

283. Hutton, Warwick. **Jonah and the Great Fish** (Margaret K. McElderry, 1984).

284. Hutton, Warwick. **Moses in the Bulrushes** (Aladdin, 1992).

285. Hutton, Warwick. **Noah and the Great Flood** (Atheneum, 1977).
With his deceptively simple watercolors, Hutton retells these well-known Bible stories.

Adam; Bible Stories; Eve; Jonah; Moses; Noah

These well-reviewed books provide an excellent introduction to a study of biblical literature.

For a Noah story from the animals' perspective, look at *Noah & the Ark & the Animals* by Ivan Gantschev and Andrew Elborn (Picture Book Studio USA, 1984).

286. Hutton, Warwick. **Persephone** (Margaret K. McElderry, 1994).

287. Hutton, Warwick. **Perseus** (Margaret K. McElderry, 1993).

288. Hutton, Warwick. **Theseus and the Minotaur** (Margaret K. McElderry, 1989).

289. Hutton, Warwick. **The Trojan Horse** (Margaret K. McElderry, 1992).
These retellings of Greek myths explain how and why Perseus killed Medusa and rescued Andromeda, and how the Greeks used a wooden horse to win the 10-year-long Trojan War.

Andromeda; Demeter; Greek Mythology; Hades; Homer; Iliad; Medusa; Military Strategy; Minotaurs; Mythology— Greek; Persephone; Perseus; Seasons; Theseus; Trojan Horse; Trojan War

These simple, but eloquent, retellings will ease students gently into more complete studies of Greek mythology. Use them as an introduction to various mythological characters.

I

290. **I Dream of Peace: Images of War by Children of Former Yugoslavia.** Children of Yugoslavia Staff (HarperCollins, 1994).
War is depicted through the art and words of children living in the former Yugoslavia. Includes an introduction by the executive director of UNICEF and a preface by Maurice Sendak.

Children and War; Civil War—Former Yugoslavia; Current Events—War; Fear; Hope; Peace; UNICEF; United Nations; War; Yugoslavia—Former

Focusing student discussions on peace is an important goal in a society that is growing increasingly more violent. Provide *The Big Book for Peace* edited by Ann Durrell and Marilyn Sachs (E. P. Dutton, 1990), *Peace Begins with You* by Katherine Scholes (Little, Brown, 1989), and *Peace Tales: World Folktales to Talk About* by Margaret R. MacDonald (Linnet Books, 1992) for elementary students; Jimmy Carter's *Talking Peace: A Vision for the Next Generation* (E. P. Dutton, 1993) for middle and high school students; and Douglas Wood's poetic fable *Old Turtle* (Pfeifer-Hamilton, 1992) for all students.

For further reading, a perfect companion book is *I Never Saw Another Butterfly: Children's Drawings and Poems from Terezin Concentration Camp, 1942-1944* edited by Hana Volavková (Schocken Books, 1993). Secondary students will also be interested in *Zlata's Diary: A Child's Life in Sarajevo* by Zlata Filipovic (Viking, 1994) and *Sarajevo: A Portrait of the Siege* by Matthew Naythons (Warner Books, 1994).

❗ = Extraordinary!   = Idea   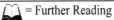 = Further Reading   = Writing $\frac{2}{4}$ = Math   = Science   = History

291. Innocenti, Roberto. **Rose Blanche** (Creative Education, 1985).

Children and War;
Concentration Camps;
Germany; Historical Fiction;
History—World War II;
Holocaust; Jews; Nazis;
Resistance; War;
World War II

Photographic realism is used to tell the story of a young German girl who discovers a Nazi concentration camp near her home. She cannot comprehend the cruelty of war and brings food to the starving children in the camp. In a cruel twist of fate she does not live to see the liberation of the camp.

Provide a selection of books detailing various aspects of the Holocaust. Consult the subject index in this book for more picture books on the Holocaust.

Innocenti says he named his book *Rose Blanche (White Rose)* because that was the name of a group of young Germans who protested the war. Have students do research to learn more about Europeans who formed resistance movements, including Rose Blanche.

292. Irving, Washington. **Rip Van Winkle.** Drawings by Gary Kelley (Creative Education, 1993).

American Literature;
Folklore—American; Irving,
Washington (1783-1859);
Laziness; Short Stories;
Supernatural

First published in 1820, *Rip Van Winkle* is the story of a man who falls asleep in the Catskill Mountains for 20 years and wakes to a much changed world.

Irving is credited with writing the first modern American short stories. Provide this book as well as other versions of *Rip Van Winkle,* such as the one illustrated by Arthur Rackham (Chancellor Press, 1985) or Thomas Locker (Dial Books for Young Readers, 1988) or even the musical version *Rip Van Winkle: Grand Romantic Opera in Three Acts* by George Frederick Bristow (Da Capo Press, 1995). In addition, provide students with other works by Irving, including versions of *The Legend of Sleepy Hollow* by Robert D. San Souci and Daniel San Souci (Doubleday, 1985) and the versions retold by Diane Wolkstein (William Morrow, 1987), Emma Harding (Henry Holt, 1995), and Will Moses (Putnam, 1995) as an introduction to Irving's body of work.

293. Isaacson, Philip M. **Round Buildings, Square Buildings, & Buildings That Wiggle Like a Fish** (Alfred A. Knopf, 1988).

Architecture; Art;
Bridges; Buildings;
Churches; Cliff Dwellings;
Fortresses; Lighthouses;
Mills; Taj Mahal; Tombs

A photo-illustrated tour of architectural styles around the world focuses on such building elements as walls, doorways, skylights, and windows while exploring structures such as bridges, lighthouses, fortresses, tombs, and cliff dwellings. Notes.

This wonderful introduction to architecture as art might motivate students to take a more detailed look at the structures featured in this book. As an alternative some students can select a specific architect for further study. Assemble an architecture book collection including the biography *The Will and the Way: Paul R. Williams, Architect* by Karen E. Hudson (Rizzoli, 1994), featuring the first African American member and Fellow of the American Institute of Architects, and the numerous references included in the *Book Links* article "Architecturally Speaking," by Augusta Scattergood [3(6):9-13, July 1994].

Interested students can go on to explore the architecture in their area. Using this book as a model, students can photograph various architectural details for research and discussion. Provide *Architects Make Zigzags: Looking at Architecture from A to Z* by Roxie Munro (Preservation Press, 1986), a picture book glossary of architectural terms.

294. Isaacson, Philip M. **A Short Walk Around the Pyramids & Through the World of Art** (Alfred A. Knopf, 1993).

Architecture; Art; Imagination; Photography; Sculpture; Visual Perception

The question "What is art?" is answered in this introduction to the world of art. This is the history of art inside and outside the walls of art museums. Isaacson invites readers to look at the world through color, shape, and artistic imagination. Discussion includes: understanding concrete and abstract components of art, looking at a variety of art forms (including sculpture, painting, pottery, photography, and everyday objects), and examining the architecture and compositions of towns and cities.

Isaacson's unusual juxtapositions of various art forms are intended to expand the viewer's perception of art and offer a new appreciation of the surrounding world. Explore your own world with students by taking a walking and talking tour of your community, focusing on "viewer perceptions."

295. Isadora, Rachel. **At the Crossroads** (Greenwillow Books, 1991).

Apartheid; Fathers; Mines; Music—African; Reunions; Segregation; Social Life and Customs—South Africa; South Africa; Townships

South African children are eager to welcome their fathers home after 10 months away working in the mines.

At the Crossroads provides a look at apartheid in South Africa. Use books like *The Anti-Apartheid Reader: South Africa and the Struggle Against White Racist Rule* edited by David Mermelstein (Grove, 1987) and *Kaffir Boy: The True Story of a Black Youth's Coming of Age in South Africa* by Mark Mathabane (NAL, 1986) to understand those times better. Compare this information with newer material about life in South Africa since the democratic election of Nelson Mandela in 1994. Consult "South Africa Beyond Apartheid" by Hazel Rochman [*Book Links* (3)3:33-38, January 1994].

Music is important to the indigenous people of South Africa. Listen to "Voices from Africa" on the soundtrack to *The Power of One* (Elektra, 1992), Paul Simon's albums *Graceland* (Warner Brothers Records, 1986) and *The Rhythm of the Saints* (Warner Brothers Records, 1990) for a greater appreciation of this unique sound.

J

296. Jackson, Ellen. **Cinder Edna**. Ill. by Kevin O'Malley (Lothrop, Lee & Shepard Books, 1994).

Cinderella Stories; Conservation; Drama; Folktales—Fractured; Fractured Folktales; Independence; Read-Aloud; Recycling; Writing

Both Cinderella and Cinder Edna live with cruel stepmothers and stepsisters, but the similarities end there. They have different approaches to life and although each ends up with the prince of her dreams, one is much happier than the other.

Students can write their own fractured folktales emphasizing today's mores and issues. For a variation on the theme take a look at *Prince Cinders* by Babette Cole (G. P. Putnam's Sons, 1987).

Theatre or drama students can develop, adapt, and script a reader's theater version of *Cinder Edna*.

297. Jackson, Ellen. **The Winter Solstice**. Ill. by Jan Davey Ellis (Millbrook Press, 1994).

Celebrations; Ceremonies; Cherokee Indians; Christmas; Folklore—Cherokee; Hanukkah; Indians of North America— Cherokee; Pourquoi Tales; Solstice—History; Winter Solstice

This book provides facts and folklore from around the world about the year's shortest day.

Jackson provides a solstice story adapted from a Cherokee tale of creation. Students can locate other such tales from a variety of cultures that explain why things happen. Also known as pourquoi or "why" tales,

---

! = Extraordinary! 　 = Idea 　 = Further Reading 　 = Writing 　 $\frac{2}{4}$ = Math 　 = Science 　 = History

these stories are found in many cultures. One example is the answer to why birds fly south for the winter found in Joseph Bruchac's *The Great Ball Game: A Muskogee Story* (Dial Books for Young Readers, 1994).

Many customs observed at Hanukkah and Christmas originate from ancient solstice celebrations. Students can further research the origins of celebrations, noting those they have in common.

298. Jakes, John. **Susanna of the Alamo: A True Story**. Designed and ill. by Paul Gacon (Harcourt Brace Jovanovich, 1986).

Alamo; Biographies; Dickenson, Susanna; Heroines; Texas—History; United States—History— 1836; War; Women—History

Susanna Dickenson, along with her baby, survived the 1836 massacre at the Alamo. Dickenson's chilling recollection provoked such rage that Santa Anna was ultimately defeated. Maps.

For further reading provide this book along with other stories of real or imagined heroines. A collection could include *Cut from the Same Cloth: American Women of Myth, Legend, and Tall Tale* by Robert D. San Souci (Philomel, 1993), *Living Dangerously: American Women Who Risked Their Lives for Adventure* by Doreen Rappaport (HarperCollins, 1991), *Getting the Real Story: Nelly Bly & Ida B. Wells* by Sue Davidson (Seal Press, 1992), *The Book of Woman: 300 Notable Women History Passed By* by Lynne Griffin and Kelly McCann (Adams Publications, 1995), *Kate Shelley: Bound for Legend* by Robert D. San Souci (Dial Books for Young Readers, 1995), and *Swamp Angel* by Anne Isaacs (Dutton Children's Books, 1994).

299. James, Betsy. **The Mud Family**. Ill. by Paul Morin (G. P. Putnam's Sons, 1994)

Anasazi; Archeology; Dolls; Droughts; Indians of North America— Southwest; Rain and Rainfall; Southwest; Water

Unless Sosi's dancing can produce rain for their endangered corn crop, the Anasazi family will have to move from the canyon.

James was inspired to write *The Mud Family* after a hike in southern Utah where she found a wall in an ancient ruin decorated with handprints, including a child's handprint, similar to the one on the last page of the book. Some students will want to learn more about the Anasazis and the ancient ruins of the Southwest; consult Caroline Arnold's *The Ancient Cliff Dwellers of Mesa Verde* (Clarion Books, 1992) among others.

The blending of the past with the present in the American Southwest can also be seen in two other picture books: *Dreamplace* by George Ella Lyon (Orchard, 1993) and *The Shepherd Boy* by Kristine L. Franklin (Atheneum, 1994).

300. Jenkins, Steve. **Duck's Breath and Mouse Pie: A Collection of Animal Superstitions** (Ticknor & Fields, 1994).

Adages; Animals— Folklore; Folklore; Read-Aloud; Superstitions

This book relates 17 superstitions (and their origins) that people have long believed could cure illnesses, change fortunes, and foretell the future. Historical notes.

Duck's Breath and Mouse Pie is a fun book to read and share aloud as well as to use for research. Consult Lila Perl's *Don't Sing Before Breakfast, Don't Sleep in the Moonlight: Everyday Superstitions and How They Began* (Houghton Mifflin, 1988) for additional folk beliefs.

 = Geography   = Art   = Music   = Drama   = Speech   = Research   = Read-Aloud

African Americans; Art—Printmaking; Bible Stories; Creation; Harlem Renaissance; Johnson, James Weldon (1871-1938); Monotypes; Poetry; Printmaking—Techniques

301. Johnson, James Weldon. **The Creation: A Poem**. Ill. by Carla Golembe (Little, Brown, 1993).

Written in 1919, this poem celebrates the biblical story of the creation.

James Weldon Johnson, author of the African American national anthem "Lift Every Voice and Sing," was a Harlem Renaissance writer in the 1920s. Other important individuals in the movement include Zora Neale Hurston, Langston Hughes, Jean Toomer, Countee Cullen, Claude McKay, Eric Waldron, Arna Bontemps, Jacob Lawrence, and Richard Wright. Interested students may wish to read biographical accounts of these African American artists and intellectuals.

Compare and contrast this poem illustrated by Golembe with the version by James Ransome (Holiday House, 1994). Golembe's illustrations are a combination of painting and printmaking called monotype. The painting is made with oil-based inks on Plexiglas and is then transferred to paper by an etching press. Often, after the print dries, oil pastels, colored pencils, or special Japanese paper are added. Students can create prints using a modified technique.

African Americans; American History; Artists; Johnson, James Weldon (1871-1938); Linocuts; Music; Oral Interpretation; Poetry; Printmaking; Songs; Speech

302. Johnson, James Weldon. **Lift Every Voice and Sing**. Ill. by Elizabeth Catlett (Walker, 1993).

The song, first performed in 1900, has been referred to as the "Negro national anthem" and celebrates triumph over adversity. The linocuts, produced independently of this book in the mid-1940s, feature poor African American men and women enduring life with dignity.

The poetic lyrics to Johnson's song combined with Catlett's linoleum prints (linocuts) make a powerful statement. Discuss the lyrics and why students think the song is qualified to be considered the "Negro national anthem." Compare this illustrated version to the one by Jan Spivey, *Lift Ev'ry Voice and Sing* (Scholastic, 1995). How do the illustrations influence the power of the lyrics?

James Weldon Johnson's poetry is excellent for students who want to give a speech in the category of poetry interpretation. For other poems consult *God's Trombones: Seven Negro Sermons in Verse* by James Weldon Johnson (Viking, 1971).

Use this book when studying African American history at the turn of the century. Musically talented students might wish to perform the song.

Art; Historical Fiction; Painting; Princesses; Spain—17th Century; Velázquez, Diego (1599-1660)

303. Johnson, Jane. **The Princess and the Painter** (Farrar, Straus & Giroux, 1994).

The five-year-old Spanish princess, Infanta Margarita, waits patiently for the unveiling of Diego Velázquez's new painting. She is surprised to discover that the friendly artist has featured her and people she knows in the painting. Note.

Las Meninas, one of Velázquez's most famous paintings, is representative of his realistic style. The story and the following note about the painting are a fine introduction to Philip IV's famous court painter. Rosabianca Skira-Venturi's *A Weekend with Velasquez* (Rizzoli, 1993) provides factual information about the artist while Elizabeth de Trevino's 1966 Newbery Award-winning *I, Juan de Pareja* (Farrar, Straus & Giroux, 1965) features the artist and his devoted Black slave.

❗ = Extraordinary!　💡 = Idea　📖 = Further Reading　 = Writing　$\frac{2}{4}$ = Math　 = Science　 = History

304. Jonas, Ann. **Reflections** (Greenwillow Books, 1987).

305. Jonas, Ann. **Round Trip** (Greenwillow Books, 1983).

A child reflects on a busy day and a trip to and from the city in these unusual "turn upside down" books.

Art—Figure—Ground;
Art—Negative Space;
Books—Unusual Designs;
Design; Escher, M. C.
(1898-1970); Imagination;
Optical Illusions; Sculpture;
Toy and Movable Books;
Visual Perception

Jonas' black-and-white illustrations in *Round Trip* are perfect for illustrating the concept "figure-ground," where you can see a pattern two different ways. You can introduce this concept to your students by showing them the classic optical illusion drawing of the vase and two faces where one can see the faces or the vase, but not both at the same time. Artists refer to *figure* (where it stands out "on top of" the ground) as a "positive shape" and *ground* (where it appears to be underneath and surrounding a figure) as a "negative shape" or "negative space." Extend student experience in looking at figure-ground (or negative-positive reversal) in art by providing pictures like M. C. Escher's *Circle Limit IV* and *Sky and Water* and sculptures where the negative is simply the empty space.

306. Jonas, Ann. **The Trek** (Greenwillow Books, 1985).

A young girl's trip to school is a simple journey through her neighborhood but a more complex journey through the "jungle" of her imagination with all its hidden animals.

Animals—Jungle;
Art—Trompe L'oeil;
Illusions; Imagination;
Jungle Animals; Literary
Recreations; Picture
Puzzles; Trompe L'oeil

Trompe l'oeil, meaning "something that deceives the eye," is the art technique employed by Jonas in this book. Trompe l'oeil was made popular by 19th-century American painters, especially William Harnett. Use Michael Capek's *Artistic Trickery: The Tradition of Trompe L'Oeil Art* (Lerner, 1995) and other examples of trompe l'oeil with students to become better versed in this art form.

307. Jordan, Martin and Tanis Jordan. **Jungle Days, Jungle Nights** (Kingfisher Books, 1993).

Set in the Amazon rain forest, this lavishly illustrated book describes much of the flora and fauna and conveys a sense of how interdependent the animals and environment are on each other.

Amazon Rain Forest;
Animals—Jungle;
Conservation; Ecology;
Environmental Issues;
Interdependence; Jungle
Animals; Jungles; Rain
Forests; Science—Ecology;
South America—
Rain Forests

This book presents detailed drawings of a variety of unique species coexisting in the Amazon rain forest. Students can select one or more of the many species mentioned and further examine their characteristics.

Scarcely a month goes by without some mention in the news of rain forest ecology. Students can select a particular area or look at the entire issue of rain forest exploitation and the struggle to preserve this natural resource.

308. Joyce, William. **A Day with Wilbur Robinson** (Harper & Row, 1990).

Spending the day at the Robinsons' house is a futuristic fantasy. While searching for Grandpa (and his missing false teeth), Wilbur and his best friend encounter weird and wacky relatives.

Art—Advertisements;
Families; Fantasy; Humor;
Inventions; Robots; Science—
Inventions; Science Fiction

Joyce's story is filled with futuristic inventions that don't really work—an "anti-gravity device" flying around the yard, a "brain augmentor" to help one think deep thoughts that aren't deep at all. Students can plan, design, and display inventions they think could improve life. Consult *The Way Things Work* by David Macaulay (Houghton Mifflin, 1988), *The Visual Dictionary of Everyday Things* (Dorling Kindersley, 1991), *Invention* by Lionel Bender (Alfred A. Knopf, 1991), *Eureka! It's an*

Airplane! by Jeanne Bendick and Robert Bendick (Millbrook, 1992), *Steven Caney's Invention Book* by Steven Caney (Workman, 1985), and *The Picture History of Great Inventors* by Gillian Clements (Alfred A. Knopf, 1994).

309. Joyce, William. **Dinosaur Bob and His Adventures with the Family Lazardo** (Harper & Row, 1988).

Adventures; Dinosaurs; Families; Fantasy; Fossils; Humor; Paleontologists; Science—Paleontology

Trouble begins for the Lazardos when they return from a trip with a friendly large green dinosaur in tow.

James Gurney's *Dinotopia: A Land Apart from Time* (Turner, 1992) and *Dinotopia: The World Beneath* (Turner, 1995) are sophisticated books for fans of dinosaur fantasies. The article "Daring Deeds, Bold Dreams, in a Land Removed from Time" by Donald Dale Jackson [*Smithsonian* 26(6):70-78, September 1995] will also be of interest to these readers.

Students interested in paleontology will be fascinated with John R. Horner and Don Lessem's *Digging Up Tyrannosaurus Rex* (Crown, 1992), which tells of the painstaking excavation of the only complete *Tyrannosaurus rex* fossil, discovered in 1990. Other books of interest for students wishing to do more research about dinosaurs and fossil discoveries include Helen Roney Sattler's *The New Illustrated Dinosaur Dictionary* (Lothrop, Lee & Shepard, 1990), John Horner's *Digging Dinosaurs* (Workman, 1988), David Norman and Angela Milner's *Dinosaur* (Alfred A. Knopf, 1989), and J. Lynett Gillette's *The Search for Seismosaurus* (Dial Books for Young Readers, 1994) among others.

310. Joyce, William. **Santa Calls** (HarperCollins, 1993).

Adventures; Brothers and Sisters; Christmas; Community Service; Fantasy; Friendship; Letters; Read-Aloud; Santa Claus; Social Action; Wishes

Three youngsters take part in an adventure to help Santa overcome evil forces at the North Pole, making Esther Aimesworth's simple Christmas wish come true.

In our materialistic world adults and children alike often wish for things that matter little in the long run. This book and Chris Van Allsburg's *The Polar Express* (Houghton Mifflin, 1985) feature children who have only modest wishes. Begin a discussion on wishes, highlighted by the sharing of letters written each holiday season by less fortunate children. These letters often appear in the local newspapers. Individual students, or a service club, can participate in local programs like "Secret Santa" to make a difference in the lives of others.

The unlikely combination of crime fighters and villains in a swashbuckling adventure helped this book capture the attention of adults and children the year it was published. It makes a great read-aloud with its simple message about wishes and friendship.

311. Jukes, Mavis. **Blackberries in the Dark**. Pictures by Thomas B. Allen (Alfred A. Knopf, 1985).

Death; Fishing; Grandfathers; Grandmothers; Grief; Intergenerational Relationships; Separation and Loss; Sports— Fly Fishing

Nine-year-old Austin has always spent the summer with his grandparents. During the first summer after his grandfather's death, he and his grandmother grieve together.

Austin's grandfather left behind some fishing flies that he had hand tied. Flies can be incredibly beautiful. Helpful how-to books include *Flies: The Best One Thousand* by Randal Scott Stetzer (Frank Amato Publications, 1992), *The Art of Fly Tying* by John van Vliet (Cy DeCosse, 1994), and *The Art of Tying the Dry Fly* by Skip Morris (Frank Amato Publications, 1993).

The important themes of grief, death, and adapting to the loss of a loved one are eloquently dealt with by Jukes. This book is excellent for readers of all ages forced to deal with separation and loss issues.

312. Jukes, Mavis. **I'll See You in My Dreams**. Ill. by Stacey Schuett (Alfred A. Knopf, 1993).

Airplanes; Death; Family; Flying; Grief; Imagination; Love; Skywriting; Terminal Illnesses; Uncles

In preparation for visiting her terminally ill uncle, a girl imagines she is a skywriter who flies over him spelling out messages of love as a final good-bye.

Children are curious, afraid, and usually inexperienced in dealing with terminal illness, death, and the grieving process. This book, "a farewell tribute to the author's brother," might help bridge that gap for many students.

313. Jukes, Mavis. **Lights Around the Palm**. Paintings by Stacey Schuett (Alfred A. Knopf, 1987).

Animals; Brothers and Sisters; Christmas; Farm Animals; Imagination; Languages; Legends; Reading

Seven-year-old Emma's older brother scoffs at the idea that she is teaching their farm animals to read and speak. On Christmas night she changes his mind.

In addition to investigating the legend that the animals spoke on the day Christ was born, provide students with *Cock a Doodle Doo!: What Does It Sound Like to You?* by Marc Robinson (Tabori & Chang, 1993) and *Who Says a Dog Goes Bow-Wow?* by Hank De Zutter (Doubleday, 1993), two cleverly done books that illustrate what animals sound like in different languages.

314. Jukes, Mavis. **Like Jake and Me**. Ill. by Lloyd Bloom (Alfred A. Knopf, 1984).

Creative Writing; Divorce; Entomology; Family Relationships; Fears; Gender Roles; Parenting Classes; Read-Aloud; Spiders; Stepfamilies

Alex and his cowboy stepfather, Jake, are not yet comfortable with each other. The barriers break down when Alex rescues a terrified Jake from a wolf spider. Newbery Honor, 1985.

Like Jake and Me was inspired by Jukes' relationship with her nine-year-old stepson and is a good discussion starter for life skills and parenting classes on stepfamily relationships.

Like Jake and Me can launch discussions on stereotyping and sex/gender roles.

Using this book's excellent description of wolf spiders as a model, students can write comparable descriptions (accompanied by original drawings) of spiders indigenous to their area.

315. Juster, Norton. **Alberic the Wise**. Ill. by Leonard Baskin (Picture Book Studio, 1965, 1992).

Art; Beauty; Proverbs; Quest; Renaissance; Stained Glass; Travel; Wisdom

Alberic journeys through the world searching for wisdom and attempting to create something of great beauty or enduring value.

The moral of this story is stated by Alberic: "It is much better to look for what I may never find than to find what I do not really want." Students can examine this moral within the context of this story or as a contemporary issue. Invite further writing or discussion.

K

316. Kalman, Maira. **Chicken Soup, Boots** (Viking, 1993).

Career Planning; Creative Writing; Humor; Occupations; Philosophy; Surrealism

By wandering past a succession of family, friends, and neighbors, Kalman creates a surreal "book about jobs," both real and imagined. Meet Eddie Lane (a composer with a great schnozzola), Mr. Pool (the recycling artist), Barney March (the eight-armed short-order cook), Dr. Smellman (inventor of the Smell-O-Meter), the writer (Kalman herself), and others.

Using *Chicken Soup, Boots* is a humorous way to introduce students to career opportunities. Read aloud selected portraits to add some levity to your class discussions.

Kalman's writing is concise, inspiring, and funny. Use the written portraits (and the way they are loosely connected) as a model for your students to create a similar class book. Each student can write about one character and link it loosely to other students' characters.

The combination of story and art is a prime example of surrealism. Use this book as an introduction to more complex books featuring this art and literary style used to express subconscious thoughts through unnatural juxtapositions or fantastic imagery.

317. Kalman, Maira. **Max in Hollywood, Baby** (Viking, 1992).

318. Kalman, Maira. **Ooh-la-la (Max in Love)** (Viking, 1991).

Creative Writing; Dogs; Hollywood; Movies; Paris; Satire; Scripts

Madcap adventures feature Max (the dreamer, the poet, the dog) and his Parisian Dalmatian bride (Crêpes Suzette) falling in love in Paris and moving to Hollywood, perhaps for stardom.

Using a movie script style similar to Kalman's, students can write a story that would include flashbacks, "cuts," stereotyping of characters, and overly affected "Hollywood" language or, perhaps, British accents.

319. Kalman, Maira. **Roarr: Calder's Circus**. Photos by Donatella Brun (Delacorte Press, 1993).

Art—Modern; Art—Sculptures; Calder, Alexander (1898-1976); Circus; Mobiles; Modern Art; Museums; Sculptures

Alexander Calder's famous circus sculptures "CRASH, BOOM, POW" into town (and into life) through Kalman's imagination.

Starting in 1926 Alexander Calder created these circus characters, christened "mobiles." Though they have been on display at the Whitney Museum of American Art in New York since 1970, Calder used to perform with them at the homes of friends. Oversee an in-depth study of Calder and his mobile sculptures. As a finale, have students create characters with scraps of material using themes such as fairs, rodeos, and flea markets, or create your own circus.

Some students might want to learn more about modern American sculpture. For those students provide books like Jan Greenberg and Sandra Jordan's *The Sculptor's Eye: Looking at Contemporary American Art* (Delacorte Press, 1993).

320. Kesey, Ken. **Little Tricker the Squirrel Meets Big Double the Bear.** Ill. by Barry Moser (Viking, 1990).

Animals; Ozarks; Read-Aloud; Storytelling; Tall Tales; Tricksters

Meet the clever little squirrel who outwits a "double-big, double-hungry grizzly bear" in the cottonwoods at Topple's Bottom.

 = Extraordinary!   = Idea   = Further Reading   = Writing $\frac{2}{4}$ = Math   = Science   = History

In the fine old tradition of storytelling, Grandma Smith first told this tall tale to novelist Ken Kesey. Pair it with other trickster tales like the Brer Rabbit stories included in this book.

 Kesey is best known for his classic *One Flew Over the Cuckoo's Nest* (Viking, 1977). In the mid-1960s he became the leader of a hippie group (the "Merry Pranksters") whose antics were included in Tom Wolfe's *The Electric Kool-Aid Acid Test* (Bantam Books, 1983). Introduce high school students to Wolfe's book and Kesey's novels and contrast them with this tall tale.

321. Kimmel, Eric A. **Charlie Drives the Stage**. Ill. by Glen Rounds (Holiday House, 1989).

Courage; Gender Equity; Historical Fiction; Stage-coaches; Tall Tales; Western Women; Women

A daring young stagecoach driver is not deterred by avalanches or floods in her efforts to deliver Senator McCorkle to the train station on time.

 With a wry twist Kimmel presents a story of the Wild West sure to delight readers of all ages. Young Charlie Drummond, the stagecoach driver, is really a girl, much to everyone's amazement. Use this book as a springboard to introduce famous Western women who may have been ignored by the history books. Consult Larry Underwood's *Love and Glory: Women of the Old West* (Media Publishers, 1991), Ruth Pelz's *Women of the Wild West: Biographies from Many Cultures* (Open Hand, 1995), or Brandon Marie Miller's *Buffalo Gals: Women of the Old West* (Lerner, 1995).

 322. Kimmel, Eric. **Hershel and the Hanukkah Goblins**. Ill. by Trina Schart Hyman (Holiday House, 1989).

Celebrations; Freedom; Goblins; Hanukkah; Judaism; Read-Aloud; Religions—Judaism; Traditions—Jewish

Hershel outwits the goblins who have been haunting the synagogue and preventing the villagers from celebrating Hanukkah. Caldecott Honor, 1990.

 Kimmel's original tale honors the freedom in celebrating Hanukkah and lighting the menorah candles as Jewish soldiers did after defeating the Ayrian army in 164 B.C. Use this tale to introduce students to the Jewish traditions included in other titles listed here. Consult the subject index in this book.

323. Kitchen, Bert. **And So They Build** (Candlewick Press, 1993).

324. Kitchen, Bert. **Somewhere Today** (Candlewick Press, 1992).

325. Kitchen, Bert. **When Hunger Calls** (Candlewick Press, 1994).

Animal Behavior; Animal Characteristics; Animals—Habits and Behavior; Animals—Habitats; Audubon, John James (1785-1851); Biology; Habitats—Animal; Parental Behavior in Animals; Predatory Animals

This trilogy focuses on animal behavior with descriptions of unusual animal architects and their buildings, unique characteristics of some animals, and strange eating habits of others.

Kitchen's dramatic wildlife portraits, including those in his *Animal Alphabet* (Dial Books for Young Readers, 1984), *Animal Numbers* (Dial Books for Young Readers, 1987), and *Gorilla/Chinchilla* (Dial Books for Young Readers, 1990), are reminiscent of Audubon's famous bird and quadruped paintings. Compare and contrast the artistic renderings of the same animals by both artists. Discuss the advantages of painting wildlife today versus 150 years ago. Peter Roop and Connie Roop's *Capturing Nature: The Writings and Art of John James Audubon* (Walker, 1993) and Joseph Kastner's *John James Audubon* (Abrams, 1992) may be useful for further study.

326. Knight, Margy Burns. **Talking Walls**. Ill. by Anne Sibley O'Brien (Tilbury House, 1992).

Berlin Wall; Caves; Cliff Dwellings; Geography; Great Wall of China; History—World; Petroglyphs; Wailing Wall; Walls

Readers are introduced to different cultures by exploring walls around the world. Map. Notes.

Use in combination with other books about walls such as Leonard Everett Fisher's *The Great Wall of China* (Macmillan, 1986) and *The Wailing Wall* (Macmillan, 1989), Eve Bunting's *The Wall* (Clarion Books, 1990), and Dr. Seuss' *The Butter Battle Book* (Random House, 1984). Examine humankind's propensity to build walls and reflect on the positive and negative results.

Students can specifically research the Berlin Wall and look at what has happened in Germany since the Wall came down.

327. Knox, Bob. **The Great Art Adventure** (Rizzoli, 1993).

Antiquities; History of Art; Humor; Museums; Parodies; Reproductions

Combining funny parodies with reproductions of paintings and artifacts from around the world, this "Museum of World Art" provides a unique introduction to art history.

Containing only brief informative captions describing each of the 11 works of art depicted, this primarily wordless book is both inventive and a fine introduction to the history of art. Have students select other art examples, produce a parody using this book as a model, and write a brief informative caption of each art piece. The finished products can be bound in a book and catalogued in your library. You could have the students limit the coverage to a certain time period or let it extend to a general history of art.

328. Kraus, Robert. **Fables Aesop Never Wrote: But Robert Kraus Did** (Viking, 1994).

Art—Collage; Collage; Fables; Humor; Irony; Literary Devices; Satire; Short Stories

Fifteen contemporary original fables tickle the funny bone.

Reminiscent of *The Stinky Cheeseman and Other Fairly Stupid Tales* by Jon Scieszka (Viking, 1992), Kraus' book provides a perfect springboard for inspiring creative writing. Read the book aloud and then have students select one of the "Morals Without Fables" about which to write their own witty creations. Clever collages (also modeled on this book) can be used to complete this activity.

329. Kroll, Steven. **By the Dawn's Early Light: The Story of the Star-Spangled Banner**. Ill. by Dan Andreasen (Scholastic, 1994).

History—United States—War of 1812; Key, Francis Scott (1779-1843); Lawyer; Poetry; Songs; United States—History—War of 1812; War of 1812

Francis Scott Key was on a British ship trying to obtain the release of a captured friend during the War of 1812. While watching the British bombardment of Baltimore, Key wrote the words to what later became the national anthem of the United States. Note. Musical score. Maps. Bibliography. Index.

Include this pictorial and written narrative in a historical study of the War of 1812.

330. Kroll, Steven. **Lewis and Clark: Explorers of the American West**. Ill. by Richard Williams (Holiday House, 1994).

Clark, William (1770-1838); Explorers; History—United States; Lewis and Clark Expedition (1804-1806); Lewis, Meriwether (1774-1809)

The two-and-a-half-year expedition of Captain Meriwether Lewis and William Clark is recounted with details about hardships, equipment, food, and fellow travelers. Map. Afterword. Chronology. Index.

🖋 = Extraordinary!   💡 = Idea   📖 = Further Reading   = Writing   ²⁄₄ = Math   ⚛ = Science   = History

Any study of the Lewis and Clark expedition will be enhanced by the information and detailed oil paintings featured in this book. Interested students can go on to read one of the many versions of Lewis and Clark's journals such as *The Journals of Lewis and Clark* by Meriwether Lewis et al. (New American Library, 1964).

331. Krupp, Robin Rector. **Let's Go Traveling** (Morrow Junior Books, 1992).

Ancient Civilization;
Civilization—Ancient;
Creative Writing;
Geography; Travel;
Wonders of the World

Travel to six ancient wonders of the world with Rachel Rose by viewing a collage of illustrations, reviewing photographs of artifacts and souvenirs, and reading Rachel's diary, postcards, lists of new words, and general impressions. Timeline.

 A companion picture book with a similar format is Susan Joyce's *Post Card Passages* (Peel Productions, 1994). Students can develop similar travelogues modeled on these books by collecting, borrowing, and creating items and artifacts—maps, coins, word lists, ticket stubs, photographs, cartoons, etc. Travel agents and friends can often help with providing materials.

 Use these six ancient wonders (the prehistoric Rouffignac caves in France, the pyramids of Egypt, the Uxmal Maya temples of Mexico, the mysterious Machu Picchu temple in Peru, Stonehenge in England, and the Great Wall of China) as a focus for a geographical and/or historical study.

 332. Kurtz, Jane. **Fire on the Mountain**. Ill. by E. B. Lewis (Simon & Schuster, 1994).

Cleverness; Creative
Writing; Ethiopia—
Folklore; Folktales—
Ethiopia; Geography;
Imagination; Read-Aloud;
Social Studies; Survival;
Trickster Tales

An Ethiopian shepherd boy outwits a cruel rich man and gains a fortune for himself and his sister. Note.

 Nearly every culture has trickster tales in which a weaker character uses pranks, lies, mischief, and wit in order to triumph over those with more power. Providing a variety of these tales is a means of introducing students to many different cultures. See this book's subject index for other trickster tales as well as Bette Bosma's *Fairy Tales, Fables, Legends, and Myths: Using Folk Literature in Your Classroom* (Teachers College Press, 1992).

 Use this book to help expand any study of Ethiopia. Kurtz uses some Ethiopian words and in the author's note explains some Ethiopian traditions. For another Ethiopian folktale see *The Lion's Whiskers: An Ethiopian Folktale* by Nancy Raines Day (Scholastic, 1995).

L

333. Lasky, Kathryn. **The Librarian Who Measured the Earth**. Ill. by Kevin Hawkes (Little, Brown, 1994).

Ancient Greece;
Astronomy—Ancient;
Biographies; Earth;
Eratosthenes (c275-c195
B.C.); Geography—Ancient;
Geometry; Librarians;
Mathematics

Lasky presents a lively biography of Eratosthenes, the ancient Greek scholar who accurately measured the circumference of the earth. Author's note. Afterword. Bibliography.

$\frac{2}{+2}\frac{}{4}$ Comparing a sectioned grapefruit with the earth, then presenting the mathematical explanation of Eratosthenes' thinking, makes the math come alive. Don't miss an opportunity to incorporate this book in appropriate math classes.

 Eratosthenes became the chief librarian at Alexandria in Egypt. Have students discover more about both this library and the museum, which were considered the best in the world.

334. Lattimore, Deborah Nourse. **The Lady with the Ship on Her Head** (Harcourt Brace Jovanovich, 1990).

Clothing—France—17th and 18th Century; Costumes; France—History—17th and 18th Century; Hats; Historical Fiction; Humor; Plays; Social Life and Customs—France—17th and 18th Century

Unaware that a ship has sailed onto her head, Madame Pompenstance competes in the annual Best Headdress Award at the Fancy Dress Ball. Note.

Students interested in fashion will enjoy Lila Perl's *From Top Hats to Baseball Caps, From Bustles to Blue Jeans: Why We Dress the Way We Do* (Clarion Books, 1990), Kathryn Lasky's *She's Wearing a Dead Bird on Her Head* (Hyperion, 1995), and L. Rowland-Warne's *Costume* (Alfred A. Knopf, 1992). Audrey Wood and Don Wood's 1986 Caldecott Honor book, *King Bidgood's in the Bathtub* (Harcourt Brace Jovanovich, 1985), is filled with characters dressed in Renaissance clothes, including a man with a ship on his head!

Lattimore's note about her art can help draw attention to the numerous elements she includes, from paintings, sculpture, and decorative arts to furniture, landscaping, and costuming that were popular in 17th- and 18th-century France. Use this book when studying that time period in history.

Students who need costume ideas for 17th- and 18th-century French clothing can get inspiration here and from the Charles Perrault edition of *Puss in Boots* (Farrar, Straus & Giroux, 1990) illustrated by Fred Marcellino.

335. Lattimore, Deborah Nourse. **The Sailor Who Captured the Sea: A Story of the Book of Kells** (HarperCollins, 1991).

Artists; Bible; Book of Kells; Heroes; Illuminations; Internet; Middle Ages; Religious Writings; Sailors; World Wide Web

This original story, set in Ireland in the year 804 A.D., features recreations of the art and designs of the ancient *Book of Kells* and tells the story of a young artist's struggle to find his voice. Historic maps. Prologue.

The *Book of Kells* is housed in the Long Room in the Old Library at Trinity College in Dublin. Interested students can investigate further by reading Bernard Meehan's *The Book of Kells: An Illustrated Introduction to the Manuscript in Trinity College Library* (Thame & Hudson, 1994) and *The Book of Kells: Reproductions from the Manuscript in Trinity College, Dublin* (Alfred A. Knopf, 1974). Excerpts, including manuscript selections and illustrations, are available for viewing via the World Wide Web on the Internet. The URL is http://library.tcd.ie/els.html.

Outstanding companion books are Elizabeth B. Wilson's *Bibles and Bestiaries: A Guide to Illuminated Manuscripts* (Farrar, Straus & Giroux, 1994), *Celtic Hand Stroke by Stroke: Irish Half-Uncial from the Book of Kells* by Arthur Baker (Dover Publications, 1983), and Jonathan Hunt's *Illuminations* (Bradbury Press, 1989).

336. Lattimore, Deborah Nourse. **Why There Is No Arguing in Heaven: A Mayan Myth** (Harper & Row, 1989).

Creation Stories; Indians of Mexico; Mayas—Legends and Myths; Mayas—Religion

Hunab Ku, the first Creator God of the Mayas, challenges the Moon Goddess and the Lizard House to create a being to worship him. They fail, but the Maize God is successful with his seeds. Author's note.

Creation stories abound in cultures throughout the world. Students can learn more by comparing creation myths. Be sure to use Virginia Hamilton's *In the Beginning: Creation Stories from Around the World* (Harcourt Brace Jovanonich, 1988) as well as others listed in the subject index in this book.

337. Lawrence, D. H. **Birds, Beasts and the Third Thing: Poems by D. H. Lawrence**. Ill. by Alice Provensen and Martin Provensen (Viking Press, 1982).

British Poetry; Lawrence, D. H. (1885-1930); Nature; Poetry—British; Poetry— Free Verse

Short Lawrence poems, primarily about the natural world, were selected by the Provensens for this collection. Introduction by Donald Hall.

Although Lawrence is known best for his "idealistic theories about sexual relations," much of his poetry is about the natural world and was written in free verse. Obtain a copy of his well-known *Birds, Beasts and Flowers* (M. Secker, 1923) and feature some of his best-known poems, such as "Fish," "Snake," and "Mountain Lion."

338. Lawrence, Jacob. **The Great Migration: An American Story** (HarperCollins, 1993).

African Americans; Art— Painting and Drawing; History—United States— Urbanization; Hope; Migration—People; Poetry; Population; Urbanization

Lawrence's 60 narrative paintings chronicle the migration of African Americans from the rural South to the industrial cities in the North between 1916 and 1919. The "journey of hope" depicted in the paintings reflects the harshness, violence, fear, courage, and dignity of the people and their struggle.

Use both the paintings and the text to focus student attention on the rural and urban lifestyles of African Americans during this period (1916-1919).

Lawrence's paintings and narrative, with Walter Dean Myers' "Migration" poem (following the last picture), provide grist for a discussion concerning this historical population shift. Also consult an interview with Jacob Lawrence, published in *Booklist*, 90(12):1048-49, February 15, 1994.

339. Lawrence, Jacob. **Harriet and the Promised Land** (Simon & Schuster, 1993).

African Americans— Biographies; Art—Narrative Painting; Biographies; Freedom; History—United States—Underground Railroad; Poetry; Read-Aloud; Slaves; Tubman, Harriet (1815?-1913); Underground Railroad

First published in 1968, Lawrence's narrative paintings and rhythmic biography celebrate Harriet Tubman's 19 trips to the South to lead fellow slaves to freedom in the North.

Jacob Lawrence is one of America's most prominent African American artists. Most of his narrative paintings celebrate the strength of the human spirit. Students can use this book in conjunction with his illustrations in Gwen Everett's *John Brown: One Man Against Slavery* (Rizzoli, 1993), Lawrence's other picture book, *The Great Migration* (HarperCollins, 1993), and the more complete *Jacob Lawrence: The Migration Series* (Rappahannock Press, 1993) by Jacob Lawrence to view more of his work. Additional research can focus on his life and his deep sense of history revealed through interviews and biographies.

Companion books featuring Harriet Tubman, and portraits of others who helped slaves escape on the Underground Railroad, include David A. Adler's *A Picture Book of Harriet Tubman* (Holiday House, 1992), Deborah Hopkinson's *Sweet Clara and the Freedom Quilt* (Alfred A. Knopf, 1993), Faith Ringgold's *Aunt Harriet's Underground Railroad in the Sky* (Crown, 1992), and Virginia Hamilton's *Many Thousand Gone, African Americans from Slavery to Freedom* (Random House, 1992). For a program that can be adapted for different age groups consult "A Harriet Tubman Celebration: Here's How We Do This Annual Mixed-Aged Project" by Gail B. Mensher [*Young Children* 50(1):64-69, November 1994]. "The Underground Railroad" book list in *Book Links* 5(1):46-48, September 1995 will also be helpful.

 = Geography　　 = Art　　 = Music　　 = Drama　　 = Speech　　 = Research　　 = Read-Aloud

340. Lawson, Julie. **The Dragon's Pearl**. Paintings by Paul Morin (Clarion Books, 1993).

China—Fairy Tales; Courage; Dragons; Droughts; Fairy Tales— Chinese; Generosity; Greed; Magic

A cheerful and dutiful son finds a magic pearl during a terrible drought, and it changes his life forever. Note.

Although dragons are a familiar element in many fairy tales and fantasies, they hold a unique place in traditional Chinese stories. The note explains that Chinese dragons are symbols of royalty and greatness. Provide students with other books specifically about Chinese dragons such as Jay Williams' *Everyone Knows What a Dragon Looks Like* (Four Winds Press, 1976) and Margaret Leaf's *The Eyes of the Dragon* (Lothrop, Lee & Shepard, 1987). Students can compare Chinese dragons with magic creatures from European mythologies.

341. Leaf, Munro. **The Story of Ferdinand**. Ill. by Robert Lawson (Viking, 1938).

Bullfighting; Bulls; Conflict Resolution; Differences—Acceptance; Individualism; Pacifism; Read-Aloud; Self-Esteem; Spain

Being himself, Ferdinand the bull refuses to fight the matador and instead enjoys smelling the flowers.

Ferdinand has great self-esteem; he's different from other bulls and not willing to fight. This classic story is perfect to use in conflict resolution classes. If your elementary school is not already involved consult the 1990 publication *Conflict Resolution: An Elementary School Curriculum* by Gail Sodalla and others (Community Board Program, Inc., 1540 Market St., #490, San Francisco, CA 94102).

For a book collection featuring pacifism consider these titles: Margaret Read MacDonald's *Peace Tales: World Folktales to Talk About* (Shoe String Press, 1993), Nathan Aaseng's *The Peace Seekers: The Nobel Peace Prize* (Lerner, 1987), Michael Nicholson's *Mahatma Gandhi: The Man Who Freed India and Led the World to Nonviolent Change* (Stevens, 1988), and *The Big Book for Peace* edited by Ann Durrell and Marilyn Sachs (Dutton Children's Books, 1990).

342. LeGuin, Ursula K. **A Ride on the Red Mare's Back**. Paintings by Julie Downing (Orchard, 1992).

Art—Woodcarving; Brothers and Sisters; Courage; Fairy Tales; Kidnapping; Loyalty; Magic; Trolls; Woodcarving

When her brother is kidnapped by trolls, a brave girl and her magic wooden horse journey into the mountains to rescue him.

Traditional tales of trolls who steal away babies have a grim fascination. Use this book along with Maurice Sendak's controversial *Outside Over There* (Harper & Row, 1981) to examine the fear of kidnapping. Older students can do a more in-depth study of the significance of fairy tales with Bruno Bettelheim's *Uses of Enchantment: The Meaning and Importance of Fairy Tales* (Random House, 1976).

Some students may be interested in woodcarving, a folk tradition and an art. For further information about wooden horse carvings consult *Painted Ponies: American Carousel Art* by William Manns (Zon International Publishers, 1986) and *Carving Carousel Animals* by H. Leroy Marlow (Sterling, 1989).

343. Leighton, Maxinne Rhea. **An Ellis Island Christmas**. Ill. by Dennis Nolan (Viking, 1992).

Christmas; Ellis Island; Emigration; Historical Fiction; History—United States—Ellis Island—1892-1924; Immigration; Poland; United States— History—1892-1924; Voyages

After having braved a stormy ocean voyage from Poland to arrive at Ellis Island on Christmas Eve, Krysia worries she won't be allowed to stay.

Seventy percent of the immigrants who arrived in the United States during the peak years of European immigration (1892-1924) entered through Ellis Island. Provide students with materials like *Ellis Island:*

| ❗ = Extraordinary! | 💡 = Idea | 📖 = Further Reading | ✏ = Writing | $\frac{2}{4}$ = Math | ⚛ = Science | 📚 = History |

Gateway to the New World by Leonard Everett Fisher (Holiday House, 1986), *Ellis Island: New Hope in a New Land* by William Jay Jacobs (Macmillan, 1990), *New Hope* by Henri Sorensen (Lothrop, Lee & Shepard, 1995), "A New Life Begins for the Island of Hope and Tears" by T. A. Bass [*Smithsonian* 21(3):88-97, June 1990], "Gateway to America" by S. L. Zuber [*Cobblestone* 12(7):6-10, July 1991], and periodic articles in *Cobblestone* for information about that period in history.

Though a picture book for younger children, Riki Levinson's *Watch the Stars Come Out* (E. P. Dutton, 1985) as well as *I Was Dreaming to Come to America: Memories from the Ellis Island Oral History Project* selected by Veronica Lawlor (Viking, 1995) are good companion books to *An Ellis Island Christmas*.

Like Ellis Island, the Statue of Liberty is a symbol of freedom. Students can learn more about this monument to freedom by examining S. H. Burchard's *The Statue of Liberty: Birth to Rebirth* (Harcourt Brace Jovavovich, 1985), Jonathan Harris' *A Statue for America* (Four Winds Press, 1985), and Leonard Everett Fisher's *The Statue of Liberty* (Holiday House, 1985).

344. L'Engle, Madeleine. **The Glorious Impossible** (Simon & Schuster, 1990).

Art—Frescoes; Churches; Frescoes; Giotto (Di Bondone) (1266?-1337); History of Art; Jesus Christ; Religious Art

The 14th-century frescoes painted by Giotto in the Scrovegni Chapel (Padua, Italy) inspired L'Engle's narrative. Twenty-four of these paintings were reproduced to enhance her text describing the life of Jesus Christ. Afterword.

Provide students with the picture book biography of Giotto, *The Boy Who Drew Sheep* by Anne Rockwell (Atheneum, 1973). Rockwell combines the few known facts about Giotto with some legends and includes information about painting techniques of Giotto's day.

The added details about Giotto and the Chapel in the afterword can help launch further study of the importance of churches in the history of art.

345. Lent, Blair. **Molasses Flood** (Houghton Mifflin, 1992).

Boston—History; Creative Writing; Floods; Historical Fiction; Molasses; Tall Tales

Lent's tall tale of a molasses explosion and flood through the streets of Boston is loosely based on a January 15, 1919, incident. Note.

Provide students with books like Donald J. Sobol's *Encyclopedia Brown's Third Record Book of Weird and Wonderful Facts* (William Morrow, 1985), *Guinness Book of World Records* edited by Donald McFarland (Bantam Books, 1991), *How Does Aspirin Find a Headache?* by David Feldman (HarperCollins, 1993), and Robin Keats' *Slime Lives! And Other Weird Facts That Will Amaze You* (Avon Books, 1995). Then have students select a factual event for the beginning of their own tall tale. Are there facts from your community that can inspire homespun tall tales?

346. Lester, Julius. **John Henry**. Ill. by Jerry Pinkney (Dial Press, 1994).

Contests; Folklore—African American; Heroes; Human Spirit; Legends; Railroads; Read-Aloud; Robotics; Science—Robotics; Tall Tales

This retelling of a popular African American legend celebrates John Henry's life from birth to his famed contest with the steam drill while building a railroad. Note. Caldecott Honor, 1995.

Compare and contrast both the texts and the illustrations of several editions of this folktale, including Ezra Jack Keats' *John Henry: An American Legend* (Pantheon Books, 1965).

The competition of "human versus machine" continues today as scientists conduct research in the field of robotics. Although a human can easily pick up a filled plastic cup, a robot has trouble doing this simple task. Why is picking up a cup a great accomplishment for a robot? What other tasks are robots learning to master? Refer to Gloria Skurzynski's *Robots: Your High-Tech World* (Bradbury Press, 1990) for further information. For another perspective on robots, consult *The Robot Zoo: A Mechanical Guide to the Way Animals Work* by John Kelly, Philip Whitfield, and Obin (Turner, 1994).

347. Levine, Arthur A. **All the Lights in the Night**. Ill. by James E. Ransome (Tambourine Books/William Morrow, 1991).

Two boys celebrate Hanukkah during their dangerous journey from Tsarist Russia to Palestine.

Brothers; Hanukkah; Immigration; Intergenerational Stories; Journeys; Judaism; Religions—Judaism; Russia— History—1914

Based on the escape of Levine's grandfather and great uncle from Dra-hitchen in 1914, this story parallels the Hanukkah miracle celebrating "Jewish resistance to oppression and the sustaining power of faith." Other picture books such as Jenny Koralek's *Hanukkah: The Festival of Lights* (Lothrop, Lee & Shepard, 1990), Karla Kuskin's *A Great Miracle Happened There: A Chanukah Story* (Willa Perlman Books/HarperCollins, 1993), and Eric A. Kimmel's *The Spotted Pony: A Collection of Hanukkah Stories* (Holiday House, 1992) deal with a similar theme.

348. Levine, Arthur A. **Pearl Moscowitz's Last Stand**. Ill. by Robert Roth (Tambourine Books, 1993).

Pearl has watched her neighborhood change many times during her lifetime. Now the neighbors, led by Pearl, refuse to let the last ginkgo tree on the block be destroyed in the name of progress.

Activism; City Life; Diversity; Government; Neighbors; Protests; Social Action; Trees

Pearl's activism is just the kind of example some students need to understand they can make a difference. Relate *Pearl Moscowitz's Last Stand* to the struggle to save the more than 400-year-old "Treaty Oak" in Austin, Texas, after someone poured liquid poison around its roots in 1989. The story of that tree is the basis of Ellen Levine's *The Tree That Would Not Die* (Scholastic, 1995). *The Kids Guide to Social Action: How to Solve the Social Problems You Choose—and Turn Creative Thinking into Positive Action* by Barbara A. Lewis (Free Spirit Publishing, 1991) and the *Cobblestone* issue "Kid Power: Changing Public Policy" [14(10), December 1993] give students helpful hints on becoming activists in many arenas—social, political, environmental.

Pearl's problem is one faced by residents of many communities as progress threatens their traditional way of life. By checking periodical indexes students can find references to the 1995 legal battle concerning the future of the several hundred years old "Friendship Oak" in Albany, Georgia. Researchers can learn about the history surrounding this tree, why it became the center of an activist crusade, the legal wrangling that occurred, and the tree's ultimate fate.

349. Lewis, J. Patrick. **The Frog Princess: A Russian Folktale**. Paintings by Gennady Spirin (Dial Books for Young Children, 1994).

This magical story with ornate illustrations tells of the youngest son of a tsar, who is forced to marry an ugly frog. Later he is astounded to learn that the frog is really the enchanted and beautiful princess Vasilisa the Wise.

Baba Yaga; Enchantment; Fairy Tales—Russian; Folk-lore—Russia; Magic; Princesses; Russia—Folk Lore; Vasilisa the Wise

The characters of Vasilisa the Wise and Baba Yaga are well known in Russian folklore. For comparison and contrast provide other stories about them such as *Vasilisa the Wise: A Tale of Medieval Russia* retold by Josepha Sherman (Harcourt Brace Jovanovich, 1988) and *Baba Yaga and Vasilisa the Brave* as told by Marianna Mayer (Morrow Junior Books, 1994).

! = Extraordinary!   = Idea   = Further Reading   = Writing $\frac{2}{4}$ = Math   = Science   = History

Gennady Spirin is one of the first Russian illustrators to be published outside his country. For further information about this artist consult "Gennady Spirin" by Barbara Elleman [*Book Links* 4(4):6-7, March 1995].

350. Lewis, Richard. **All of You Was Singing**. Art by Ed Young (Atheneum, 1991).

Aztec Mythology; Creation Stories; Music; Mythology— Aztec; Oral Interpretation; Poetry; Speech

This Aztec creation myth describes the beginnings of the earth and the advent of music.

Match this poetic creation story with James Weldon Johnson's *The Creation: A Poem* (Little, Brown, 1993).

Use Lewis' creation myth to contrast and compare with other creation stories from a variety of cultures. Some of these are *The Origin of Life on Earth: An African Creation Myth* by David L. Anderson (Sights Productions, 1991), *The Woman Who Fell from the Sky: The Iroquois Story of Creation* by John Bierhorst (William Morrow, 1993), *The Fire Children: A West African Creation Tale* by Eric Maddern (Dial Books for Young Readers, 1993), *The Children of the Morning Light: Wampanoag Tales* by Medicine Story and Mary F. Arquette (Macmillan, 1994), and *The Story of the Creation: Words from Genesis* by Jane Ray (Dutton Children's Books, 1993).

Provide this stunning book for students looking for material for oral interpretation events.

351. Lindbergh, Reeve. **View from the Air: Charles Lindbergh's Earth and Sky**. Photographs by Richard Brown (Viking, 1992).

Airplanes; Environment— Human Impact; Flight; Lindbergh, Charles A. (1902- 1974); Nature; New England; Pilots; Spatial Relations; Visual Perspectives

Along with photographs taken during a series of flights Lindbergh made over New England in 1971 and 1972, his daughter shares his perspective on his "lifetime of flying and his commitment to preserving the wildness he loved." Introduction.

Other picture books with interesting visual perspectives and spatial relations are Istvan Banyai's *Zoom* (Viking, 1995) and *Re-Zoom* (Viking, 1995), as well as Lynne Cherry's *The Armadillo from Amarillo* (Harcourt Brace Jovanavich, 1994) and *Looking Down* by Steve Jenkins (Houghton Mifflin, 1995). A photographic look at the earth from outer space is available in Patricia Lauber's *Seeing Earth from Space* (Orchard, 1990).

As noted in the introduction, Lindbergh was concerned with human impact on nature. Interested students can seek out some of Lindbergh's articles about protecting the earth.

352. Littlechild, George. **This Land Is My Land** (Children's Book Press, 1993).

Artists; Canada; Collage; Cree Indians; Cultures; Indians; Symbolism

Canadian artist Littlechild pays tribute to his ancestors, thanking them for surviving the difficult times since Columbus' arrival, while documenting their struggles in a calm, healing, conversational tone.

Littlechild uses a multilayered collage technique, permeated with Indian symbolism. Students can use his collage technique while incorporating their own personal or cultural symbolism to illustrate a subject that is meaningful to them such as family, environment, computers, etc.

The portrait gallery of Littlechild's ancestors can be used to inspire students to learn more about some of their relatives. Students can produce their own uniquely illustrated family trees.

353. Lobel, Arnold. **Fables** (Harper & Row, 1980).

Creative Writing; Fables; Morals; Truths

These 20 original fables feature animals and unusual morals. Caldecott Medal, 1981.

Use Lobel's one-page *Fables* as a model for students to write their own fables. Similar brief fables can be found in Jacob Lawrence's *Aesop's Fables* (Windmill Books, 1970).

354. Locker, Thomas. **Miranda's Smile** (Dial Books for Young Readers, 1994).

355. Locker, Thomas. **The Young Artist** (Dial Books for Young Readers, 1989).

Apprentices; Artists; Dutch Masters; Ethics; Fathers and Daughters; History of Art; Painting; Portraits; Realism

Both books feature portrait artists. In *Miranda's Smile,* Miranda's father struggles with her portrait, especially her smile, after her front tooth falls out. In *The Young Artist*, the artist must make a difficult decision. Commanded to paint the royal courtiers, his integrity is threatened when his subjects insist on being painted as they wished they looked.

Sharing these books, studying the Dutch Masters, and inviting a portrait artist to visit will provide students with an excellent introduction to portrait painting. Locker used the style of the Dutch Masters in *The Young Artist*, as he also did in *The Boy Who Held Back the Sea* (Dial Press, 1987). Another picture book of interest is Diane Stanley's *The Gentleman and the Kitchen Maid* (Dial Books for Young Readers, 1994), which contains numerous paintings reproduced by Dennis Nolan in the styles of famous European portrait artists.

356. Locker, Thomas. **Snow Toward Evening: A Year in a River Valley: Nature Poems Selected by Josette Frank** (Dial Books for Young Readers, 1990).

Artists—Hudson River School; Geography—United States; Hudson River Valley— New York; Landscape Painting; Nature; Paintings— Landscapes; Poetry; Read-Aloud; Seasons

Thirteen poems, one for each month and one for beginning the New Year, were selected by Locker (a noted landscape painter) to celebrate the changing seasons outside his studio.

Snow Toward Evening is nicely complemented by Diane Siebert's three poetic celebrations of other American landscapes: *Heartland* (Thomas Y. Crowell, 1989), *Mojave* (Thomas Y. Crowell, 1988), and *Sierra* (HarperCollins, 1991). Together they give a geographic overview of the United States.

This poetic and artistic celebration of nature can be shared at the beginning of each month, especially in the Northeast.

357. Locker, Thomas. **Where the River Begins** (Dial Books for Young Readers, 1984).

Artists—Hudson River School; Camping; Grandfathers; History of Art; Landscape Painting; Paintings—Landscapes

A grandfather and his two grandsons hike to the source of the river that flows beside their home.

The most powerful aspect of this book, along with Locker's *The Mare on the Hill* (Dial Books for Young Readers, 1985) and *Sailing with the Wind* (Dial Books for Young Readers, 1986), is the art that is done in the style of the Hudson River School painters of the 19th century. Introduce students to this school of artists by sharing the romantic, sometimes melodramatic landscapes painted by Thomas Cole (1801-1848), Asher Durand (1796-1886), Frederic Church (1826-1900), or Sandford Gifford (1823-1880).

358. Loewen, Nancy. **Poe: A Biography**. Photographic interpretation by Tina Mucci (Creative Education, 1993).

Biographies; Poe, Edgar Allan (1809-1849); Writers

Poe, an impressionistic photobiography of Edgar Allan Poe, features standard biographical information, excerpts from his poetry and stories, and dramatized scenes that complete a picture of the relationship between his life and his works.

 This visual and literary biography can influence student attitude about perennial biography assignments. Don't let the book's lack of bibliography, index, and source notes deter readers from finding out more about Poe. Provide books such as Suzanne LeVert's *Edgar Allan Poe* (Chelsea, 1992) and Kathleen Krull's *Lives of the Writers: Comedies, Tragedies (and What the Neighbors Thought)* (Harcourt Brace Jovanovich, 1994), as well as some of Poe's own writings. *Poe* is sure to appeal to reluctant readers in search of biographies.

359. Loewen, Nancy. **Walt Whitman**. Ill. by Rob Day (Creative Education, 1994).

Biographies; Poetry; Whitman, Walt (1819-1892)

Selections from Whitman's *Leaves of Grass* combined with other poetry, historical notes, and photographs create a unique biography. Index.

 Leaves of Grass was revised by Whitman throughout his lifetime and has been continuously in print since the first edition in 1855. This biography is terrific for introducing or complementing a study of Whitman and his ideals honoring nature, individualism, and democracy.

360. London, Jonathan. **The Eyes of Gray Wolf**. Ill. by Jon Van Zyle (Chronicle Books, 1993).

Current Events—Wolves; Endangered Species; Fears; Nature; Wildlife; Wolves— Reintroduction

Surveying his territory on a cold northern night, gray wolf comes upon an unknown wolf pack where a young female steps out to join him. Note.

 A book collection about wolves could include Seymour Simon's *Wolves* (HarperCollins, 1993), Candace Savagis' *Wolves* (Sierra, 1989), R. D. Lawrence's *Wolves* (Sierra/Little, Brown, 1990), *There's a Wolf in the Classroom!* by Bruce Weide and Patricia Tucker (Carolrhoda Books, 1995), and Sylvia A. Johnson and Alice Aamodt's *Wolf Pack: Tracking Wolves in the Wild* (Lerner, 1985). Consult "Wolves— Wicked or Wonderful?" by Marilyn Carpenter [*Book Links* 3(5):14-18, May 1994] for an extensive listing of resources and activities. A recent novel based on wolf reintroduction is Dorothy Hinshaw Patent's *Return of the Wolf* (Clarion Books, 1995).

Both the note from the author about the history and status of wolves, and the list of organizations working to help preserve and reintroduce wolves into their native habitats will be helpful in a study of these majestic animals. Students can trace the controversial reintroduction of wolves into Yellowstone National Park by accessing periodicals through indexes.

361. London, Jonathan. **Hip Cat**. Ill. by Woodleigh Hubbard (Chronicle Books, 1993).

Fame; Jazz; Musicians; Saxophones; Success

A jazzy rhythmic story tells of a "Hip Cat" seeking fame and fortune in the big city. Although it's hard to make ends meet, the cat learns it's important to "do what you love to do and do it well."

Perfect companion picture books include Chris Raschka's *Charlie Parker Played Be Bop* (Orchard, 1992) and *Ben's Trumpet* by Rachel Isadora (Greenwillow Books, 1979).

 = Geography = Art = Music = Drama = Speech = Research = Read-Aloud

Morgan Monceaux's *Jazz: My Music, My People* (Alfred A. Knopf, 1994) is an excellent introduction to the jazz musicians who have left their mark on this uniquely American genre of music. Many recordings by older artists are available on compact discs. Be sure to play as many as you can. Does your school system have a jazz band? If so, invite them to give a live performance.

362. Longfellow, Henry Wadsworth. **Paul Revere's Ride**. Ill. by Ted Rand (Dutton Children's Books, 1990).

American Revolution; Colonies—America; History— American Revolution—1775; Poetry; Revere, Paul (1735-1818); Revolutionary War; United States—History— Revolution—1775

The drama and suspense of the "midnight ride" featured in Longfellow's historic poem is enhanced by Rand's paintings. Note.

Students will immediately be drawn into the drama of Longfellow's poem by Rand's paintings. The endnote includes historic information about the actual ride. Another version of the poem, illustrated by Nancy Winslow Parker (Greenwillow Books, 1985), can be used for comparison purposes. Further research can focus on the real life of Paul Revere, folk hero of the American Revolution.

363. Lowe, Steve. **Walden**. Ill. by Robert Sabuda (Philomel, 1990).

Biographies; Environment—Human Impact; Environmental Action; Forests; Nature; Solitude; Thoreau, Henry David (1817-1862); Walden Pond

Selected excerpts from *Walden* accompanied by linoleum prints describe Thoreau's retreat into the woods and his discovery of the wonders of nature and joy of solitude.

This is an excellent profile of the life and work of Henry David Thoreau. The introduction provides a fine biographical sketch students can use to launch a more in-depth study. For another picture book biography of Walden see Robert Burleigh's *A Man Named Thoreau* (Atheneum, 1985).

A controversy over preserving Walden Pond and its legacy has developed 150 years after Thoreau first retreated there. Students can research periodicals to learn more about the status of the pond, the Walden Woods Project, and the Thoreau Society. Some students might be interested in investigating the commercializing of environmental crusades.

364. Lucht, Irmgard. **The Red Poppy** (Hyperion Books for Children, 1994).

Botany; Flowers; Life Cycles—Flowers; Nature; Plants; Poppies—Life Cycle; Science—Botany

The life cycle and intricate environment surrounding the red poppy is beautifully presented. Notes.

Books featuring other beautiful illustrations of flowers include Ken Robbins' *A Flower Grows* (Dial Books for Young Children, 1990), Anita Lobel's *Alison's Zinnia* (Greenwillow Books, 1990), and Jerome Wexler's *Jack-in-the-Pulpit* (Dutton Children's Books, 1993).

Blooming for only one day, the red poppy must be fertilized at that time to ensure seed production and the hope for future plants. Use *The Red Poppy* in introductory botany classes at any age or grade level.

365. Luenn, Nancy. **Song for the Ancient Forest**. Ill. by Jill Kastner (Atheneum, 1993).

Conservation; Forests— Old Growth; Logging; Nature; Pacific Northwest; Trees; Trickster Tales

Long ago Raven (the Trickster) dreamed of the destruction of the ancient forest. Though he warned others for centuries, no one believed him or understood him until he met Marni, the daughter of a logger.

Stage a debate about the logging and environmental issues addressed in *Song for the Ancient Forest*. Use the classic debate requirement of having students prepare to argue both sides of the issue. Have your students research all aspects of old-growth forest, timber industry

---

 = Extraordinary!   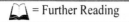 = Idea   = Further Reading   = Writing   = Math   = Science   = History

economics, and endangered species, as well as job training and career placement programs for displaced loggers. Student debate should be so effective that listeners find it difficult to support one position over the other. Helpful books include Richard Manning's *Last Stand: Logging, Journalism, and the Case for Humility* (Peregrine Smith, 1991), Steven Lewis Yaffee's *The Wisdom of the Spotted Owl: Policy Lessons for a New Century* (Island Press, 1994), Ruth Loomis' *Keeping the Forest Alive* (All About Us Canada, 1993), and Barbara Bash's *Ancient Ones: The World of the Old-Growth Douglas Fir* (Sierra Club Books, 1994). Journal articles under the topic heading "Forests and Forestry—the Pacific Northwest" can provide information on both sides of the issue.

366. Lyon, George Ella. **Cecil's Story**. Paintings by Peter Catalanotto (Orchard, 1991).

Civil War (1861-1865); Families; Fear; Historical Fiction; History—United States—Civil War (1861-1865); Letters; United States— History—Civil War (1861-1865); War

A boy worries as he waits at a neighbor's farm for his wounded father to return from the Civil War.

Letters written to loved ones during wartime accurately and emotionally reflect the toll a war takes, including the trauma of separation and fear. Students can examine collections of letters to gain a new perspective on their study of the Civil War. Perhaps they can carry on a correspondence with a historic letter writer selected from the following books. Books that include letters written throughout the Civil War include *The Brother's War: Civil War Letters to Their Loved Ones from the Blue and the Gray* edited by Annette Tapert (Times Books, 1988), *All for the Union: The Civil War Diary and Letters of Elisha Hunt Rhodes* edited by Robert Hart Rhodes (Orion, 1991), *Letters in American History: Words to Remember* by Jack Lang (Crown, 1982), *Letters from a Slave Girl: The Story of Harriet Jacobs* by Mary E. Lyons (Charles Scribner's Sons, 1992), *Becca's Story* by James D. Forman (Charles Scribner's Sons, 1992), and *Women as Letter Writers* by Richard Ingpen (Telegraph Books, 1981).

M

367. Macaulay, David. **Baaa** (Houghton Mifflin, 1985).

Allegory; Art—Cartoons; Cartoons; Civilization; Creative Writing; Satire; Societies

When the last person is gone from the earth, sheep take over. However, they make the same mistakes as humankind, and they too eventually vanish.

An allegory is defined as a "story in which people, things, and events have a symbolic meaning, often instructive." Often this literary concept is difficult for students to understand. Using Macaulay's book as an example, students can write an allegory about something important in their lives or their futures.

Cartoon artists Garry Trudeau (*Doonesbury*) and Bill Watterson (*Calvin and Hobbes*) regularly satirize our dependence on television, our blind trust in leaders, and our tendency to want to be like everyone else. Using cartooning techniques, students can spoof or satirize school, local, or state politics.

368. Macaulay, David. **Black and White** (Houghton Mifflin, 1990).

Art; Book Design— Unique; Humor; Literary Devices; Narratives—Nonlinear; Nonlinear Narratives; Perspective

Four stories work both independently and together as people, trains, cows, newspapers, and humor intertwine in a nonlinear fashion. Caldecott Medal, 1990.

Each quarter section of the page layout contains a distinct voice, plot, and illustration style. Focus student attention on the unchanging perspective of the upper right, the figure-ground visual play in the lower right, and the variety of voice in the narratives.

Architecture; Castles;
Construction; Medieval
Period; Middle Ages;
Social Life and Customs—
Medieval Period; Wales

369. Macaulay, David. **Castle** (Houghton Mifflin, 1977).

The planning and construction of a 13th-century Wales castle and adjoining town is explained through the text and detailed drawings. Although an imaginary castle, its design and specifications are based on several castles of that period and location. Caldecott Honor, 1978.

 The plans and information in these books make it possible for students to build miniature castles themselves.

 Use this book, Christopher Gravett's *Castle* (Alfred A. Knopf, 1994), Sarah Howarth's *The Middle Ages* (Viking, 1993), and the section about castles in *Stephen Biesty's Incredible Cross-Sections* by Richard Platt (Alfred A. Knopf, 1992) to enhance a study of the medieval period or medieval architecture. For additional information consult books recommended in "The Middle Ages" by Stanley Steiner and Linda Marie Zaerr [*Book Links* 4(2):11-15, November 1994] and watch the excellent PBS documentary narrated by Macaulay, *Castle* (PBS Video, 1983).

370. Macaulay, David. **Cathedral: The Story of Its Construction** (Houghton Mifflin, 1973).

371. Macaulay, David. **Pyramid: The Story of Its Construction** (Houghton Mifflin, 1975).

Architecture; Churches;
Construction; Gothic
Architecture; Pyramids;
Social Life and Customs—
Ancient Egypt; Social Life
and Customs—
Europe—1200s-1400s

Clear narratives accompanied by detailed drawings and architectural diagrams follow the long and complex construction of imaginary buildings—a 13th-century Gothic cathedral and an Egyptian pyramid. *Cathedral* was a Caldecott Honor Book, 1974.

 The real cathedrals built during the Gothic period in Europe are a testament to the artistry and hard work of the craftsmen and the desire of the citizenry to "thank God for His kindness." Be sure to include *Cathedral* in a European history class focusing on the 13th through 15th centuries. George Ancona's *Cutters, Carvers and the Cathedral* (Lothrop, Lee & Shepard, 1995), a photo essay of the construction of the Cathedral of Saint John the Divine in New York City, is an interesting companion book.

372. Macaulay, David. **Motel of the Mysteries** (Houghton Mifflin, 1979).

Archeology; Careers;
Creative Writing; Future;
Humor; Satire

Macaulay provides a look into the future at a 4022 A.D. discovery and investigation of the ancient ruins of a motel (circa 1985 A.D.) in a country known as Usa.

 Written as a parody on Howard Carter and his discovery of King Tut's tomb, *Motel of the Mysteries* is nevertheless a wonderful introduction to the field of archeology. Provide books that highlight actual discoveries and investigations such as Nicholas Reeves' *Into the Mummy's Tomb: The Real Life Discovery of Tutankhamen's Treasures* (Scholastic, 1992), John W. Hackwell's *Digging to the Past: Excavations in Ancient Lands* (Charles Scribner's Sons, 1986), and Jane McIntosh's *Archeology* (Alfred A. Knopf, 1994). A related book that curious readers will enjoy is Penny Colman's *Toilets, Bathtubs, Sinks, and Sewers: A History of the Bathroom* (Atheneum, 1994).

 This sophisticated book appeals to adults and older students. Use it as a satiric model for student writing and speeches where "artifacts" can be used for visual humor.

---

373. Macaulay, David. **Ship** (Houghton Mifflin, 1993).

Adventures; Archeology; Caribbean; Exploration; History—15th Century; Journals; Ships; Shipwrecks

Follow marine archaeologists as they recover a caravel, sunken in the Caribbean, and discover a journal describing the construction of these long-lost ships that were used for coastal and transatlantic exploration. Although fictional, this story is based on recent work by archaeologists and historians.

Macaulay's *Motel of the Mysteries* (Houghton Mifflin, 1979) and *Ship* can be used to pique interest in the field of archeology. Invite an archaeologist to share information about his or her chosen career.

Caravels were ships that served as "space shuttles of the fifteenth century." Use *Ship* as an introduction to a study of exploration during this time period. Some students may want to focus their research efforts on the different ships of various countries.

374. Macaulay, David. **The Way Things Work** (Houghton Mifflin, 1988).

Inventions; Machines; Physics; Science; Technology

Much of the world's technology is explored in this visual guide filled with line drawings and highlighted with watercolors. Hundreds of devices and machines are arranged under four categories: the mechanics of movement (e.g., levers, screws, friction), harnessing the elements (e.g., heat, wind, water), working with waves (e.g., light, sound, telecommunications), and electricity and automation (e.g., electricity, magnetism, computers).

This is a "must" reference source for any classes studying technology, machines, and/or physics. An excellent companion book is *The Random House Book of How Things Work* by Steve Parker (Random House, 1991).

375. MacGill-Callahan, Sheila. **And Still the Turtle Watched**. Ill. by Barry Moser (Dial Books for Young Readers, 1991).

Artifacts; Creative Writing; Ecology; Environment—Human Impact; Graffiti; Museums; Pollution; Sculptures; Turtles

A turtle, carved into a rock long ago, watches as humankind encroaches on nature and begins to destroy the area with pollution, neglect, and graffiti.

This original story was inspired by a statue at the New York Botanical Garden. Visit a museum, or provide pictures of a variety of sculptures, and have students write stories about the past life of one of those pieces of art. Display a picture of the sculpture along with the story.

This story can serve as an introduction to how and where museums get their artifacts.

376. Maestro, Betsy and Giulio Maestro. **A More Perfect Union: The Story of Our Constitution** (Lothrop, Lee & Shepard, 1987).

Bill of Rights; Constitution; Documents; Government—United States; History—United States—1787; United States—History—1787

The Maestros present the four-year story of the Constitution (the foundation of the U.S. government) from the opening of the Constitutional Convention to the ratification of the Bill of Rights. Additional information includes the preamble, a summary of the Articles of the Constitution and the amendments, notes on the delegates, a chronology, and other assorted facts of interest.

Use this basic presentation with students who are confused over the series of events that took place at the Constitutional Convention and/or are unsure about facts related to the Constitution and the Bill of Rights.

377. Mahy, Margaret. **17 Kings and 42 Elephants**. Ill. by Patricia MacCarthy (Dial Books for Young Readers, 1987).

Alliteration; Art—Batiks; Assonance; Batiks; Creative Writing; Imagery; Jungle Animals; Literary Devices; Poetry; Read-Aloud

Kings and elephants journey through a wild, wet jungle night with other animals moving to their beat.

Teachers looking for examples of alliteration, assonance, and imagery should read aloud this infectious, rollicking poem.

 = Geography   = Art   = Music   = Drama   = Speech   = Research   = Read-Aloud

Where have the kings and elephants come from? Where are they going? Students can write more about this "wild, wet jungle night."

378. Manson, Christopher. **Two Travelers** (Henry Holt, 1990).

Charlemagne (742-812 A.D.); Elephants; France—8th Century; Friendship; Geography; Hannibal (247-183 B.C.); Peace; Travel

The elephant Abulabaz (a gift of peace to the emperor Charlemagne of France from the Caliph of Baghdad) and ambassador Isaac become friends during their arduous journey to France. Afterword.

Use elephants as a study theme. In addition to this story, have students research Hannibal taking elephants over the Alps in his campaign against the Romans during the Second Punic War and the killing of the elephants in the Tokyo Zoo in World War II. Consult Yukio Tsuchiya's *Faithful Elephants: A True Story of Animals, People and War* (Houghton Mifflin, 1988). Another picture book that involves the gift of an elephant from royalty is *The Stolen White Elephant* by Mark Twain (P.I.C. Pty Ltd., 1987).

Using the story, based on a true event in 787 A.D., students can plot the possible route Abulabaz and Isaac took from Baghdad to France.

379. Martin, Rafe. **The Boy Who Lived with the Seals**. Ill. by David Shannon (G. P. Putnam's Sons, 1993).

Art—Carving; Canoes; Chinook Indians—Legends; Indians of North America; Legends; Memories; Seals; Storytelling

Hope is never abandoned for the boy lost along the great river. When he is spotted swimming with the seals, he is captured and brought back to the People. Although he loves his parents, his home under the sea calls him back. Note.

Both the People of the Northwest Coast and their art are distinctively portrayed in this book. Students can discover more about their past and present lives, art, cultural motifs, and stories through research. The author's note is a good beginning point. The *Cobblestone* issue "Indians of the Northwest Coast" [13(9), November 1992] will be of help, as will *The Prince and the Salmon People* by Claire Rudolf Murphy (Rizolli International Publications, 1993).

380. Maruki, Toshi. **Hiroshima No Pika** (Lothrup, Lee & Shepard, 1980).

Art—Visual Literacy; Atomic Bomb; Children and War; Hiroshima; History—World War II— Japan; Japan—History— World War II; Peace; Visual Literacy; World War II

The 1945 bombing of Hiroshima is told through the experience of a mother and her daughter. Notes.

Use this title with *My Hiroshima* by Junko Morimoto (Viking, 1987) and *Sadako* by Eleanor Coerr (G. P. Putnam's Sons, 1993) to explore the issue of war through an individual's experience. Provide John Hersey's *Hiroshima* (Alfred A. Knopf, 1985) for a look at what life was like for six individuals in Hiroshima the day the atomic bomb was dropped. Use picture books that depict other cultures and places during World War II (see the subject index) and provide *On the Wings of Peace: Writers and Illustrators Speak Out for Peace in Memory of Hiroshima and Nagasaki* (Clarion Books, 1995). What common emotional experiences did young people of this period share?

Visual literacy can be enhanced by an in-depth study of picture book art. Have students study the illustrations in *Hiroshima No Pika*. Discuss how the artist makes the shock, terror, and suffering become personal. Notice how the illustrations fill the page with swirling fire, dark masses, and figures defined by bleeding watercolor lines.

381. Mason, Cherie. **Wild Fox: A True Story**. Ill. by Jo Ellen McAllister Stammen (Down East Books, 1993).

Animals—Foxes;
Environmental Action;
Foxes; Life Cycles; Maine;
New England—Maine;
Trapping; Wildlife

A young fox, disabled by a steel-jawed trap, is befriended by the author. Always remaining wild (coming and going when he chooses, hunting his own food, and interacting with other foxes), the fox develops an unusual relationship with Mason for half a year.

 The use of steel-jawed traps, like the one that injured this fox, are outlawed in more than 65 countries. Students might investigate more about these traps and why they are still used legally in some parts of the United States.

Many children find human-wild animal relationships fascinating. Help those students find other books, such as Joseph Bruchac's *Fox Song* (Philomel, 1993), to discover more true animal-human adventures.

382. Mattingley, Christobel. **The Angel with a Mouth-Organ**. Ill. by Astra Lacis (Holiday House, 1984).

Angels; Christmas;
Families; Harmonicas;
Historical Fiction; History—
World War II—Europe;
Music; Refugees; Survival;
World War II—Europe

Placing the angel on the Christmas tree is the inspiration for the mother to retell the story of her family's survival as refugees during World War II.

Focusing on one family's struggle to survive as war refugees can make more of an impact than hard facts on students beginning to study World War II. Use this book for that endeavor.

383. Mattingley, Christobel. **The Miracle Tree**. Ill. by Marianne Yamaguchi (Harcourt Brace Jovanovich, 1985).

Atomic Bomb; Christmas;
Creative Writing; Gardening;
Historical Fiction; History—
Japan—World War II;
Japan—History—World
War II; Literary Devices;
Love; Nagasaki; Origami

In Japan, during World War II, a husband, his beautiful and beloved wife, and her mother are separated by the bombing of Nagasaki. It is the nurturing of a tree that eventually reunites them one Christmas.

 A woman known only as Shizuka watches the growth of the tree from her window across the street. She is a victim of the bombing; her memory is gone, she is scarred and frail. She watches the tree in the sunlight, the moonlight, blowing in the wind, and covered with raindrops, and she is inspired to write poetry. What might some of her poems be? Students can write examples.

The literary device *simile* is defined as an explicit comparison of one unlike thing to another when they share some common similarity. *The Miracle Tree* is rich with similes such as "skin as smooth as a camellia petal," "hair as shiny as a crow's wing," "eyes sparkled like pools in the sun," "voice rang like a bell." Students can locate these and other similes and build an understanding of the power of this literary device.

 384. Maupassant, Guy de. **The Necklace**. Ill. by Gary Kelley (Creative Editions, 1993).

Despair; Greed; Irony; Liter-
ary Devices; Literature—
French; Maupassant, Guy de
(1850-1893); Read-Aloud;
Short Stories; Vanity

Discontented with her dreary life, Madame Loisel borrows a diamond necklace for a party. After she loses it, she and her husband devote 10 years working to replace the necklace only to discover that it was costume jewelry.

Long recognized as a classic short story writer, Guy de Maupassant is required reading in many literature classes. Provide this elegantly illustrated version to pique interest, and watch students devour the rest.

This timeless story is a classic example of irony, a literary device that is sometimes missed by readers. Use it, along with the illustrated version of O. Henry's *The Gift of the Magi* (Picture Book Studio, 1982), to explain irony.

Daughters; Family Relationships; Fathers; Jealousy; Magritte, René (1898-1967); Single Parent Families; Surrealism

385. McAfee, Annalena and Anthony Browne. **The Visitors Who Came to Stay** (Viking, 1984).

Surreal illustrations reflect the changes in Katy's life when her single father's friend Mary and her son come to visit.

For a further look at surrealism, provide *Dinner at Magritte's* by Michael Garland (E. P. Dutton, 1995), a fascinating surreal visit with René Magritte and Salvador Dali and a fine introduction to the work of these artists.

Much of illustrator/author Anthony Browne's work is influenced by the surreal French artist René Magritte. In fact, there are direct references to Magritte in *The Visitors Who Came to Stay*. Provide students with *Magritte: The True Art of Painting* by Harry Torczyner (Henry N. Abrams, 1985). Look for tributes to these paintings by Magritte: "The Red Model," "Personal Values," "Time Transfixed," "The Explanation," and "The Reckless Sleeper."

Architecture; Folklore—Indians of North America; Indians of North America; Mythology—Pueblo; Pueblo Indians; Religions—Pueblo Indians; Spirits

386. McDermott, Gerald. **Arrow to the Sun: A Pueblo Indian Tale** (Harcourt Brace Jovanovich, 1974).

A young man sets out to prove he is the son/spirit of the Lord of the Sun in this retelling of an ancient Pueblo myth. Caldecott Medal, 1975.

The sun has played an important role in many religions and myths throughout time. For further reading provide other stories about the sun, including McDermott's *Raven: A Trickster Tale from the Pacific Northwest* (Harcourt Brace Jovanovich, 1993) and the Greek myth of Prometheus stealing fire from heaven.

Pueblo art, architecture, and religion are featured in McDermott's stylized paintings. Further study can center on the wide variety of Pueblo pottery; religious ceremonies, including the use of kivas; and the Pueblo style of architecture. Consult "The Art of Gerald McDermott" by Dona Helmer [*Book Links* 4(5):20-24, May 1995], especially the section entitled "Coyote: An Illustrator's Notes" (pp. 22-23), for more information about McDermott's incorporation of Pueblo designs in his work. Other books about Pueblo life include *Pueblo Boy: Growing Up in Two Worlds* by Marcia Keegan (Cobblehill, 1991) and *Pueblo Storyteller* by Diane Hoyt-Goldsmith (Holiday House, 1991).

387. McDermott, Gerald. **Coyote: A Trickster Tale from the Southwest** (Harcourt Brace Jovanovich, 1994).

388. McDermott, Gerald. **Papagayo: The Mischief Maker** (Harcourt Brace Jovanovich, 1992).

389. McDermott, Gerald. **Raven: A Trickster Tale from the Pacific Northwest** (Harcourt Brace Jovanovich, 1993).

390. McDermott, Gerald. **Zomo the Rabbit: A Trickster Tale from West Africa** (Harcourt Brace Jovanovich, 1992).

Amazon; Folklore—African; Folklore—Indians of North America; Folklore—South America; Humor; Indians of North America; Legends; Rain Forests; South America—Folklore; Storytelling; Trickster Tales; West Africa

Each title in McDermott's series of trickster tales features a traditional story from a different culture and country. Coyote wheedles feathers from crows, Papagayo saves the moon from being eaten in the Amazon, Raven finds the sun in the Pacific Northwest, and Zomo finds wisdom in West Africa. *Raven: A Trickster Tale from the Pacific Northwest* received a Caldecott Honor Book award in 1994.

 = Extraordinary! = Idea = Further Reading = Writing $\frac{2}{4}$ = Math = Science = History

On the back side of each title page, McDermott includes information about the featured tricksters. These stories are perfect for comparison studies with other trickster tales. Consider "Anansi" tales from Africa, "Iktomi" stories from the Plains Indians, and others.

Have students read *Zomo* and the Brer Rabbit "Jump" stories adapted by Van Dyke Parks (Harcourt Brace Jovanovich). Brer Rabbit's roots come from Zomo and can spark a discussion of traditional storytelling before this century.

391. McDermott, Gerald. **Daughter of Earth: A Roman Myth** (Delacorte Press, 1984).

Ceres; Kidnapping; Mythology—Roman; Myths; Pluto; Porsepina; Roman Mythology; Seasons

When Pluto wrongly takes Porsepina to be his bride in the Underworld, Ceres, Mother of Porsepina and Goddess of Earth, withdraws to mourn and refuses to allow crops to grow. Note.

Introduce Roman myths that students can compare and contrast with Greek myths. Provide picture book versions of Greek myths such as those by Warwick Hutton.

392. McDonald, Megan. **The Potato Man**. Ill. by Ted Lewin (Orchard, 1991).

Antique Cars; Christmas; Historical Fiction; History—United States—1920s; Kindness; Peddlers; Setting; Social Life and Customs—United States—1920

A grandfather tells of a time when peddlers sold their wares from wagons and he was befriended by the potato man whom he had been taunting.

This book is excellent for understanding "setting" within stories. Students can discover the approximate time period of this story by researching the production dates for the heyday of the Stanley Steamer featured in the story. If available, also use the author's *The Great Pumpkin* (Orchard, 1992).

393. McDonough, Yona Zeldis. **Eve and Her Sisters: Women of the Old Testament**. Paintings by Malcah Zeldis (Greenwillow Books, 1994).

Bible Stories; Bible Studies; Biblical History; Literature—Bible; Women

Brief accounts of 14 women mentioned in the Old Testament are presented, stressing the human aspects of their stories.

Use this book for a study of the Bible as literature. Students can select other well-known women (from biblical or other times) and write about them in human terms.

 394. McGugan, Jim. **Josepha: A Prairie Boy's Story**. Ill. by Murray Kimber (Chronicle Books, 1994).

Canada—History—1900s; Friendship; Historical Fiction; History—Canada—1900s; History of Art; Immigrants; Isolation; Pioneer Life; Schools

Forced to sit with the little children until he learns English, Josepha is an outcast. Despite cultural and language barriers, one strong friendship emerges before he must leave school to help support his family.

Using *Three Names* by Patricia MacLachlan (Charlotte Zolotow Books, 1991) helps complete the picture of what it was like to attend a one-room school on the prairie at the turn of the century, while Jo Bannatyne-Cugnet's *A Prairie Alphabet* (Tundra, 1992) presents a modern-day perspective of prairie life.

Middle school students will feel the power and sorrow in this understated and intense story of friendship that transcends cultural and language barriers. This book is perfect for introducing a study of immigration to North America at the turn of the century. *Peppe the Lamplighter* by Elisa Bartone (Lothrop, Lee & Shepard, 1993), *New Hope* by Henri Sorensen (Lothrop, Lee & Shepard, 1995), and *Watch the Stars Come Out* by Riki Levinson (E. P. Dutton, 1985) are related books of interest.

 = Geography   = Art   = Music   = Drama   = Speech Q = Research   = Read-Aloud

Kimber's illustrations contain subtle references to specific movements and artists in 20th-century painting including the styles of Thomas Hart Benton (1782-1858), Henri Matisse (1869-1954), and Fauvism. Advanced art history students can identify these movements and artists and locate reproductions with similar elements.

395. McKissack, Patricia C. and Fredrick L. McKissack. **Christmas in the Big House, Christmas in the Quarters**. Ill. by John Thompson (Scholastic, 1994).

An 1859 Christmas celebration is portrayed in a big Virginia plantation house and in the slave quarters. The book includes holiday customs, recipes, poems, and songs. Endnotes.

Christmas—19th Century; Freedom; History—United States—1775-1865; Plantation Life; Slaves; Social Life and Customs—Southern States— 19th Century; Southern States—History—19th Century

Joan Anderson's *A Williamsburg Household* (Clarion Books, 1988) features two households in 1770 (the white homeowners and their slaves) while John Goodall's *Great Days of a Country House* (Margaret K. McElderry, 1992) shows festivities and everyday events at a mythical British country house from 1485 to the present. Focusing on the 18th and 19th centuries, compare and contrast the social life and customs featured in all three books.

The McKissacks weave together events and topics of the United States in the 19th century. Complement this narrative with research and reading about John Brown's raid, slave uprisings, the issue of secession, war, and other historical events.

396. Meeks, Arone Raymond. **Enora and the Black Crane** (Scholastic, 1991).

Enora, a young man living in the rain forest, changes his life forever when he kills a crane to prove to his people that he has seen a bird with colors.

Aborigines; Art— Aborigines; Australia; Birds; Folktales—Aboriginal; Painting—Aboriginal Style; Rain Forests—Australia; Social Studies; Spirits; Wildlife Conservation

Meeks, an Aboriginal artist, illustrated this book in the traditional style of the Aborigines. Compare his illustrations with Bronwyn Bancroft's in Oodgeroo Nunukul's *Dreamtime* (Lothrop, Lee & Shepard, 1994) for a greater understanding of the style.

Meeks is a member of the Kokoimundji tribe and grew up on the Australian coast near Dunk Island. Use Jeanie Adams' *Going for Oysters.* (Whitman, 1994), a picture book featuring a contemporary Aborigine family on a weekend fishing and oyster hunting trip; Richard Nile's *Australian Aborigines* (Raintree, 1993), Jan Reynolds' *Down Under: Vanishing Cultures* (Harcourt Brace Jonanovich 1992), Jeannie Baker's *Where the Forest Meets the Sea* (Greenwillow Books, 1987); and other titles to commence a study on the Australian Aboriginal culture.

397. Mellecker, Judith. **Randolph's Dream**. Ill. by Robert Andrew Parker (Alfred A. Knopf, 1991).

An English boy, sent away from London during the bombing, dreams he saves his father, who is on duty in the North African desert.

Africa—North; Bombs; Children and War; Dreams; England—History—World War II; Fathers and Sons; Historical Fiction; History— England—World War II; World War II—England

During World War II thousands of British children were evacuated to the British countryside as well as to the United States, Canada, Australia, New Zealand, and South Africa. Students may wish to do further research on this topic and time period; one particular event worth examining is the tragic sinking of *The City of Benares,* which brought an end to the evacuations. Numerous fictional accounts are also available depending on student interest and reading levels; consult a librarian.

❗ = Extraordinary! 💡 = Idea 📖 = Further Reading   = Writing $\frac{2}{4}$ = Math   = Science   = History

398. Melville, Herman. **Catskill Eagle**. Paintings by Thomas Locker (Philomel, 1991).

Paintings accompany a passage about nature excerpted from Melville's *Moby-Dick,* written in 1851.

Catskill Mountains; Eagles; Endangered Species; Environment—Human Impact; Literature—American; Melville, Herman (1819-1891); Moby-Dick; Nature— Appreciation

The text for this book is a passage from Chapter 96 in Herman Melville's *Moby-Dick; or, The Whale* (World's Classics Series, 1988). Locker's introductory note concerning Melville's visit to Kaaterskill Clove in the Catskill Mountains is essential to share with students. This Melville/Locker picture book is a surefire way to begin, or reinvigorate, discussions about Melville and his writing.

The 100 years that separated Melville's and Locker's visits to Kaaterskill Clove in the Catskill Mountains makes their appreciation for nature even more dramatic. Use *Catskill Eagle* for beginning a study on the tenuous survival of various eagle species as humankind invades its natural habitat.

399. Mendez, Phil. **The Black Snowman**. Ill. by Carole Byard (Scholastic, 1989).

A dirty city snowman, draped with the magic kente cloth, comes to life and reveals to Jacob and Peewee the importance of their African heritage. He also brings to Jacob, particularly, needed self-esteem.

African Americans; Ashanti Tribe; Black History Month; Creative Writing; Heritage; Magic; Self-Esteem; Storytelling

The magic kente cloth brings *The Black Snowman* to life with a powerful blending of realism, history, and fantasy. Using this ancient cloth (which came from Africa with the slaves) as a vehicle, students can write the next episode in the "life" of this magic cloth.

This story, along with Dakari Hru's *Joshua's Masai Mask* (Lee & Low Books, 1993), can be included in a multicultural study featuring Black history.

 400. Merrill, Jean. **The Girl Who Loved Caterpillars**. Ill. by Floyd Cooper (Philomel, 1992).

Resisting the pressures of her family and Japanese society to conform, a 12th-century girl maintains her passion for caterpillars. Afterword.

Caterpillars; Conduct of Life—Women; Gender Roles; Japan—History—12th Century; Social Life and Customs—Japan—12th Century; Women

Although this book is based on a 12th-century scroll, it dramatizes the struggle for independence that many capable and strong young women face in many cultures today. A classroom library or a book list with titles by and about women who have succeeded might include *I Know Why the Caged Bird Sings* by Maya Angelou (Random House, 1970), *Beloved* by Toni Morrison (Alfred A. Knopf, 1987), *Having Our Say: The Delany Sisters' First 100 Years* by Sarah Louis Delany and Annie Elizabeth Delany (Kodansha International, 1993), *The Color Purple* by Alice Walker (Harcourt Brace Jovanovich, 1982), *Shabanu* by Suzanne Fisher Staples (Alfred A. Knopf, 1989), *Wise Child* by Monica Furlong (Alfred A. Knopf, 1987), *American Women, Their Lives in Their Words* edited by Doreen Rappaport (HarperCollins/Thomas Y. Crowell, 1990), *The Autobiography of Miss Jane Pittman* by Ernest Gaines (Doubleday, 1971), and *The Woman Warrior: Memoirs of a Girlhood Among Ghosts* by Maxine Hong Kingston (Alfred A. Knopf, 1976). Another picture book that depicts a strong woman is Robert N. Munsch's *The Paper Bag Princess* (Annick Press, 1980).

401. Micklethwait, Lucy, devised and selected by. **I Spy: A Lion—Animals in Art** (Greenwillow Books, 1994).

402. Micklethwait, Lucy, devised and selected by. **I Spy: An Alphabet in Art** (Greenwillow Books, 1992).

403. Micklethwait, Lucy, devised and selected by. **I Spy Two Eyes—Numbers in Art** (Greenwillow Books, 1993).

Alphabet Books; Animals; Art Galleries; Counting Books; Games; History of Art; Literary Recreations; Museums; Paintings; Picture Puzzles; Visual Perception

Organizing paintings by theme is the focus of these art appreciation books with partially hidden animals, alphabetical objects, or groups of objects from 1 to 20.

 Complementary art books include the out-of-print but superb *Beasts: An Alphabet of Fine Prints* by Catherine Leuthold Fuller (Little, Brown, 1968), *Animals Observed: A Look at Animals in Art* by Dorcas MacClintock (Charles Scribner's Sons, 1993), and Gladys S. Blizzard's *Come Look with Me: Enjoying Art with Children* (Thomasson-Grant, 1990).

Older students can prepare in-depth oral or written reports about the art and artists featured in any of these art books, or from the "gallery of reproductions" project below, to further enhance knowledge and art appreciation.

Exploring fine art is made fun with these books. Students can search the reproductions, which often include whimsical details, for the partially hidden objects. Create your own classroom "gallery of reproductions" by using Micklethwait's organizational themes (animals, alphabet, or numbers) or other general ones like colors, buildings, music, etc. Students can select appropriate reproductions from fine art books or from circulating library collections.

404. Mikolaycak, Charles. **Orpheus** (Harcourt Brace Jovanovich, 1992).

Allegory; Death; Eurydice; Greek Mythology; Grief; Love; Music; Mythology; Orpheus

With explicit illustrations, Mikolaycak retells the tragic myth of Orpheus and his eternal love for the doomed Eurydice. Note. Bibliography. Discography.

The note at the conclusion of the book lists a variety of information about the Orpheus story and further retellings in various forms—opera, ballads, poetry, paintings, and films. Provide students with some of these versions for further study.

High school students studying Greek myths, or the tale of Orpheus in particular, will be absorbed by this retelling. The artwork is elaborate and detailed; the text, including the songs of Orpheus, is poetic and melodic.

405. Miller, Debbie S. **A Caribou Journey**. Ill. by Jon Van Zyle (Little, Brown, 1994).

Arctic; Caribou; Environmental Action; Environments— Arctic; Life Cycles

In narrative form *Caribou Journey* presents the life cycle of the caribou and the seasonal changes in the Arctic environment.

Students may be interested in knowing about the project to restore woodland caribou in Maine, which received some funds from the sale of Mary Beth Owens' *A Caribou Alphabet* (Dog Ear Press, 1988). This picture book includes a compendium with additional facts concerning caribou and their habits and habitats. Students can research the "Maine Audubon—Caribou fund" and/or the current status of caribou herds in North America, northern Europe, and Asia.

*Africa—East
Droughts; Folklore—
Africa; Geography;
Magic; Masai (African
People); Planets—Venus;
Pourquoi Stories*

406. Mollel, Tololwa M. **The Orphan Boy**. Ill. by Paul Morin (Clarion Books, 1990).

The old man's insatiable curiosity about an orphan boy's ability to feed and water the animals despite the drought breaks the trust and magic that had existed between the two. The "orphan boy," known to the Masai as the planet Venus ("Kileken"), returns to the sky.

 Weather experiments and activities for middle-grade students can be found on "Daily Planet," the home page of the Department of Atmospheric Sciences at http://faldo.atmos.uiuc.edu/TUA_/Home.html.

 Pourquoi tales answer the question "Why?" or explain "how" an animal, plant, star, etc., was created or came to have certain characteristics. Other pourquoi tales include Barbara Knutson's *How the Guinea Fowl Got Her Spots: A Swahili Tale of Friendship* (Carolrhoda Books, 1990), Ann Dixon's *How Raven Brought Light to People* (Margaret K. McElderry/Macmillan, 1992), and Sherry Garland's *Why Ducks Sleep on One Leg* (Scholastic, 1993).

 Droughts periodically plague different areas of the world, and East Africa is no exception. The paintings in this book highlight the extreme differences between the land when it is drought stricken and when it is lush with vegetation. Further study can focus on weather patterns, specific natural phenomena (e.g., droughts, hurricanes, tornadoes), and/or the economics of weather-related disasters. Recommended resources are listed in "Changing Weather Patterns" by Barbara Elleman [*Book Links* 3(2):29-32, November 1993]. Another picture book for older readers that deals with droughts is *Drylongso* by Virginia Hamilton (Harcourt Brace Jovanovich, 1992).

 The photo-realistic paintings give the modern reader a connecting bridge to this Masai pourquoi story from East Africa. Other folktales such as Judy Sierra's *The Elephant's Wrestling Match* (Dutton/Lodestar Books, 1992), Blaise Cendrars' *Shadow* (Charles Scribner's Sons, 1982), Gerald McDermott's *Zomo the Rabbit: A Trickster Tale from West Africa* (Harcourt Brace Jovanovich, 1992), Verna Aardema's *Why Mosquitoes Buzz in People's Ears: A West African Tale* (Dial Press, 1975), and John Steptoe's *Mufaro's Beautiful Daughters: An African Tale* (Lothrop, Lee & Shepard, 1987) can help give a picture of the rich cultural heritage of the region.

*Biographies; Jazz;
Musicians—Biographies;
Musicians—Jazz*

407. Monceaux, Morgan. **Jazz: My Music, My People** (Alfred A. Knopf, 1994).

Personal recollections, biographies, and paintings tell the story of the people who created and influenced jazz. Foreword. Glossary. Index.

This history of jazz begins with Buddy Bolden (1868-1931), the legendary trumpet player who formed the first jazz band. While sharing the stories of these musicians, provide students with jazz recordings to hear. In recent years numerous historic recordings have been rereleased on compact discs and are available for purchase and through library collections.

 = Geography   = Art   = Music   = Drama   = Speech   = Research   = Read-Aloud

Art—Visual Literacy;
Atomic Bomb; Children
and War; Hiroshima;
History—Japan—World War
II; Japan—History—World
War II; Visual Literacy;
War; World War II—
History—Japan

408. Morimoto, Junko. **My Hiroshima** (Viking, 1987).

Written in memory of the author's many friends, Morimoto vividly retells her experience as a young girl growing up in Hiroshima before and after the dropping of the first atomic bomb. Notes.

Contrast this title with *Hiroshima No Pika* by Toshi Maruki (Lothrup, Lee & Shepard, 1980). Both present the bombing from a child's perspective. How else are they similar? How do they differ in text and visuals?

Line and watercolor illustrations are combined with photographs at the end of the book to describe the first use of an atomic bomb in warfare. Observe how the artist changed the line quality, color scheme, and depiction of the air to communicate the changes in one child's life and world. Discuss how these artistic devices strengthened the impact of the story.

Cows; Dairy Farms;
Farm Life; Memories;
Social Studies; Stories—
Families; Storytelling; Time

409. Morris, Linda Lowe. **Morning Milking**. Ill. by David Deran (Picture Book Studio, 1991).

While helping her father with the milking, a girl discovers the "way to stop time" is to turn loving family memories into stories.

Family farms are disappearing as corporate farms buy up smaller operations. Several picture books can be used to present a historic look at family farms: Donald Hall's *Ox-Cart Man* (Viking, 1979) and *The Farm Summer 1942* (Dial Books for Young Readers, 1994), Thomas Locker's *Family Farm* (Dial Books for Young Readers, 1988), Tony Johnston's *Yonder* (Dial Books for Young Readers, 1988), Candace Christiansen's *Calico and Tin Horns* (Dial Books for Young Readers, 1992), and Patricia MacLachlan's *All the Places to Love* (HarperCollins, 1994). *Born to the Land: An American Portrait* by Brent K. Ashabranner (G.P. Putnam's Sons, 1989), *The American Family Farm* by Joan Anderson (Harcourt Brace Jovanovich, 1989), *Portrait of a Family Farm* by Raymond Bial (Houghton Mifflin, 1995), and *Voices from the Field: Children of Migrant Farm Workers Tell Their Stories* by S. Beth Atkin (Little, Brown, 1993) present farming information for reports.

Accidents;
Ballads; Ghosts; Hunting
Safety; Love; Music;
Read-Aloud; South;
Tragedies; Trials;

410. Moser, Barry. **Polly Vaughn** (Little, Brown, 1992).

Inspired by a traditional British ballad, Moser sets this tragic story in the Deep South. It features two sweethearts whose love is interrupted by a hunting accident. Afterword.

Although hunting and hunting safety is a small thread in this story, it can act as a springboard for a look at hunting accidents and prevention methods.

In the afterword Moser explains why he was interested in retelling this song. Interested students can obtain the verses of other ballads, such as the familiar "Barbara Allen," and experiment with story versions in various settings.

 = Extraordinary!   = Idea    = Further Reading   = Writing   = Math   = Science   = History

411. Moser, Barry, retold by. **The Tinderbox** (Little, Brown, 1990).

412. Moser, Barry. **Tucker Pfeffercorn: An Old Story Retold** (Little, Brown, 1994).

Moser retells the "The Tinderbox" by Hans Christian Andersen and "Rumpelstiltskin" by the Brothers Grimm, both set in the American South.

Andersen, Hans Christian (1805-1875); Evil; Fairy Tales; Folklore—Germany; Foreshadowing; Greed; Grimm, Brothers; Lies; Literacy Devices; Read-Aloud; Rumpelstiltskin; Soldiers— Confederate; South

The afterword to *The Tinderbox* explains why Moser used a more modern setting. Compare this retelling to others set more traditionally such as *The Tinderbox* illustrated by Warwick Hutton (Macmillan, 1988). Does the Moser retelling seem more frightening than the others because of the contemporary setting?

The use of Tucker Pfeffercorn's silhouette on the book cover sets the stage for the story and serves as a fine example of foreshadowing. Show it to students as a concrete example of this literary device. For a beautifully illustrated traditional version of this story use *Rumpelstilt-skin* retold and illustrated by Paul O. Zelinsky (E. P. Dutton, 1986) or *Rumpelstiltskin* retold by Alison Sage (Dial Press, 1991).

413. Mullins, Patricia. **V for Vanishing: An Alphabet of Endangered Animals** (HarperCollins, 1994).

In this book, featuring information on 25 species faced with possible extinction and a page of those already extinct, Mullins highlights animals in their natural environment.

Alphabet Books; Conservation; Endangered Species

Alphabet books have been published since the 16th century and often are not intended to teach children the letters of the alphabet. Instead they have been used for teaching morality ("In Adam's fall we sinned all"), for fun (Graeme Base's *Animalia* [Harry N. Abrams, 1986]), and for information, like *V for Vanishing: An Alphabet of Endangered Animals*. Provide a variety of alphabet books for students to peruse. A collection of informational alphabet books would not be complete with at least some of these: *Ashanti to Zulu: African Traditions* by Margaret Musgrove (Dial Press, 1976), *Away from Home* by Anita Lobel (Greenwillow Books, 1994), *Jambo Means Hello: Swahili Alphabet Book* by Muriel Feelings (Dial Press, 1985), *Illuminations* by Jonathan Hunt (Bradbury Press, 1989), *The ABC Exhibit* by Leonard Everett Fisher (Macmillan, 1991), *The Z Was Zapped: A Play in Twenty-Six Acts* by Chris Van Allsburg (Houghton Mifflin, 1987), and *Hieroglyphs for A to Z: A Rhyming Book with Ancient Egyptian Stencils for Kids* by Peter Der Manuelian (Rizzoli, 1991).

Another alphabet picture book that features endangered or extinct animals is Ann Jonas' *Aardvarks, Disembark!* (Greenwillow Books, 1990). Structure a study of these animals by having students select those featured in these books. Consult the May 1993 edition of *Book Links* 2(5):58-62 for "Endangered Animals" by Carolyn Wiseman, which offers additional suggestions.

414. Munro, Roxie. **The Inside-Outside Book of London** (E. P. Dutton, 1989).

415. Munro, Roxie. **The Inside-Outside Book of New York** (Dodd, Mead, 1985).

416. Munro, Roxie. **The Inside-Outside Book of Paris** (E. P. Dutton, 1992).

417. Munro, Roxie. **The Inside-Outside Book of Washington, D.C.** (E. P. Dutton, 1987).

Architecture; Buildings; Chambers of Commerce; Geography; London; New York; Paris; Perspectives; Tourism; Travel Guides; Washington, D.C.

These brief visual introductions to famous buildings are presented from two perspectives—looking at the buildings and looking out from the buildings.

Include these books in geography and social studies units. They are like beginning travel guides and can serve as models for students developing a similar guide for your community. Let students select buildings to photograph or illustrate the inside-outside perspective. The final project could be displayed at the local Chamber of Commerce or public library. *My New York* by Kathy Jakobsen (Little, Brown, 1993) is a nice companion book for the New York City book.

418. Murphy, Claire Rudolf. **The Prince and the Salmon People**. Ill. by Duane Pasco (Rizolli International Publications, 1993).

Anthropology; Artifacts— Indian; Conservation; Ecology; Indians of North America—Legends; Legends— Tsimshian Indians; Pollution; Salmon; Tsimshian Indians— Legends

A prince is born in a Northcoast Indian village where life is dependent on the salmon. Based on anthropologic research, this legend is told with illustrations interspersed with photographs of Tsimshian artifacts. Map. Notes.

Murphy retold this story because it contains a powerful and timely message. She is concerned about the plight of the North Pacific salmon. Students can research this controversial issue, noting arguments from all sides. For further information provide *Salmon Story* by Brenda Z. Guiberson (Henry Holt, 1993) and have students search for current articles through indexes.

419. Musgrove, Margaret. **Ashanti to Zulu: African Traditions**. Ill. by Leo Dillon and Diane Dillon (Dial Press, 1976).

Africa; Alphabet Books; Ethnology—Africa; Social Life and Customs—Africa; Social Studies—Africa; Tribes—African

Customs and traditions of 26 African tribes are presented alphabetically. The text describes ceremonies, celebrations, and day-to-day customs while most illustrations include "a man, a woman, a child, their living quarters, an artifact, and a local animal." Caldecott Medal, 1977.

This book is a celebration of both the diversity and the homogeneity between these African tribes. *Ashanti to Zulu* is essential to any study of the indigenous peoples of Africa.

420. Myers, Walter Dean. **Brown Angels: An Album of Pictures and Verse** (HarperCollins, 1993).

African Americans—Early 1900s; Art—Photography; Autobiographies—Writing; Collections; Creative Writing; Photography—Portraits; Poetry

Turn-of-the-century photographs, accompanied by Myers' poems, celebrate the lives of African American children from long ago.

Walter Dean Myers' *Glorious Angels: A Celebration of Children* (HarperCollins, 1995) is the companion volume to *Brown Angels*.

Students can select photographs from their childhood to help them write their memoirs. If well done, this writing exercise can be used for biographical portions of applications, including those for colleges.

Myers searched antique shops for years as he developed this collection. Students can study and practice portrait photography by examining these pictures and gathering further information from books such as David Cumming's *Photography* (Raintree, 1990), Terri Morgan and Samuel Thaler's *Photography: Take Your Best Shot* (Lerner, 1991), and Laurie Lawlor's *Shadow Catcher: The Life and Work of Edward S. Curtis* (Walker, 1994). Select a theme like senior citizens, babies, classmates, etc., and let students experiment with portrait photography for a class project. Display the results.

! = Extraordinary! **🕯** = Idea **📖** = Further Reading **✍** = Writing   = Math   = Science   = History

N

421. Nichol, Barbara. **Beethoven Lives Upstairs**. Ill. by Scott Cameron (Orchard, 1993).

Ten-year-old Christopher writes letters to his uncle describing life with Beethoven, a difficult tenant. Christopher's initial reactions to the eccentric boarder are anger and embarrassment, but these later evolve to compassion and admiration.

Beethoven, Ludwig van (1770-1827); Biographies; Composers; Deafness; Historical Fiction; Letters; Music; Uncles

Any book about a composer is a fine reason to expose students to alternative music. Play Beethoven's music in class, offer extra credit for symphony attendance, or invite a chamber orchestra to perform.

Combine drama and music by staging a reading of this book with musical vignettes composed by Beethoven and played by student musicians.

This fictional biography is a great tie-in to a study of other composers and their idiosyncrasies. Did their brilliance make them eccentric, or is the reverse true? Look at the greatness of notable individuals from the present and the past to answer this question. A video version of *Beethoven Lives Upstairs* is available from The Children's Group, Inc., 1992.

422. Norworth, Jack. **Take Me Out to the Ballgame**. Ill. by Alec Gillman (Four Winds Press, 1993).

The lyrics of this old familiar song are brought to life by illustrations depicting the 1947 World Series games between the Dodgers and the Yankees and played on the old Brooklyn Ebbets Field. Notes. Music.

Advertisements; Baseball; Consumer Awareness; Historical Fiction; Music; Songs; World Series—1947

Baseball fans will be delighted to discover this simple baseball book with many notes of interest—information about the composers, Ebbets Field and the 1947 World Series, and the original verses and music.

"Buy me some peanuts and Cracker Jacks. . . ." Just how long has Cracker Jacks been sold as a commercial product? Students can keep a list of actual commercial products mentioned in their readings for a period of time. Then they can investigate them and examine their advertising practices for a consumer awareness project. Provide books like *The Want Makers: The World of Advertising: How They Make You Want to Buy* by Eric Clark (Viking, 1989).

423. Noyes, Alfred. **The Highwayman**. Ill. by Neil Waldman (Harcourt Brace Jovanovich, 1990).

Dramatic paintings accompany this classic romantic poem where Bess takes her own life in an attempt to warn her beloved of the soldiers lying in wait.

Love; Narrative Poetry; Noyes, Alfred (1880-1958); Poetry; Read-Aloud; Robbers and Outlaws; Romance

Use this illustrated edition of *The Highwayman* along with the ones illustrated by Charles Mikolaycak (Oxford University Press, 1987) and Charles Keeping (Oxford University Press, 1981) to introduce narrative poetry. The drama of the story is enhanced by the illustrations and can help reluctant students bridge the gap often created by an unfamiliar language. The element of romance offers appeal. Paul B. Janeczko's collection of narrative poetry in *The Music of What Happens: Poems That Tell Stories* (Orchard, 1988) is a nice addition.

424. Nunukul, Oodgeroo, **Dreamtime**. Ill. by Bronwyn Bancroft (Lothrop, Lee & Shepard, 1994).

Aborigines; Art—Aborigines; Australia—Aborigines; Dreams; Folklore—Aborigines; Memoirs; Painting; Short Stories—Australian; Storytelling

Thirteen stories from Nunukul's childhood and 14 folktales provide a unique look at Australian Aboriginal life and heritage.

Provide students with *Dream Time,* edited by Toss Gascoigne et al. (Houghton Mifflin, 1991), a 16-story anthology by some of the best Australian authors, to further acquaint them with Australian culture and lifestyle. "Dream time," a uniquely Australian concept of dreams, fantasies, and illusions, is the unifying theme of the stories and essential for understanding the culture. A historical look at Australian life can be found in *My Place* by Nadia Wheatley and Donna Rawlins (Collins Dove, 1987).

Bancroft, an Aboriginal textile designer and painter, combined the traditional Aboriginal dots with a contemporary look while at the same time adhering to the time-honored style. Find examples of traditional Aboriginal art to compare with these illustrations.

O

425. Oakley, Graham. **Graham Oakley's Magical Changes** (Atheneum, 1979).

Art—Bookmaking; Book Design—Unique; Changes; Imagination; Surrealism; Wordless Books

Thirty-two paintings on split pages let the reader mix and match scenes in surreal ways with a British twist of humor and history.

Using the concept of central columns to unify the split pictures, students (individually or in groups) can create a similar book. Provide some of John Goodall's split-page books to give students more experiences with book designs.

426. Oakley, Graham. **Henry's Quest** (Atheneum, 1986).

Archeology; Chivalry; Future; Humor; Knights; Quests

Henry, who lives in a small kingdom based on the principles of King Arthur's Round Table, goes on a quest seeking a legendary substance called gasoline.

Like David Macaulay's funny and futuristic *Motel of the Mysteries* (Houghton Mifflin, 1979), *Henry's Quest* examines contemporary frailties by offering a glimpse at future interpretations. Students can look at their own surroundings and imagine later excavations.

427. Olson, Arielle North. **The Lighthouse Keeper's Daughter**. Ill. by Elaine Wentworth (Little, Brown, 1987).

Bravery; Gardens; History—United States—1850s; Lighthouses; Science—Meteorology; United States—History—1850s; Weather

Miranda keeps the lighthouse working on their barren island when her father is kept ashore on the mainland during four weeks of brutal winter weather.

The author's note following the story indicates that the mid-1850s was a period of time when tremendous storms plagued the Maine coast. Students can learn more about weather, weather patterns, and weather forecasting by using some of the following materials: Seymour Simon's *Weather* (Morrow Junior Books, 1993), Vicki McVey's *The Sierra Club Book of Weatherwisdom* (Little, Brown/Sierra Club Books, 1991), the "Weather Tracker's Kit" (Running Press, 125 S. 22nd St., Philadelphia, PA 19103), and "The WeatherCycler Slide Chart" (Weather School, 5075 Lake Rd., Brockport, NY 14420-9750). The issue of global warming and its possible effect on the weather can also be explored through books, periodicals, and resources listed in "Changing Weather Patterns" by Barbara Elleman [*Book Links* 3(2):29-32, November 1993].

! = Extraordinary!   = Idea   = Further Reading   = Writing $\frac{2}{4}$ = Math   = Science   = History

This book is a fictional account of Abbie Burgess, who really kept the lamps in the Matinicus Rock lighthouse burning for four weeks by herself. Lighthouses once dotted coastlines to warn ships of danger. Now electronic technology has made these structures obsolete but nonetheless interesting and historical. Using periodical guides and other research tools, students can delve into the history of lighthouses. Many lighthouses are open to the public and are well worth a field trip.

428. Oppenheim, Shulamith Levey. **Iblis.** Ill. by Ed Young (Harcourt Brace Jovanovich, 1994).

Adam—Biblical Figure; Devil; Eve—Biblical Figure; Islam; Religions—Islam

This is a presentation of an Islamic version of Adam and Eve's fall from Paradise. Note.

 This story, based on the work of an Islamic scholar in the 9th century, has been retold for thousands of years and is a fine introduction to Islamic religion and the sacred Koran.

P

429. Paek, Min. **Aekyung's Dream** (Children's Book Press, 1988).

Bilingual Books; Daily Life; Friendship; Immigration; Korean Americans; Languages— Korean

A young Korean immigrant learns to adapt to her new American life. Note.

 Like Molly, the young Russian Jewish immigrant in Barbara Cohen's *Molly's Pilgrim* (Lothrop, Lee & Shepard, 1983), Aekyung struggles to fit into everyday life in her new home while not letting go of her Korean culture. Invite an immigrant to speak about cultural adaptation or encourage students to interview individuals or families who are new to the United States.

 Written in English and Korean, *Aekyung's Dream* offers an opportunities for students to experience the Korean language. Obtain Korean language audiotapes such as *The Easy Way to Korean Conversation* by Pong Kook Lee (Holly Corporation, 1984).

430. Panzer, Nora, ed. **Celebrate America in Poetry and Art** (Hyperion Books for Children, 1994).

America—Poetry; Art— American; Artists; Folk Art; History of Art; Museums; Poetry

Published in association with the National Museum of American Art, this collection of American poetry celebrates more than 200 years of American life and history as illustrated by works of art from the National Museum's collection. Biographical notes. Index.

 This wonderful book is an excellent introduction to many of America's most well known poets and artists. Use this in conjunction with Laura Whipple's *Celebrating America: A Collection of Poems and Images of the American Spirit* (Philomel, 1994), Lee Bennet Hopkins' *Hand in Hand: An American History Through Poetry* (Simon & Schuster, 1994), *Children of Promise: African-American Art for Young People* edited by Charles Sullivan (Harry N. Abrams, 1991), and Shorito Begay's *Navajo Visions and Voices Across the Mesa* (Scholastic, 1995).

431. Paraskevas, Betty. **Junior Kroll.** Ill. by Michael Paraskevas (Harcourt Brace Jovanovich, 1993).

Children; Family Relationships; Feelings; Newspapers; Poetry

This is a collection of wacky, offbeat poems and illustrations about the pranks and adventures of a young boy.

 These offbeat poems appeared for several years in a weekly Long Island, New York, newspaper, *Dan's Papers*, and are good for initiating discussions on family relationships and feelings.

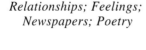 = Geography   = Art   = Music   = Drama   = Speech   = Research   = Read-Aloud

Animals; Creative Writing; Nature; Seasons; Snow; Winter

432. Parnall, Peter. **Alfalfa Hill** (Doubleday, 1985).
Alfalfa Hill and its animal residents prepare for and experience the arrival of winter.

 Writing about and illustrating examples of nature's effect on animals and the landscape is Parnall's forte. Using this book as an example, encourage students to select a hill or other local area and describe how weather affects it and its inhabitants.

433. Parnall, Peter. **Apple Tree** (Macmillan, 1987).
434. Parnall, Peter. **The Rock** (Macmillan, 1991).
435. Parnall, Peter. **Winter Barn** (Macmillan, 1986).

Barns; Creative Writing; Imagery; Life Cycles; Literary Devices; Nature; Personification; Seasons; Simile

Each book describes interactions between the plant and animal life and the surrounding world of hills, trees, rocks, and barns. Each has a historical thread—the apple tree is the only one left in the orchard planted by an early German settler, the winter barn was built by a Hessian soldier, and so forth.

 Parnall's sophisticated language used in combination with line drawings creates excellent examples to illustrate literary devices. Use these books in creative writing classes to present concrete samples of similes, personification, and imagery.

436. Parnall, Peter. **The Mountain** (Doubleday, 1971).

Ecology; Environment; Litter; National Park Service; Recycling; Satire; Science—Ecology

Based on the structure of the cumulative tale "This Is the House That Jack Built," the brief text and color illustrations show "the mountain that stood in the West." Using less and less color, Parnell goes on to depict the demise of the mountain as it is loved to death by visitors.

 This book provides grist for discussion, and follow-up action, for units on Earth Day, litter, and recycling.

 Students can investigate the origins of the U.S. National Park Service and what steps are being taken to help solve the problem of loving our parks to death. Focus on individual parks, or even monuments, especially those close to your area.

437. Passes, David. **Dragons: Truth, Myth, and Legend**. Ill. by Wayne Anderson (Western, 1993).

Animals—Mythical; Dragons; Dragons— Folklore; Mythical Creatures

Dragon myths and legends from throughout the world are discussed and accompanied by intricate drawings. Index.

Many people love dragons and dragon lore. In addition to the Passes book, include some of the following in a dragon book collection: *The Flight of Dragons* by Peter Dickinson (HarperCollins, 1979); *A Book of Dragons* by Hosie Baskin and Leonard Baskin (Alfred A Knopf, 1985); *Dragons and Dreams* by Jane Yolen, Martin H. Greenberg, and Charles G. Waugh (HarperCollins, 1986); *Dragons, Gods and Spirits from Chinese Mythology* by Geraldine Harris (Schocken Books, 1983); Demi's *Dragons and Fantastic Creatures* (Henry Holt, 1993); and *The Truth About Dragons* by Rhoda Blumberg (Four Winds Press, 1980).

---

438. Paterson, Katherine. **The King's Equal**. Ill. by Vladimir Vagin (Harper-Collins, 1992).

Fairy Tales; Gender Equity; Governments—Monarchies; Kings; Magic; Monarchies; Peace; Queens; Read-Aloud; Wolves

An arrogant prince must find a bride who is his equal if he wants to wear the crown of his kingdom. After searching far and wide he finds someone far better than he.

Princes and princesses must have a difficult time finding a proper spouse. Use this book as a springboard to examine the problems with marriages in the current British monarchy. Students may wish to speculate about the future of this form of government.

439. Paulsen, Gary. **Dogteam**. Ill. by Ruth Wright Paulsen (Delacorte Press, 1993).

Dog Sledding; Dogs; Iditarod Race; Night; Racing—Sled Dogs; Sled Dogs; Sports—Sled Dog Racing; Wolves

Based on firsthand experience, the author portrays the excitement, beauty, emotions, and danger of a night run with a sled dog team.

For middle-grade readers, this book can serve as a visual companion to the many adventure books featuring dog sledding including Gary Paulsen's *Woodsong* (Bradbury Press, 1990) and *Dogsong* (Bradbury Press, 1985), as well as John Reynolds Gardiner's *Stone Fox* (Harper & Row, 1980), and Scott O'Dell's *Black Star, Bright Dawn* (Houghton Mifflin, 1988).

Paulsen has run the Iditarod race between Anchorage and Nome, Alaska. This annual contest will interest many students. Race information can be found in periodicals, newspapers covering the race, and in *Race Across Alaska: First Woman to Win the Iditarod Tells Her Story* by Libby Riddles and Tim Jones (Stackpole Books, 1988).

440. Paxton, Tom. **Aesop's Fables**. Ill. by Robert Rayevsky (Morrow Junior Books, 1988).

441. Paxton, Tom. **Androcles and the Lion and Other Aesop's Fables**. Ill. by Robert Rayevsky (Morrow Junior Books, 1991).

442. Paxton, Tom. **Belling the Cat and Other Aesop's Fables**. Ill. by Robert Rayevsky (Morrow Junior Books, 1990).

443. Paxton, Tom. **Birds of a Feather and Other Aesop's Fables**. Ill. by Robert Rayevsky (Morrow Junior Books, 1993).

Aesop's Fables; Creative Writing; Fables; Morals; Poetry; Truths

Selected Aesop fables, 10 per book, are retold in verse.

These excellent collections are perfect for launching a study of fables, their purposes, and history. Books such as Barbara Bader's *Aesop and Company* (Houghton Mifflin, 1991) include the origins of these fables and their uses throughout history. For a more complete study of historical fables, include some originally translated by Jean de LaFontaine.

Most students will be inhibited about writing original fables in verse form. Don't discourage budding poets; introduce Arnold Lobel's 1981 Caldecott Medal book, *Fables* (Harper & Row, 1980), with short one-page stories, as another model for students writing their own fables.

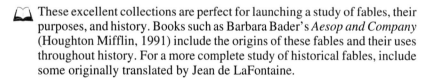

444. A Peaceable Kingdom: The Shaker Abecedarius. Ill. by Alice Provensen and Martin Provensen (Viking, 1978).

This rollicking animal verse, including both real and imagined creatures, was first published in the Shaker Manifesto in July 1882. Afterword.

Alphabet Books; Animals; Art—Primitive; Hicks, Edward (1780-1849); History—Shakers; Museums; Primitive Art; Religion— Shakers; Shakers

Brought to the United States by Ann Lee and eight followers in 1774, the Shaker movement reached its peak around 1860. Provide Raymond Bial's *Shaker Home* (Houghton Mifflin, 1994) and Nancy O'Keefe and Sallie G. Randolph's *Shaker Villages* (Walker, 1993) for more information concerning this industrious communal group who are well known today for their furniture, handicrafts, and inventions such as the flat broom, clothespin, packaged seeds, and the washing machine. Consult the article "The Gift of Sarah Barker" by Pat Scales [*Book Links* 4(5):40-43, May 1995] for activities and other materials supporting further study of the Shakers. *Shaker Boy* by Mary Lyn Ray (Browndeer Press/Harcourt Brace Jovanovich, 1994), a picture book about a boy's life among the Shakers, includes seven songs (words and music) from Shaker collections.

The animals who escape from the Brooklyn Museum's *The Peaceable Kingdom* painting to the Brooklyn Botanical Garden are featured in Ewa Zadrzynska's satirical picture book *The Peaceable Kingdom* (Metropolitan Museum of Art Books, 1994). This book lists the 18 museums that have a variation of the painting. If one is nearby, arrange a class visit.

The primitive artist Edward Hicks is known for his more than 100 versions of *The Peaceable Kingdom*. He was a preacher and member of the Society of Friends (Quakers) but helped to support himself by his paintings. It is fitting for the Provensens to have used this cover illustration because the Shaker movement originated in a Quaker revival in 1747. Using several versions of *The Peaceable Kingdom* painting as a model, student artists can paint their own versions employing the primitive style. Display the finished products along with information about Edward Hicks and the Shakers.

445. Pilkey, Dav. **Dogzilla** (Harcourt Brace Jovanovich, 1993).

446. Pilkey, Dav. **Kat Kong** (Harcourt Brace Jovanovich, 1993).

The town of Mousopolis is terrorized by the dreaded Dogzilla, who emerges from a volcano, and later by a monster cat unwittingly captured by the mouse residents.

Art—Photographic Collage; Collage; Dogs; Humor; Mice; Monsters; Puns; Read-Aloud

While students of all ages will appreciate the humor and the puns, artists may wish to create their own stories using Pilkey's photographic collage style. Provide old magazines for clippings.

447. Pinkney, Andrea Davis. **Alvin Ailey**. Ill. by Brian Pinkney (Hyperion Books for Children, 1993).

This narrative biography (with dialogue "to weave the story together") introduces readers to Ailey, creator of a modern dance company that explored the African American cultural experience and gained international fame.

African Americans; Ailey, Alvin (1931-1989); Biographies; Blues; Choreographers; Dancers; Gospel Music; Modern Dance; Music

Introduce students to modern dance in a variety of ways. Invite a modern dancer to perform routines, demonstrate moves, and answer questions. Also play the music Ailey danced to: "Revelations" (his masterpiece), "Blue Suite," as well as gospel music such as "Rock-My-Soul" and "Rumba with a Little Jive Mixed In," which captured his soul.

❗ = Extraordinary!   💡 = Idea   📖 = Further Reading = Writing $\frac{2}{4}$ = Math = Science = History

This biography, with additional facts following the text, can help start student researchers on a unit concerning the contributions of African Americans to the arts.

448. Pittman, Helena Clare. **A Grain of Rice** (Hastings House, 1986).

Chinese—Folklore; Cleverness; Factorials; Folklore—Chinese; Love; Mathematics— Factorials; Rice; Royalty

A Chinese Emperor, who treasures his daughter more than all the rice in China, is outwitted by a clever and hardworking farmer's son who wins her hand in marriage.

$\frac{2}{\frac{+2}{4}}$ This charming folktale provides a concrete example of the mathematical concept *factorial.* Use this as well as Mitsumasa Anno's *Anno's Multiplying Jar* (Philomel, 1983) and *The Rajah's Rice: A Mathematical Folktale from India* adapted by David Barry (W. H. Freeman, 1994) as an introduction to this sometimes confusing idea.

449. Platt, Richard. **Stephen Biesty's Cross-Sections: Castle**. Ill. by Stephen Biesty (Dorling Kindersley, 1994).

Adventure; Architecture; Castles; Construction; Drawing; Literary Recreations; Medieval Period; Visual Perception

Readers visit 10 cross sections, representing a mythical historical castle, as they view soldiers protecting the villagers and the fortification from enemy attack.

Students can locate the hidden characters—the stowaway in the warship and the spy in the castle.

Using other castle books indexed in this book, students can build a castle to scale, design a modern castle, or develop castle blueprints.

450. Platt, Richard. **Stephen Biesty's Cross-Sections: Man-of-War**. Ill. by Stephen Biesty (Dorling Kindersley, 1993).

Construction; Great Britain—History—18th Century; History—Great Britain—18th Century; Man-of-War; Napoleonic Era; Naval Battles

Biesty takes the reader on a tour of an 18th-century 100-gun British warship by dissecting this ship in cutaway sections from bow to stern. The illustrations are based on the 1765 plans of the H.M.S. *Victory* (British Admiral Horatio Nelson's flagship), and the text and anecdotal notes come from historical accounts of life at sea. Glossary. Index.

This is a fine reference book for studying the historic naval battles of the Napoleonic era. Fans of fictional works, such as Patrick O'Brien's "Aubrey-Maturin" series (W. W. Norton), set in the same period will also find this a useful guide for understanding the complexities of these ships.

451. Platt, Richard. **Stephen Biesty's Incredible Cross-Sections**. Ill. by Stephen Biesty (Alfred A. Knopf, 1992).

Architecture; Construction; Drawing— Techniques; Medical Technology; Science— Computer Technology; Visual Perception

The inside views of a medieval castle, an oil rig, a car factory, an opera house, and a space shuttle, among other things, are accompanied by informative, detailed text. The cutaway drawings reveal the inner workings of real machines and buildings. The foldout pictures of the *Queen Mary* and the steam train are more than three feet long.

This is a great companion to David Macaulay's *Castle, Pyramid, Cathedral,* and *Mill* titles.

Use the cutaway sections to help students understand the medical imaging produced by CAT scan and MRI machines. Invite a radiologist to share some images from computer-enhanced machines that students can compare with book's cutaway sections.

452. Pochocki, Ethel. **Rosebud & Red Flannel**. Ill. by Mary Beth Owens (Henry Holt, 1991).

Clothes; Courage; Creative Writing; Farms; Literary Devices; Love; Personification; Romance

A shy pair of long johns and a snobby lace nightgown find true love after being blown off the clothesline during a snowstorm.

Rosebud & Red Flannel is an excellent example of personification. This book, with its romantic theme, is especially fitting for use with secondary students as a writing model featuring this literary device.

An earlier version of this story was published in *Cricket Magazine* [16(5):10+, January 1989]. Introduce students to magazine writing by using this book and other books such as Olaf Baker's *Where the Buffaloes Begin* (Warne, 1981), which first was published in *St. Nicholas Magazine* [42(4):291+ February 1915]. Several magazines such as *Stone Soup, Read Magazine, Virginia Writing, Voices of Youth, How on Earth!, Writing!,* and the two editions of *Merlyn's Pen* publish articles and artwork by students. More information about magazines that publish readers' work can be found in *Magazines for Kids and Teens: A Resource for Parents, Teachers, Librarians, and Kids!* edited by Donald R. Stoll (Educational Press Association of America/International Reading Association, 1994).

453. Polacco, Patricia. **Just Plain Fancy** (Bantam Books, 1990).

Amish; Eggs; Farms; Peacocks; Pennsylvania— Lancaster County; Religions—Amish

Taking to heart the Amish tradition of simplicity and austerity, 10-year-old Naomi becomes very concerned about the "fancy" chick that hatches from an unusual egg.

This book and Barbara Mitchell's picture book *Down Buttermilk Lane* (Lothrop, Lee & Shepard, 1993) can be used to introduce students to the hardworking, simple ways of the Amish. References are made to a "working bee," getting "your white cap," being "shunned," "Ordnung" (laws), and quilting. Resources that will help expand student knowledge of the Amish include Doris Faber's *The Amish* (Doubleday, 1991), Raymond Bial's *Amish Home* (Houghton Mifflin, 1993), Richard Ammon's *Growing Up Amish* (Atheneum, 1989), and various periodicals.

454. Polacco, Patricia. **The Keeping Quilt** (Simon & Schuster Books for Young Readers, 1988).

Family History; Immigration; Memories; Jews; Judaism; Quilts; Religions—Judaism; Traditions

The keeping quilt, passed on through four generations of the author's family, is filled with memories of enduring love and faith.

A real sense of family history is conveyed through this personal story. To help bring history alive to your students encourage them to bring a family item (or a drawing or photograph) to class and tell its story. Students may want to write their own family story as a gift for a family member.

Be sure to include geography and map skills with the project.

455. Polacco, Patricia. **Meteor!** (Dodd, Mead, 1987).

Astronomy; Country Life; Falling Stars; Gossip; Meteors; Miracles; Science—Astronomy

Polacco's book, inspired by a true story, tells how a quiet, rural community is dramatically changed when a meteor crashes into the Gaws' front yard.

Use *Meteor!* along with nonfiction books about meteors. Students can research meteor crashes into the earth and report their findings.

As the news about the meteor passes through the town, it becomes more and more exaggerated, much like the popular game of "Gossip" or "Telephone." Start a story in your classroom and see where it ends up. A fun companion book is Jan Pienkowski's pop-up *Gossip* (Price Stern Sloan, 1983).

 = Extraordinary!   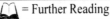 = Idea   = Further Reading   = Writing $\frac{2}{4}$ = Math   = Science   = History

456. Polacco, Patricia. **Pink and Say** (Philomel, 1994).

Black Soldiers; Boy Soldiers; Bravery; Civil War (1861-1865)—United States; Death; Fear; Friendship; Historical Fiction; History—United States—Civil War (1861-1865); Oral History; Read-Aloud; Reading—Power of; Slavery; United States—History—Civil War; War

Left for dead, Say Curtis is rescued and befriended by Pinkus Aylee who was separated from his Black regiment. This Civil War story of these two boy soldiers on opposing sides was passed down from generation to generation in Polacco's family.

It was forbidden for slaves to learn to read, but because Pink's master liked being read to, he was willing to break the law. Obtaining the magical power of reading was difficult for most slaves. Gary Paulsen's *Nightjohn* (Delacorte Press, 1993) is a dramatic story of such a struggle. This short novel is perfect for sharing with all but the youngest elementary students. A related fictionalized picture book biography about Booker T. Washington, which also features the theme of the power of reading, is *More Than Anything Else* by Marie Bradby (Orchard, 1995).

This is an excellent book to use in conjunction with a study of the Civil War in U.S. history classes. Other materials related to boy soldiers and Black soldiers include Jim Murphy's *The Boys' War: Confederate and Union Soldiers Talk About the War* (Clarion Books, 1990) with authentic photographs; Mark Twain's satire "The Private History of the Campaign That Failed" in *The Unabridged Mark Twain* edited by Lawrence Teacher (Running Press, 1976); Clinton Cox's *Undying Glory* (Scholastic, 1991); and the videos *Glory* (RCA/Columbia Pictures, 1990), the story of the first Black regiment to fight in the Civil War, and *The Massachusetts 54th Colored Infantry* (PBS Video, 1992).

Numerous references to outstanding books and audiovisuals are included in "The Civil War, Part I: Update" by Barbara Chatton [*Book Links* 5(1):42-50, September 1995] and "The Civil War, Part II: Update" by Barbara Chatton and Michael O'Laughlin [*Book Links* 5(2):39-46, November 1995].

457. Polacco, Patricia. **Tikvah Means Hope** (Doubleday, 1994).

Cats; Fear; Fires—California; Hope; Judaism—Customs; Neighbors; Religions—Judaism; Sukkoth

During a celebration of Sukkoth, the Jewish harvest holiday, thousands of homes in Oakland, California, are destroyed in a devastating fire. A lost cat, Tikvah, survives, symbolizing hope for a neighborhood. Based on a true incident.

 Compare and contrast Polacco's book about the 1991 Oakland, California, fires with Eve Bunting's Caldecott Medal-winning *Smoky Night* (Harcourt Brace Jovanovich, 1994), also based on a real event—the 1992 Los Angeles riots. In both books cats and neighbors are important symbols. How do these picture books capture the emotion of these events?

458. Prelutsky, Jack. **The Dragons Are Singing Tonight**. Ill. by Peter Sis (Greenwillow Books, 1993).

Dragons; Fantasy; Poetry

This book features 17 original poems about dragons, including "If You Don't Believe in Dragons."

 Dragon lovers, who by their very nature transcend age groups, would love to find this book among the offerings in a dragon book collection.

459. Price, Leontyne, retold by. **Aïda**. Ill. by Leo Dillon and Diane Dillon (Harcourt Brace Jovanovich, 1990).

Ancient Egypt; Careers; Love; Music; Opera; Performing Arts; Tragedy; Verdi, Giuseppe (1813-1901)

Having frequently performed Verdi's *Aïda*, Leontyne Price brings a unique experience to the retelling of this tragic story. The enslaved Ethiopian princess is torn between her loyalty for her father and country, and her love for the captain of the enemy army.

Present this fine retelling of Verdi's *Aïda* before listening to one of Price's recorded performances. Because there are few picture books that feature classic performing arts, take this opportunity to introduce students to another one, such as Margot Fonteyn's retelling of *Swan Lake*, illustrated by Trina Schart Hyman (Gulliver Books, 1989), or *Behind the Curtain* by Christian Thee (Workman, 1994), an interactive book featuring the magic of the theater.

Several out-of-print opera picture books could provide additional material for study. These include John Updike's retelling of Wagner's *The Ring* (Alfred A. Knopf, 1964), Stephen Spender's *The Magic Flute* (Putnam, 1966), and Doris Orgel's *Lohengrin* (Putnam, 1966). Also consider using Jane Rosenberg's *Sing Me a Story: The Metropolitan Opera's Book of Opera Stories for Children* (Thames & Hudson, 1989).

460. Prokofiev, Sergei. **Peter and the Wolf**. Ill. by Erna Voigt (Godine, 1979).

Folklore; Music; Musical Instruments; Opera; Wolves

Prokofiev composed the music for this classic tale. Peter and a few animal friends capture the wolf and are victorious. Each character in the story is introduced by an instrument from the orchestra.

Music for each character is provided in this rendition. Invite musicians to bring the featured instruments and demonstrate their sounds. Obtain a full version of *Peter and the Wolf* to play for your students such as the audiocassette and book version translated by Maria Carlson (Live Oak Media, 1987). Provide other versions of this story such as *Peter and the Wolf* retold and illustrated by Michel Lemieux (Morrow Junior Books, 1991) or *Peter and the Wolf Pop-Up Book* illustrated by Barbara Cooney (Viking, 1986). A CD-ROM interactive version is Chuck Jones' *Peter and the Wolf* (Times Warner Interactive, 1994). This well-reviewed computer game provides students an opportunity to learn about and listen to an astounding spectrum of instruments.

461. Provensen, Alice. **The Buck Stops Here: The Presidents of the United States** (HarperCollins, 1990).

Art—Posters; History— Presidents; Poster Art; Presidents—United States; United States—History

The first 41 U.S. presidents (from Washington to Bush) are featured in posterlike portraits with banners, maps, and sidebars filled with familiar and obscure facts about their lives. Notes.

Add excitement to perennial middle school presidential units by launching the study with these full-page illustrations and the interesting facts, especially the obscure ones. Students will enjoy learning about the human side of the presidents. *Presidents* (HarperCollins, 1995) by Martin W. Sandler is a perfect companion for other glimpses into the lives of these famous men.

462. Provensen, Alice. **Punch in New York** (Viking, 1991).

Cartoons; Drama; Humor; Italy; Punch and Judy; Puppets; Theater; Tricksters

A typical "Punch and Judy" adventure (with less wickedness than Punch is noted for) ensues after the puppet is stolen at the airport. Notes.

This book is a tribute to the traditional Italian secular dramas, "commedia dell'arte," in which Punch and Judy performed for hundreds of years in Europe. Students can investigate more about these dramas, famous characters, and the folk tradition behind them by beginning with the informational notes at the end of the book. A cumulative activity would include a Punch and Judy show.

 = Extraordinary!   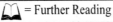 = Idea   = Further Reading   = Writing $\frac{2}{4}$ = Math   = Science   = History

There is a direct link from the Punch and Judy shows to *Punch* (the famous English comic magazine) and to the meaning of "cartoon" as a form of illustration. Interested students can investigate this relationship, then look at and critique current *Punch* and American cartoon illustrations.

463. Provensen, Alice and Martin Provensen. **The Glorious Flight: Across the Channel with Louis Blériot** (Viking, 1983).

Airplanes—Designs; Aviation History; Biographies; Blériot, Louis (1872-1936); English Channel; Flying; Pilots; Social Life and Customs— France—1900s

This illustrated biography profiles Louis Blériot, a Frenchman who designed and built an airplane and flew across the English Channel in 1909. Caldecott Medal, 1984.

Explore the history of the early years of aviation with the following books: Don Berliner's *Before the Wright Brothers* (Lerner, 1990), Andrew Nahum's *Flying Machines* (Alfred A. Knopf, 1990), David Jefferis' *Epic Flights* (Franklin Watts, 1988), Robert Burleigh's *Flight: The Journey of Charles Lindbergh* (Philomel, 1991), Russell Freedman's *The Wright Brothers: How They Invented the Airplane* (Holiday House, 1991), and Barry Moser's *Fly: A Brief History of Flight* (HarperCollins, 1993).

464. Provensen, Alice and Martin Provensen. **Shaker Lane** (Viking, 1987).

Cautionary Tales; Changes; City and Town Life; Community; Law; Neighbors; Real Estate Development; Reservoirs

The residents of Shaker Lane did little to care for their property and decided to move away rather than fight when the town decided to build a reservoir on their land.

This cautionary tale of real estate development is an excellent introduction to changes in American society. The Provensens were inspired to write *Shaker Lane* by a real event that took place in upstate New York. Their paintings and text are a great discussion starter on the subject of communities losing to "advances" in society.

Provide Uri Shulevitz's picture book *Toddlecreek Post Office* (Farrar, Straus & Giroux, 1990), which also illustrates changes from a rural to urban society.

R

465. Rabin, Staton. **Casey Over There**. Ill. by Greg Shed (Harcourt Brace Jovanovich, 1994).

Art—Posters; Brothers; Families; Historical Fiction; Letters; Posters; Presidents; Uncle Sam; War; World War I (1914-1918)

Seven-year-old Aubrey is too young to join the army and fight in the Great War with his older brother, Casey. Instead, Aubrey keeps in touch through letters and packages while he wonders and waits.

In this fictional story President Wilson answers the letter Aubrey wrote to the "Honorable Uncle Sam." In real life, too, children correspond with political figures. Students can read about Grace Bedell urging Abraham Lincoln to grow a beard in Russell Freedman's *Lincoln: A Photobiography* (Ticknor & Fields, 1987) and Samantha Smith's correspondence with Yuri Andropov (then the leader of the Soviet Union) in her *Samantha Smith: Journey to the Soviet Union* (Little, Brown, 1985). Students can learn about writing great letters from *How to Write a Letter* by Mischel Florence (Franklin Watts, 1988) and *Sincerely Yours: How to Write Great Letters* by Elizabeth James and Carol Barkin (Clarion Books, 1993).

When Aubrey doesn't hear from Casey for more than three months, he writes to the "Honorable Uncle Sam." The classic "I Want You" Uncle Sam posters were known by everybody during World War I. Students can learn more about "Uncle Sam" and his posters from "One Thousand and One Ways of Saying Uncle" by Sam Connery [*Smithsonian* 26(4):70-73, July 1995].

 = Geography   = Art   = Music   = Drama   = Speech   = Research   = Read-Aloud

466. Raimondo, Lois. **The Little Lama of Tibet** (Scholastic, 1994).

Biographies; Buddhism; Ling Rinpoche (1988-); Monasteries; Religions—Buddhism; Tibet

This photo-illustrated book describes the day-to-day life of six-year-old Ling Rinpoche, whom many believe to be the reincarnation of a revered Buddhist monk. Map. Notes.

Students interested in more information about this community and religion can read *Little Buddha,* a novel by Gordon McGill (Berkley, 1994) based upon the movie screenplay of *Little Buddha.* The novel and film center on a child from the United States who is believed to be a reincarnation of a holy monk.

This interesting look at the Tibetans' attempt to preserve their culture while in exile can be used in any study of Tibet. Students can also research attempts being made to eliminate Buddhism and Tibetan culture. According to the book's notes more than 100,000 Tibetans are now living as refugees in India and Nepal.

467. Ramachander, Akumal. **Little Pig**. Ill. by Stasys Eidrigevicius (Viking, 1992).

Art—Photography; Betrayal; Death; Fables; Masks; Morality; Photography; Pigs; Trust

The pig farmer, Mary, befriends Little Pig (building him a special house and bringing him gifts), then tricks him into getting in a van going to market.

This haunting story can be used with Raymond Briggs' *When the Wind Blows* (Schocken Books, 1982) and Robert Innocenti's *Rose Blanche* (Creative Education, 1986) for discussing the issues of trust, betrayal, and death.

The unusual illustrations in this book—photographs of a person holding up different masks—deserve attention. Supply books like the following for a historical study of masks: *Mummies, Masks and Mourners* by Margaret Berrill (E. P. Dutton, 1990), *Masks Tell Stories* by Carol Gelber (Millbrook, 1993), and *Masks* by Lyndie Wright (Franklin Watts, 1990) and "Round and Round the World, Life Is a Masquerade" by Marlane A. Liddell [*Smithsonian* 25(9):94-99, December 1994]. For a final project, students can fashion masks in Eidrigevicius' style, which can also be seen in *The Hungry One* by Kurt Baumann (North-South Books, 1993).

468. Randall, Brian. **The B Book** (Warner Books, 1994).

Allegory; Art; Cautionary Tales; Charity; Good Versus Evil; Greed; Literary Devices; Mythology—Modern; Photography

Randall uses color plates of elaborate costumes and sets, along with minimal text, to tell the story of Miss Bee, who represents an American child who discovers the downfall of greed.

This allegory can be used as an example for students who are studying this literary device. The contemporary illustrations will appeal to students who are interested in studying popular culture.

The lavish costumes and sets, as well as the unbelievable characters, embellish this story much like special effects embellish many music videos. Students can illustrate or photograph their own myth or provide illustration for the lyrics of a popular song.

469. Rankin, Laura. **The Handmade Alphabet** (Dial Press, 1991).

Alphabet Books; American Sign Language; Communication; Disabilities; Hearing Impaired; Speech

Each page has a life-sized illustration of a hand forming a letter of the manual alphabet used in American Sign Language. The hand sign links an illustration of a word beginning with that letter to the corresponding letter symbol printed on the corner of the page.

 = Extraordinary!   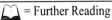 = Idea   = Further Reading   = Writing $\frac{2}{4}$ = Math   = Science   = History

Use *The Handmade Alphabet* to focus students' attention on the hearing impaired and as an introduction to the manual alphabet of the American Sign Language. Companion books include Remy Charlip and Mary Beth Miller's *Handtalk: An ABC of Finger Spelling & Sign Language* (Four Winds Press, 1980) and *Handtalk Birthday: A Number & Story Book in Sign Language* (Four Winds Press, 1987), as well as George Ancona and Mary Beth Miller's *Handtalk Zoo* (Four Winds Press, 1989) and *Handtalk School* (Four Winds Press, 1991). *You Don't Need Words! A Book About Ways People Talk Without Words* by Ruth Belov Gross (Scholastic, 1991) expands on the topic of nonverbal communication.

 Students can translate a poem or story into sign language and present it.

Allusions; Bears; Circuses; Dwarves; Freedom; Friendship; Loneliness; Outcasts; Social Issues; Voyages and Travels

470. Rascal. **Oregon's Journey**. Ill. by Louis Joos (BridgeWater Books, 1993).

A lonely clown and a bear search for freedom and a nonpolluted idyllic home as they trek across the country.

 The characters in this book—a clown, the bear (visible only to the clown), the Black man—are loners on the edge of society. Two companion books that can help students focus on society's less visible members are Cynthia Rylant's *An Angel for Solomon Singer* (Orchard, 1992) and Ethel Pochocki's *The Mushroom Man* (Green Tiger Press, 1993). All three books provide grist for discussion.

 Challenge students to find allusions to Snow White, Robert Frost's "Stopping by the Woods," and Van Gogh's landscapes in Rascal's story.

African Americans; Biographies; Choral Reading; Historical Fiction; Jazz; Music; Musicians; Parker, Charlie (1920-1955); Read-Aloud; Speech; Storytelling

471. Raschka, Chris. **Charlie Parker Played Be Bop** (Orchard, 1992).

Readers can hear Charlie Parker's music in this book! His classic bebop style, his saxophone, and cat (waiting at home) are all here. Caldecott Honor, 1994,

 Bill Martin Jr.'s *The Maestro Plays* (Henry Holt, 1994) is a nice companion book that successfully describes music through images and words.

 Bebop was a major influence in the development of rap music. Students can research both bebop and rap, unique forms of American music, with books such as Leslie Gourse's *Dizzy Gillespie and the Birth of Bebop* (Atheneum, 1994), Nelson Havelock and Michael A. Gonzales' *Bring the Noise: A Guide to Rap Music and Hip-Hop Culture* (Harmony Books, 1991), and Maurice K. Jones' *Say It Loud! The Story of Rap Music* (Millbrook, 1994).

Don't let this simple-looking book dissuade you from using it as an introduction to Charlie Parker's special brand of jazz. With practice readers can make it sound so much like music it can be performed for storytelling or dramatic reading contests. Mouth noises and other sounds can be added for a choral reading presentation. Be sure to play some of Parker's classic recordings.

 Students might also like to do readings from the raps in *Nathaniel Talking* by Eloise Greenfield (Writers and Readers Publishing, 1988) and the poems for two readers in Paul Fleischman's *Joyful Noise: Poems for Two Voices* (Harper & Row, 1988).

472. Raschka, Chris. **Yo! Yes?** (Orchard, 1993).

Body Language; Communication; Drama; Friendship; Plays

A single-word conversation between two shy boys blossoms into a jubilant friendship.

This very short book, featuring one-syllable dialogue, is perfect to read aloud and can be adapted into a great mini one-act play. The illustrations give all the posturing clues that students can use to elaborate on the sparse dialogue.

473. Rattigan, Jama Kim. **Dumpling Soup.** Ill. by Lillian Hsu-Flanders (Little, Brown, 1993).

Bilingual Books; Celebrations; Food; Hawaii; Languages— Korean; New Year's; Social Life and Customs— Korean; Traditions

A young Hawaiian girl tries to make dumplings for her family's New Year's celebration. Set in Hawaii, this book is a rich mix of language, food, and customs from a variety of cultures. Glossary includes English, Japanese, Hawaiian, and Korean words.

Using a multiethnic cookbook such as *The Multicultural Cookbook for Students* by Carole Lisa Albyn (Oryx Press, 1993), students can prepare and share an ethnic dish or meal.

Students can investigate another culture represented in their community and identify various traditions and customs.

474. Ray, Jane. **Noah's Ark: Words from the Book of Genesis** (Dutton Children's Books, 1990).

Animals; Art—Folk; Bible Stories; Genesis; Noah

Excerpts, adapted and rearranged from Genesis of the Authorized (King James) Version of the Bible, combined with folk art and primitive motifs, tell the classic story of Noah's ark.

Other versions of this story include *Noah and the Great Flood* by Warwick Hutton (Atheneum, 1977) and *Noah & the Ark & the Animals* by Ivan Gantschev and Andrew Elborn (Picture Book Studio USA, 1984). For more books and activities about Noah consult "Noah's Continuing Voyage" by Kathy Piehl [*Book Links* 3(2):35-38, November 1993].

475. Reading Is Fundamental. **Once Upon a Time . . . Celebrating the Magic of Children's Books in Honor of the Twentieth Anniversary of Reading Is Fundamental** (G. P. Putnam's Sons, 1986).

Author and Illustrator Studies; Books and Reading; Children's Literature— Appreciation; Illustrators— Books and Reading; Read-Aloud; Short Stories

A rich variety of anecdotes, memories, and stories by 28 writers and illustrators of children's books celebrate the joy of reading. Introduction.

These short gems are perfect for sharing with students and/or parents to help inspire them to explore the magical world of reading. Read entries at parent meetings or to introduce studies on authors or illustrators. More information about these professionals can be found in the multivolume series *Something About the Author*, published since 1971 by Gale Research.

476. Reiner, Annie. **A Visit to the Art Galaxy** (Green Tiger Press, 1990).

Art—Modern; Artists; History of Art; Modern Art; Museums; Paintings; Sculptors; Sculptures

An ordinary visit to a museum turns into a fantasy flight to the "Land of Modern Art." Notes.

This narrative introduction to Henri Matisse, Pablo Picasso, Mark Rothko, Franz Klein, Alberto Giaometti, and Chris Burden explores concepts of beauty, ways of seeing things, and art that comes from real-life experiences. Expand a study of modern art with this book and others.

 = Extraordinary!    = Idea   = Further Reading   = Writing   = Math   = Science   = History

477. Rice, Tim and Andrew Lloyd Webber. **Joseph and the Amazing Technicolor® Dreamcoat**. Ill. by Quentin Blake (Holt, Rinehart & Winston, 1982).

Bible; Drama; Jealousy; Joseph (Son of Jacob); Librettos; Old Testament; Opera; Plays

This is an operatic telling of the Old Testament story of Joseph (son of Jacob) and his brothers.

This story, written in verse by Tim Rice and scored by the famed Andrew Lloyd Webber (*Cats, Phantom of the Opera,* etc.), is perfect for theater productions. The music is available, but it also can be performed as a play instead of a libretto.

478. Ringgold, Faith. **Aunt Harriet's Underground Railroad in the Sky** (Crown, 1992).

African Americans; Brothers and Sisters; Flying; Freedom; Motifs; Slavery; Symbolism; Tubman, Harriet (1820?-1913); Underground Railroad

Cassie and her brother (from *Tar Beach*) meet Harriet Tubman on a flight of fantasy peppered with historical facts as the children follow the route of the Underground Railroad. Note. Map. Bibliography.

Use the symbolic motif of flying in *Aunt Harriet's Railroad in the Sky* as an introduction to identifying symbolism in literature and art.

Consult the Jacob Lawrence entry of *Harriet and the Promised Land* (Simon & Schuster, 1993) in this book (entry 339) for a listing of other books about Harriet Tubman and her trips to the South to lead slaves to freedom.

479. Ringgold, Faith. **Dinner at Aunt Connie's House** (Hyperion Books for Children, 1993).

African Americans; Art— Coming to Life; Art— Portraits; Courage; Families; Fantasy; Feminism; History— Women; Portraits; Women

Family dinners at Aunt Connie's house are always wonderful, but this particular time Melody and Lonnie are playing hide-and-seek and hear strange voices coming from the attic. The 12 beautiful portraits of famous African American women that Aunt Connie painted talk to Melody and Lonnie about their courageous lives.

Ringgold intended her original story for adults to prompt recollections of childhood memories. Students can interview adults in their lives and collect their memories in text or illustration.

As demonstrated by Ringgold's artistic style, portraits need not be traditional. Important people in a student's life can be immortalized in art and displayed in a portrait gallery. Perhaps they too can "speak" via a reader's theatre or original radio play. For a biographical portrait of Ringgold, see *Faith Ringgold* by Robyn Montana Turner (Little, Brown, 1993).

Through research students can learn more about the African American women featured in the portraits. As an extension of the "famous people at dinner" theme, older students might want to learn about the women featured in Judy Chicago's renowned exhibition *The Dinner Party* and featured in her book *The Dinner Party: A Symbol of Our Heritage* (Anchor Press, 1979). This monumental feminist artwork centers on a triangular table that is set with, among other things, 39 oversize plates, each of which represents a woman in history.

480. Ringgold, Faith. **Tar Beach** (Crown, 1991).

African Americans; Art—Needlework; Dreams; Flying; Harlem; Museums; Needlework; New York City; Quilts

In this story, based on the author's "Tar Beach" quilt, a young girl claims all she sees for her and her family as she dreams of flying over parts of New York City. Notes.

 = Geography   = Art   = Music   = Drama   = Speech   = Research   = Read-Aloud

"Tar Beach" was the first of Ringgold's quilts in her "Woman on a Bridge" series, which is owned by the Guggenheim Museum. Students interested in learning more about needlework as art can consult the notes Ringgold included in *Tar Beach,* Judy Chicago's *The Birth Project* (Doubleday, 1985), and Roderick Kiracofe's *Cloth & Comfort: Pieces of Women's Lives from Their Quilts and Diaries* (Crown, 1994).

Invite quilters to share their creations. Some students might be interested in doing a small sample pattern or a class quilt. Books of interest include *Eight Hands Round: A Patchwork Alphabet* by Ann Whitford Paul (HarperCollins, 1991), which contains the origins of 26 Early American quilting patterns; *Stitching Stars: The Story Quilts of Harriet Powers* by Mary Lyons (Charles Scribner's Sons, 1993); and *The Quilt-Block History of Pioneer Days: With Projects Kids Can Make* by Mary Cobb (Millbrook, 1995).

481. Robbins, Ken. **A Flower Grows** (Dial Books, 1990).

Art—Photographs; Botany; Flowers; Life Cycles—Flowers; Nature; Photographs; Plants; Science—Botany

From a nondescript bulb bursts to life a spectacular Apple Blossom amaryllis, which then fades to its inevitable death to await a rebirth. Note.

This deceptively simple book about the life cycle of bulbs is perfect for botany classes. Examine a real amaryllis that mirrors the cycle depicted in Robbins' book.

Look again! This book contains hand-tinted black-and-white photographs, a trademark of Robbins. With the help of a professional artist, study the process of hand tinting and the effect it creates. Compare and contrast hand-tinted photos with standard color photos. Some students might want to experiment with this technique; creating an exhibit of flower photography would be a nice accompanying activity to this book. Other books Robbins has illustrated with the hand-tinted technique include *Earth: The Elements* (Henry Holt, 1995) and *Water: The Elements* (Henry Holt, 1994).

482. Rockwell, Anne. **The Robber Baby: Stories from the Greek Myths** (Greenwillow Books, 1994).

Atalanta; Daedalus; Demeter; Greek Mythology; Hermes; Mythology— Greek; Pandora

Rockwell retells and illustrates 15 tales from Greek mythology. Note. Pronunciation guide.

Use this as an excellent, though simple, introduction to Greek mythology along with other picture book myths such as those by Warwick Hutton, Leonard Everett Fisher, and Aliki.

483. Rodari, Florian. **A Weekend with Picasso** (Rizzoli, 1991).

Art—Modern; Artists; Biographies; History of Art; Modern Art; Picasso, Pablo (1881-1973)

Rodari weaves factual information, art explanations, photographs, and reproductions into a weekend visit with Picasso as the guide. Chronology. Museum and illustration directories.

Books such as *Introducing Picasso* by Juliet Heslewood (Little, Brown, 1993), *Pablo Picasso* by John Beardsley (Harry N. Abrams, 1991), and *What Makes a Picasso a Picasso?* by Richard Muhlberger (Metropolitan Museum of Art/Viking, 1993) will complement a study of Picasso as the most famous and influential of all modern artists.

484. Rohmann, Eric. **Time Flies** (Crown, 1994).

Birds; Creative Writing; Dinosaurs; History; Imagination; Museums; Time Travel; Wordless Books

In this wordless tale a bird flying around a dinosaur exhibit in a natural history museum has an unsettling experience when the dinosaur seems to come to life and view the bird as a potential meal. Caldecott Honor, 1995.

♥ = Extraordinary!   💡 = Idea   📖 = Further Reading   ✍ = Writing $\frac{2}{4}$ = Math   ⚛ = Science   📚 = History

Time Flies provides a framework for students to study history by going back in time. Have students research your community's history. What happened there 50, 100, 150, 200, 500, and 1,000 years ago? Other picture books with this same theme include *Under the Moon* by Dyan Sheldon (Dial Books for Young Readers, 1993), *The Backyard* by John Collier (Viking, 1993), *Home Place* by Crescent Dragonwagon (Macmillan, 1990), *The House on Maple Street* by Bonnie Pryor (William Morrow, 1987), *Time Train* by Paul Fleischman (HarperCollins, 1991), and *Dreamplace* by George Ella Lyon (Orchard, 1993).

 The concept of going back in time is intriguing to many. As an extension activity, students can write the text they imagine would accompany *Time Flies,* or write and possibly illustrate an original adventure that takes place in the past. As a further extension, provide students with some of the many time travel novels for recreational reading.

 485. Romanova, Natalia. **Once There Was a Tree**. Ill. by Gennady Spirin (Dial Books for Young Readers, 1985).

Cautionary Tales; Crafts; Ecology; Environment; Fables; Life Cycle; Nature; Science—Ecology; Trees

The interrelationship between a tree and a diverse group of animals celebrates nature and its connection to all life.

 The relationship between human and tree in this book is quite different from that in *The Giving Tree* by Shel Silverstein (Harper & Row, 1964). Focus student attention on humans' relationship with nature. Are either of these stories a cautionary tale?

 During a study in ecology, students can focus on a ecosystem similar to the one supported by the stump in Romanova's book. Be sure to have students notice how each small system relates to a larger one. Use Alvin Tresselt's *The Gift of the Tree* (Lothrop, Lee & Shepard, 1992) as a companion book.

 Provide Mortez E. Sohi's *Look What I Did with a Leaf!* (Walker, 1993), which provides explicit directions and illustrations for creating art from leaves. This book can serve as inspiration for a myriad of art projects involving natural objects.

486. Rosen, Michael J. **The Greatest Table: A Banquet to Fight Against Hunger**. Ill. by various artists (Harcourt Brace Jovanovich, 1994).

487. Rosen, Michael J. **Home** (HarperCollins, 1992).

Book Design—Unique; Charity; Philanthropy; Poetry; Social Action; Social Issues—Homeless; Social Issues—Hunger

In *The Greatest Table,* 16 artists illustrate Rosen's "poem of grace and thanksgiving" in a 12-foot-long accordion book format. Rosen's *Home* features 17 illustrators and 13 authors who celebrate the places and things that make up a home. Both books support the nonprofit organization Share Our Strength's (SOS) fight against homelessness and hunger.

 The proceeds from the sale of these books benefit SOS programs. Interested students can discover what programs are available to serve the homeless and the hungry in their communities. For further information about SOS, write to Share Our Strength, 1511 K Street, N.W., Suite 600, Washington, D.C. 20005.

 = Geography   = Art   = Music   = Drama   = Speech   = Research   = Read-Aloud

488. Rosen, Michael J., ed. **Speak! Children's Book Illustrators Brag About Their Dogs.** Ill. by various artists (Harcourt Brace Jovanovich, 1993).

Artists; Creative Writing; Dogs; Humane Societies; Pets; Philanthropy; Social Issues—Responsible Pet Ownership

This treasury of dog poems, shaggy dog stories, hilarious (doggie) tales, and touching memories is written and illustrated by 43 children's book artists. The royalties and a portion of the publisher's profits are donated to The Company of Animals Fund, a philanthropic organization that provides grants to agencies promoting the humane treatment of animals.

Speak! can help focus attention on responsible pet ownership, especially when combined with class presentations by veterinarians or humane society officials. Some students may wish to become involved with their local humane society.

In a similar fashion, students can illustrate and write about their pets, and display the works in a classroom, library, or school gallery. Related books include *Unleashed Poems by Writers' Dogs* edited by Amy Hempel and Jim Shepard (Crown, 1995) and *A Dog's Life* by Peter Mayle (Alfred A. Knopf, 1995), both of interest to older adolescents. Those interested specifically in cats can take a look at Rosen's *Purr . . . Children's Book Illustrators Brag About Their Cats* (Harcourt Brace, 1996).

Students can investigate philanthropic organizations and their value to society.

489. Roth, Susan L. **Buddha** (Doubleday, 1994).

Art—Collage; Buddha; Buddhism; Collage; Gautama Buddha (563?-483? B.C.); Religions— Buddhism; Siddhartha; Spiritualism

Using collage Roth tells the story of a prince named Siddhartha who was born into luxury but began a spiritual journey after witnessing the suffering of others. Afterword.

This book is a fine introduction to Siddhartha Buddha and Buddhism at an elementary level. Materials such as Peggy Morgan's *Being a Buddhist* (Batsford, 1990), Huston Smith's *The World's Religions,* rev. ed. (Harper & Row, 1991), and John Snelling's *Buddhism* (Bookwright, 1986) will be useful.

Buddhism, a major world religion, has more than 250 million followers. Students studying comparative religion will benefit from this straightforward introduction to the story of Siddhartha. Older students can go on to read the well-known *Siddhartha* by Herman Hesse (New Directions, 1951).

490. Roth, Susan L. **Marco Polo: His Notebook** (Doubleday, 1990).

China—13th Century; Explorers; History—13th Century; Italy—13th Century; Journeys; Polo, Marco (1254-1323?); Trade; Voyages and Travels

Using fictional journal entries accompanied by prints, photographs, and maps from museum collections, this book tells of Marco Polo's 13th-century travels, which took him from Italy to China and back. Notes. Map.

This picture book was based on Polo's *The Travels of Marco Polo* (Grosset & Dunlap, 1931), which was written more than 700 years ago. Use it to launch a study of Marco Polo, his travels, the lands he visited, and/or the establishment of trade routes between Asia and Europe. *The Travels of Marco Polo,* still a popular travel book, would be of interest to secondary students. Younger students can refer to Richard Humble's *The Travels of Marco Polo* (Franklin Watts, 1990).

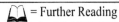 = Extraordinary!   = Idea   = Further Reading   = Writing $\frac{2}{4}$ = Math   = Science   = History

491. Rylant, Cynthia. **All I See**. Paintings by Peter Catalanotto (Orchard, 1988).
A shy child and an artist become friends and paint together, despite "seeing" different things.

Artists; Creative Writing; Friends; Painting; Seeing; Senses; Whales

How we use our senses for observation, imagination, and to "see" is a topic in several books. Use this Rylant book with Byrd Baylor's *The Other Way to Listen* (Charles Scribner's Sons, 1978) to foster discussions—and perhaps original writings or paintings! Advanced students will enjoy Diane Ackerman's in-depth look at the senses in *A Natural History of the Senses* (Random House, 1990).

  492. Rylant, Cynthia. **An Angel for Solomon Singer**. Paintings by Peter Catalanotto (Orchard, 1992).
Loneliness haunts Solomon Singer as he wanders the streets of New York City and lives by himself in a hotel. But, beginning with the chance encounter and smile from the waiter at the Westway Cafe, life begins to change.

Aging; City Life; History of Art; Hopper, Edward (1882-1967); Loneliness; Metaphor; Outcasts; Read-Aloud; Senior Citizens; Social Action

An Angel for Solomon Singer is a fine discussion starter concerning society and how we ignore citizens living on its fringes. How can students participate in community efforts to provide assistance and kindness to those individuals who are alone? Invite a spokesperson to talk about ways students can help.

Catalanotto's illustrations are reminiscent of the American artist Edward Hopper (1882-1967), especially the one modeled on Hopper's 1942 painting *Nighthawks,* in which Hopper painted "the loneliness of a large city." In fact, Hopper portrayed the loneliness of American life in much of his work. Have students investigate more about Hopper, his paintings, the theme of loneliness, and his emphasis on qualities of light. Refer to *Edward Hopper: An Intimate Biography* by Gail Levin (Alfred A. Knopf, 1995).

493. Rylant, Cynthia. **Appalachia: The Voices of Sleeping Birds**. Ill. by Barry Moser (Harcourt Brace Jovanovich, 1991).

 494. Rylant, Cynthia. **The Relatives Came**. Ill. by Stephen Gammell (Macmillan, 1985).

495. Rylant, Cynthia. **When I Was Young in the Mountains**. Ill. by Diane Goode (E. P. Dutton, 1985).
Rylant shares her childhood memories of the land, the people (especially families), and their customs in West Virginia with readers of these books. Caldecott Honor, 1983.

Appalachia; Families; Historical Fiction; Mining—Coal; Photographs; Read-Aloud; Setting; Social Life and Customs—Appalachia

 All of these picture books feature an Appalachian setting. These books can serve as an example of how authors ground readers to a time and place.

Use these books to introduce Rylant's autobiography, *But I'll Be Back Again* (Orchard, 1989).

  496. Rylant, Cynthia. **The Dreamer**. Ill. by Barry Moser (Blue Sky Press, 1993).
An artist creates the world (the earth, sky, trees, and all the planet's creatures) from his dreams.

Artists; Creation; Dreamers; Genesis; God; Read-Aloud

 An Artist by M. B. Goffstein (Harper & Row, 1980) is a perfect book for comparing and contrasting with *The Dreamer*. Goffstein's artist wants to work like God to make his paint sing. Discuss the word *artist*.

This modern creation story with a new twist can be compared to creation myths from around the world. Be sure to use Virginia Hamilton's *In the Beginning: Creation Stories from Around the World* (Harcourt Brace Jovanonich, 1988) as well as others listed in the subject index for this book.

497. Rylant, Cynthia. **Soda Jerk**. Paintings by Peter Catalanotto (Orchard, 1990).
A teenaged soda jerk observes the people in his small town and comments in poetry.

Oral Interpretation; Poetry; Small Town Life; Speech; Poetry

 Use this book to introduce students to Rylant's poetry collection titled *Something Permanent* (Harcourt Brace Jovanovich, 1994). These poems are accompanied by the poignant photographs of Walker Evans, a photographer known for his Depression-era work.

Rylant's poetry flows effortlessly, and *Soda Jerk* speaks with an authentic young adult voice. It is perfect for oral interpretation events.

S

498. Sabuda, Robert. **Saint Valentine** (Atheneum, 1992).
This recounting of Saint Valentine, a physician in ancient Rome, features his treatment and prayers for a young blind girl. Note.

Ancient Rome; Art— Mosaics; Christian Martyrs; Christianity; Legends— Valentine's Day; Mosaics; Saints; Valentine, Saint (??-270); Valentine's Day

 Aspects of the life and customs of Ancient Rome are seen throughout the story, as well as in dramatic mosaics that are representative of the time period. Other books of interest include John D. Clare's *Classical Rome* (Harcourt Brace Jovanovich, 1993) and Simon James' *Ancient Rome* (Alfred A. Knopf, 1990).

Students can research the origins and traditions of Valentine's Day (which doesn't originate solely from Valentine's message to the blind girl).

499. San Souci, Daniel. **N. C. Wyeth's Pilgrims** (Chronicle Books, 1991).
This book presents the early Pilgrim years through San Souci's text and the 14-panel mural done by Wyeth for the Metropolitan Life Insurance Company in the early 1940s. Note.

Art—Murals; History— United States—Pilgrims; Murals; Pilgrims; Wyeth, N. C. (1882-1945)

 The obvious curriculum extension is to include this book with the others mentioned in the entry for Gary Bowen's *Stranded at Plimoth Plantation 1626* (HarperCollins, 1994).

N.C. Wyeth is renowned for his illustrations in children's classics such as *Treasure Island* (Charles Scribner's Sons, 1981), *Robin Hood* (Running Press, 1993), *The Last of the Mohicans* (Charles Scribner's Sons, 1986), and *Rip Van Winkle* (Morrow Junior Books, 1987). These murals present a romantic perspective, which is a trademark of Wyeth's work. Students can learn more about the artist and his paintings. Consult *An American Vision: Three Generations of Wyeth Art* by James H. Duff et al. (Little, Brown, 1987).

500. San Souci, Daniel. **North Country Night** (Doubleday, 1990).
This book is virtually an artist's catalog of nocturnal northern woodland animals and their winter activities.

Animals—Nocturnal; Ecosystems; Winter; Woodlands

 Further study of the featured animals (great horned owl, gray coyote, fox, mountain lion, porcupine, cottontail rabbit, bobcat, beaver, weasel, raccoon, and mule deer) and their interdependent relationships can help students better understand this ecosystem.

! = Extraordinary!   ▽ = Idea   📖 = Further Reading   ✎ = Writing $\frac{2}{4}$ = Math   🔬 = Science   📕 = History

501. San Souci, Robert D. **Larger Than Life: The Adventures of American Legendary Heroes.** Ill. by Andrew Glass (Doubleday, 1991).

Adventure; Folk Heroes; Heroes—Folk; Humor; Legends; Oral Tradition; Storytelling; Tall Tales

Five stories, handed down from generation to generation, feature American folk heroes. The adventurous and funny stories feature John Henry, Old Stormalong, Slue-Foot Sue and Pecos Bill, Strap Buckner, and Paul Bunyan and Babe the Blue Ox.

The stories in this book provide good material for storytelling. Students may wish to host a festival for their parents, peers, or younger students.

Compare and contrast these retellings with others such as Paul Robert-Walker's *Big Men, Big Country* (Harcourt Brace Jovanovich 1993), Ezra Jack Keats' *John Henry: An American Legend* (Pantheon Books, 1965), Julius Lester's *John Henry* (Dial Press, 1994), and an original tall tale featuring a woman—*Swamp Angel* by Anne Isaacs (Dutton Children's Books, 1994).

502. San Souci, Robert D. **The Talking Eggs**. Pictures by Jerry Pinkney (Dial Books for Young Readers, 1989).

Creole—Folktales; Folktales—Creole; Folktales—United States; Kindness; Magic; Punishment; Read-Aloud; Rewards; Selfishness; South; Storytelling; Supernatural; Witches

This folktale of the American South tells the story of one sweet daughter, Blanche, and one selfish daughter, Rose. When Blanche is kind to an old witch, she is rewarded. Rose ridicules the old woman, and her rewards match her behavior. Caldecott Honor, 1990.

This Creole folktale is perfect for learning and performing in a storytelling competition or performance. Children and adults will enjoy the just desserts!

503. Sara. **Across Town** (Orchard, 1990).

Art—Collage; Art—Visual Literacy; Cats; City Life; Collage; Creative Writing; Friendship; Loneliness; Visual Literacy; Wordless Books

In this strikingly stark book, a lonely man befriends a cat while walking in the dark city night.

Sara notes that *Across Town* was inspired by her observation of a tramp who befriended a cat. Both the topic and the art technique make it a perfect companion to compare and contrast with Libby Hathorn's *Way Home* (Crown, 1994).

Show and discuss Peter Catalanotto's paintings in *An Angel for Solomon Singer* (Orchard, 1992) without reading Cynthia Rylant's text. After reading the text have the students write their own story to accompany the illustrations in *Across Town*. Both books have striking illustrations and feature the theme of loneliness.

This wordless book is an excellent example of the power of art. Discuss the sense of loneliness and emotion evoked by the illustrations. Define and discuss whether or not the illustrations qualify as "minimal art." An art discussion "Paint, Cut, Tear, Compose: The Elements of Collage" by Dilys Evans [*Book Links* 1(1):38-41, September 1991] presents specifics about *Across Town* and other books created in a similar manner.

504. Sart, Jean de. **Scary Animals**. Ill. by Jean-Marie Winants (Charlesbridge, 1994).

Animals; Bats; Boars; Extinction; Fear; Habitats; Lynx; Snakes; Toads; Vultures; Wasps; Wolves

Nine animals that humans typically fear are portrayed and discussed with descriptions and information about location, habitat, behavior, food, reproduction, and threat of extinction.

Use this book with any study of animals, particularly those that provoke strong reactions. Students can select an animal that they fear, or are interested in, and conduct further research.

505. Say, Allen. **El Chino** (Houghton Mifflin, 1990).

Bill Wong was a Chinese American civil engineer who wanted to be a great athlete. He eventually became a famous bullfighter in Spain.

American Dream; Athletes; Biographies; Bullfighting; Chinese Americans; Dreams; Spain; Sports—Bullfighting; Wong, Bong Way

Bullfighting is a sport about which most Americans know little. Provide interested students with books such as Maia Wojciechowska's 1965 Newbery Award winner *Shadow of a Bull* (Atheneum, 1964), Munro Leaf's picture book *The Story of Ferdinand* (Viking, 1936), and the paintings and drawings in Michael Batterberry and Ariane Ruskin's *Children's Homage to Picasso* (Harry N. Abrams, 1970).

506. Say, Allen. **Grandfather's Journey** (Houghton Mifflin, 1993).

Say's account of his grandfather's immigration to the United States, followed years later by his return to Japan, portrays the feeling of someone from two countries who is always homesick. Caldecott Medal, 1994.

Adventures; Autobiographies; Grandfathers; Historical Fiction; Home; Homesickness; Immigration; Japan; Japanese Americans; Oral Histories; Voyages

Grandfather's Journey is a fine companion to *The Bicycle Man* (Houghton Mifflin, 1982) and *Tree of Cranes* (Houghton Mifflin, 1991), Say's autobiographical books about his childhood in Japan. Launch an oral history project with these books. Read Say's Caldecott Medal acceptance speech [*Horn Book* 70(4):427-31, July-August 1994] for additional insights into his childhood.

Use this book to begin a study of current U.S. immigration policy. Share *Who Belongs Here? An American Story* by Margy Burns Knight (Tilbury House, 1993). What do your students think of the current policy and quotas?

507. Say, Allen. **Lost Lake** (Houghton Mifflin, 1989).

When a father and son journey to Lost Lake only to discover others already there, they search for a new secluded spot in the mountains. They find both the perfect spot and the beginning of a better relationship.

Backpacking; Camping; Creative Writing; Fathers and Sons; Loneliness; Plot; Sports—Backpacking

This story gives students an idea of what backpacking entails. Invite a backpacker to bring her or his equipment to your school to discuss what is needed and how one prepares for a trip. Perhaps it would be possible to arrange a backpacking trip for interested students through a city recreation program or some other organization.

This book can be used to help students understand the development of parallel stories—the backpacking trip to a secluded lake and the developing relationship between the father and son.

508. Schoenherr, John. **Bear** (Philomel, 1991).

A young bear's struggle for survival begins when he wakes up one morning to find his mother gone.

Alaska; Bears; Fear; Nature; Survival; Wilderness

This coming-of-age story of a wild animal shows respect for the natural world and is a refreshing departure from presentations that are frequently anthropomorphic. The video *The Bear* (Tri-Star Pictures, 1989), which deals with the survival of a grizzly cub, is another accurate portrayal. Have students discuss the pros and cons of realistic versus fairy tale presentations of the natural world.

❗ = Extraordinary!   💡 = Idea   📖 = Further Reading   ✍ = Writing $\frac{2}{4}$ = Math   ⚛ = Science   📕 = History

509. Schroeder, Alan. **Ragtime Tumpie**. Ill. by Bernie Fuchs (Little, Brown, 1989).

African Americans; Baker, Josephine (1906-1975); Biographies; Dancing; Historical Fiction; Jazz; Music—History; Ragtime; World War II

Based on true events from Josephine Baker's childhood, this fictional account celebrates her love of ragtime music and dancing. The poverty surrounding her life was secondary to her determination to succeed as a dancer.

Musical terms and phrases from popular songs are sprinkled throughout this story. To initiate a study of ragtime music, identify those words and investigate their meaning and connection to this special brand of jazz.

"Tumpie" grew up to become the famous entertainer Josephine Baker. The author's note following the story might spur some students to learn more about this woman who appeared on Broadway, starred in the "Ziegfeld Follies," became a French citizen, and worked in the French Resistance during World War II.

510. Schur, Maxine Rose. **Day of Delight: A Jewish Sabbath in Ethiopia**. Ill. by Brian Pinkney (Dial Books for Young Readers, 1994).

Africa—Ethiopia; Art— Scratchboard Paintings; Beta Israel; Ethiopia; Jews—Ethiopia; Judaism; Religions—Judaism; Sabbath; Scratchboard Paintings

This book presents a portrait of the vanishing Sabbath activities that were traditionally practiced by Ethiopian Jews by focusing on one village family. Note. Pronunciation guide. Glossary.

Award-winning artist Brian Pinkney uses scratchboard paintings in many of his books. An explanation of the process is included in this book: "a technique that requires a white board covered with black ink. The ink is then scraped off with a sharp tool to reveal the white, which is painted over with oil pastels, oil paints, and gouache." Create a collection of Pinkney's books to study this technique. Invite an artist to answer questions and demonstrate this process.

Using the author note, students can learn more about the plight of the Ethiopian Jews who call themselves "Beta Israel."

511. Schwartz, David M. **Supergrandpa**. Ill. by Bert Dodson (Lothrop, Lee & Shepard, 1991).

Aging; Bicycle Racing; Grandfathers; Health; Physical Conditioning; Social Issues—Aging; Sports—Bike Racing; Sweden

Barred from entering the 1,761-kilometer Tour of Sweden bike race, 66-year-old Gustav bikes the 600-mile race unofficially and finishes first. Note.

This story is based on Gustav Hakansson's actual 1951 Tour of Sweden bike race. One of the four-member teams participating in the "Race Across America" in the summer of 1995 consisted of three men in their sixties and one in his seventies. Use stories about people like these to discuss life expectancy, "old age," the role of genes in aging, health and fitness, and physical conditioning.

512. Scieszka, Jon. **The Book That Jack Wrote**. Paintings by Daniel Adel (Viking, 1994).

Children's Literature; Creative Writing; Cumulative Tales; Humor; Nursery Rhymes; Parody; Poetry; Surrealism

This surreal and wacky variation of the cumulative rhyme ("The House That Jack Built") is filled with references to children's literature and humorous visual details.

Have students identify the characters (the Cheshire Cat, the Mad Hatter, the cow jumping over the moon, the pie man at the fair, and Humpty Dumpty) in this story who appear in other children's books. Then take this opportunity to read aloud Lewis Carroll's *Alice's Adventures in Wonderland & Through the Looking Glass* (Bantam Books, 1984). Use *The Annotated Alice: Alice's Adventures in Wonderland* edited by Martin Gardner (C. N. Potter, 1960) with older students and explore many of the interesting notes.

 = Geography = Art = Music = Drama = Speech = Research = Read-Aloud

The short, concise nature of this parody makes it a good selection for students to use as a model for writing their own parodies.

513. Scieszka, Jon. **The Frog Prince Continued.** Paintings by Steve Johnson (Viking, 1991).

Creative Writing; Folktales—Fractured; Fractured Folktales; Frogs; Happiness; Magic; Royalty; Witches

Scieszka (rhymes with *fresca*) explains what happens after the princess kisses the frog and they supposedly live "happily ever after."

Provide students with a selection of familiar fairy tales and invite them to write a continuation. What happens next?

514. Scieszka, Jon. **The Stinky Cheeseman and Other Fairly Stupid Tales.** Ill. by Lane Smith (Viking, 1992).

Art; Creative Writing; Fairy Tales—Fractured; Fractured Folktales; Humor; Read-Aloud; Satire

Scieszka and Smith combine talents to create 11 fractured versions of familiar tales with titles such as "The Princess and the Bowling Ball," "The Really Ugly Duckling," and "Cinderumpelstiltskin." Caldecott Honor, 1993.

Lane Smith's illustrations do not depict the cheerful characters we are used to seeing. Instead they are grotesque and distorted—perfectly suited to the irreverent handling of the stories by Scieszka. Some believe this book is a must for any student of fairy tales at any level. Without question it is a guaranteed success for a read-aloud session with any age group, including adults.

Like Scieszka's other books, this one lends itself well as a model for creative writing students. Provide a selection of well-known tales and challenge students to write their own twisted versions. Art students can be invited to supply the illustrations, à la Lane Smith.

515. Scieszka, Jon. **The True Story of the 3 Little Pigs by A. Wolf.** Ill. by Lane Smith (Viking, 1989).

Drama; Folktales— Fractured; Fractured Folktales; Humor; Point of View; Read-Aloud; Reader's Theater

Claiming he was framed and merely out to borrow a cup of sugar, Alexander T. Wolf relates this "true" telling of the age-old "Three Little Pigs" story. Even teens who are not thrilled by folklore will love this.

This tongue-in-cheek story will appeal to listeners of all ages. Read it aloud, present it as a reader's theater, or act it out. (It's very easy to adapt to a script.)

Let justice be served! Have students develop and stage a mock trial using Alexander T. Wolf's written account and the evidence hidden in the illustrations.

516. Scott, Ann Herbert. **Cowboy Country.** Ill. by Ted Lewin (Clarion Books, 1993).

Cowboys; Heroes— Popular; History—United States—19th Century; Music— Songs; Old West; Songs

An old-time buckaroo tells about his life as a modern-day cowboy and why he would choose that life again.

Complement this realistic portrayal of cowboy life with books that explore the myth and the history of the American cowboy. Some good choices are Linda Grandfield's *Cowboy: An Album* (Ticknor & Fields, 1994), Martin Sandler's *Cowboys: A Library of Congress Book* (Harper-Collins, 1994), Russell Freedman's *Cowboys of the Wild West* (Clarion Books, 1985), and David Murdoch's *Cowboy* (Alfred A. Knopf, 1993).

Songs of the Wild West (Metropolitan Museum of Art and Simon & Schuster, 1991) has handsome art reproductions and musical selections, providing another perspective on the lifestyle of the American cowboy.

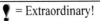 = Extraordinary!   = Idea 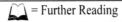 = Further Reading   = Writing   = Math   = Science   = History

517. Seltzer, Isadore. **The House I Live In: At Home in America** (Macmillan, 1992).

Architecture; Buildings; Dwellings; Homes; Houses

This simple introduction to architecture explains why and how people built where they did.

A variety of building styles common in the United States are presented in this book. Another picture book showing different architecture styles is Arthur Dorros' *This Is My House* (Scholastic, 1992), in which the text and illustrations depict different types of houses lived in by children all over the world.

518. Sendak, Maurice. **Outside Over There** (Harper & Row, 1981).

Artists; Daydreams; Goblins; Heroes; Heroines; Kidnapping; Responsibility

Ida faces pressures and responsibilities as her mother pines for Ida's absent, seafaring father and the goblins steal her baby sister. Caldecott Honor, 1982.

This perplexing and haunting story provides plenty of opportunity for discussion among older students. Who is the intended audience? Is the story Ida's daydream and escape because her mother can't seem to cope with her absent husband? What are the meanings of the subplots seen in the windows, in the pastoral landscapes? Expand the discussion to include Sendak's other controversial books: *We Are All in the Dumps with Jack and Guy* (HarperCollins, 1993), *Where the Wild Things Are* (Harper & Row, 1963), and *In the Night Kitchen* (Harper & Row, 1970). John Cech's *Angels and Wild Things: The Archetypal Poetics of Maurice Sendak* (Pennsylvania State University, 1995) will aid those interested in analyzing Sendak's art and writing.

Use *The Art of Maurice Sendak* by Selma G. Lanes (Harry N. Abrams, 1980) for launching a study of the artist's work.

519. Service, Robert. **The Cremation of Sam McGee**. Ill. by Ted Harrison (Greenwillow Books, 1986).

520. Service, Robert. **The Shooting of Dan McGrew**. Paintings by Ted Harrison (Godine, 1988).

Arctic; Ballads; Cremation; Death; Klondike Gold Rush; Poetry; Read-Aloud; Yukon Territory

Ted Harrison, a celebrated Yukon Territory artist, illuminates two classic ballads by Robert Service. Accompanying the lines and illustrations of *The Cremation of Sam McGee* are informational passages explaining life and survival in this cold environment.

These poems are examples of the ballad, a narrative form of poetry. Select other ballads such as Jane Yolen's *Tam Lin* (Harcourt Brace Jovanovich, 1990) to further study this literary form.

Gather books such as Michael Cooper's *Klondike Fever: The Famous Gold Rush of 1898* (Clarion Books, 1989) for further study of the history of this period.

521. Seuss, Dr. **The Butter Battle Book** (Random House, 1984).

Allegory; Arms Race; Bombs; Creative Writing; Literary Devices; Metaphor; Peace; Walls; War; Weapons

The Yooks and the Zooks' long-running war escalates to the point of mutual annihilation as each develops bigger and more destructive weapons.

Use this book to begin student investigations into the 20th-century arms race. Develop a time line to indicate the pivotal historical events for both arms increases and the agreements for mutual arms reduction.

 = Geography   = Art   = Music   = Drama   = Speech   = Research   = Read-Aloud

Real walls built to defend countries from attack are part of the history of the world. Have students create a "Wall of Information" gallery featuring Hadrian's Wall, the Great Wall of China, the Berlin Wall, and less well known fortifications such as the Maginot Line, Offa's Dike, and some of the walled cities of Europe.

522. Seuss, Dr. **The Lorax** (Random House, 1971).

Creative Writing; Deforestation; Environmental Action; Environmental Issues—Deforestation; Forest; Literary Devices; Metaphor; Pollution; Trees

"I am the Lorax, I speak for the trees, I speak for the trees, for the trees have no tongues." But after the trees are destroyed only the Once-ler is left to describe the local environmental problems.

In today's society groups and individuals are searching for the balance between business profit and environmental concerns. Using *The Lorax* as a springboard, students can focus on the difficulties in achieving that balance. What companies, local and national (such as Ben & Jerry's ice cream), are proactive in this area? What are they doing? Like Walter in Chris Van Allsburg's *Just a Dream* (Houghton Mifflin, 1990), students can become active. For student activities consult *Our Earth, Ourselves: The Action-Oriented Guide to Help You Protect and Preserve Our Planet* by Ruth Caplan (Bantam Books, 1990), *Saving the Earth: A Citizen's Guide to Environmental Action* by Will Steger and Jon Bowermaster (Random House, 1990), *Design for a Livable Planet: How You Can Help Clean Up the Environment* by Jon Naar (Perennial Library, 1990), and *The Global Ecology Handbook: What You Can Do About the Environmental Crisis* by Walter H. Corson (Beacon Press, 1990).

Seuss and other picture book authors/artists address serious topics using appealing, nonthreatening formats. Provide students with Dr. Seuss' *The Butter Battle Book* (Random House, 1984) as well as Bill Peet's *The Wump World* (Houghton Mifflin, 1970) and Barbara Emberley's *Drummer Hoff* (Prentice-Hall, 1967) for thought-provoking reading and discussion. In the same fashion students can write in a metephorical sense about current issues using imaginary characters and places.

523. Seuss, Dr. **Oh, the Places You'll Go!** (Random House, 1990).

Graduation; Humor; Percentages; Philosophy; Poetry; Success

A brief graduation speech from Dr. Seuss encourages each and everyone to find success from within despite the ups and downs of life. "And will you succeed? Yes! You will, indeed! (98 and 3/4 percent guaranteed.)"

For a humorous interlude while studying percentages, read aloud this book as well as Dr. Seuss' *Horton Hatches the Egg* (Random House, 1940).

524. Seymour, Tres. **Pole Dog**. Ill. by David Soman (Orchard, 1993).

Abandonment; Animals— Treatment; Dogs; Humane Society; Pets—Responsible Ownership; Social Action— Responsible Pet Ownership

Suffering through hunger, inclement weather, and shooting guns, an abandoned old dog waits faithfully by the roadside for his owners to return.

This dramatically simple story focuses attention on the numerous pets abandoned each and every day. Discussions can center on such topics as responsible pet ownership, animal control, and the role of the Humane Society. How bad is this situation in your community? Is there a public education program? Some of your students might want to become involved. See the entry for Michael J. Rosen's *Speak! Children's Book Illustrators Brag About Their Dogs* (Harcourt Brace Jovanovich, 1993) for further suggestions.

! = Extraordinary!   = Idea   = Further Reading = Writing = Math = Science = History

525. Seymour, Tryntje Van Ness. **The Gift of Changing Woman** (Henry Holt, 1993).

Apache Indians; Coming of Age; Creation Stories; Dances; Geography; Indians of North America— Legends; Legends—Apache Indians; Prayers; Women

Using original art by Apache painters, the author describes the traditional coming-of-age ceremony for young Apache women. Changing Woman, the legendary ancestor of their people, is celebrated through special dances and prayers used to reenact the Apache story of creation.

For other creation stories consult Virginia Hamilton's 1989 Newbery Honor Book, *In the Beginning: Creation Stories from Around the World* (Harcourt Brace Jovanonich, 1988).

Identify other Native American tribes of North America and locate them on a map.

526. Shannon, David. **How Georgie Radbourn Saved Baseball** (Blue Sky Press, 1994).

Baseball; Corruption; Creative Writing; Fantasy; Freedom; Greed; Power; Propaganda; Seasons; Tall Tales; Tyranny

When the tyrannical Boss forbade baseball it was forever winter in America, until the birth of Georgie Radbourn, who saved baseball and brought back spring.

This book will remind readers of the baseball strike of 1994 when baseball did disappear for a time. Interested students can research this occurrence, noting the reasons for the strike, the outcome, and the residual effect on the sport.

Present this wonderfully illustrated story along with other traditional tall tales to inspire students to write their own modern exaggerations with similar sophisticated themes. Consider including these tall tales of Baron Munchausen by Adrian Mitchell: *The Baron Rides Out* (Philomel, 1987), *The Baron on the Island of Cheese*, (Philomel, 1987), and *The Baron All at Sea* (Philomel, 1987).

527. Shulevitz, Uri. **The Secret Room** (Farrar, Straus & Giroux, 1993).

Artists; Cleverness; Envy; Jealousy; Journeys; Kings; Riddles

The old man's clever answer to a king's question ("Why is your head gray and your beard black?") grows in meaning as this original folktale progresses.

An interesting companion book pondering jealousy and the consequences of envy is Demi's *The Artist and the Architect* (Henry Holt, 1991).

Shulevitz has written about the artistry of picture books and how readers use visual code in *Writing with Pictures: How to Write and Illustrate Children's Books* (Watson-Guptill, 1985). Explore books with your students using Shulevitz's book as a guide.

528. Shulevitz, Uri. **Toddlecreek Post Office** (Farrar, Straus & Giroux, 1990).

Changes; Post Offices; Rural Life; United States Postal Service; Urban Society; Villages

The Toddlecreek post office was an important village gathering spot (not merely a place to buy stamps, mail packages, and purchase mail orders) until the postal inspector closed it.

Hail to Mail (Henry Holt, 1990), a 1927 poem written by Samuel Marshak of the Soviet Union, is a humorous tribute to mail carriers around the world.

Study the history of the U.S. Postal Service. Use resources such as Cherly Weant McAffee's *The United States Postal Service* (Chelsea, 1987).

Although there may be a few small rural post offices left, this story is clearly an elegy to an America that was. Students can discuss changes in society, both positive and negative. What other books can they find that illustrate changes in our society from a rural to urban orientation?

529. Siebert, Diane. **Heartland**. Paintings by Wendell Minor (Thomas Y. Crowell, 1989).

530. Siebert, Diane. **Mojave**. Paintings by Wendell Minor (Thomas Y. Crowell, 1988).

531. Siebert, Diane. **Sierra**. Paintings by Wendell Minor (HarperCollins, 1991).

Desert; Farms; Geography—United States; Maps; Midwest; Mountains; Nature; Poetry; Social Studies—United States

These poetic celebrations of three American landscapes (the Midwest farmland, the Mojave Desert, and the Sierra Nevada Mountains) speak of how nature reigns and the inhabitants coexist.

Celebrating America: In Poetry and Art edited by Nora Panzer (Hyperion, 1994) is a natural companion for these three books.

All three books are naturals for enhancing social studies and geography units. Don't miss the opportunity to work on mapping skills; include the unique regional presentations in *The Eyewitness Atlas of the World* (Dorling Kindersley, 1994).

532. Silver, Donald M. **One Small Square Cave**. Ill. by Patricia J. Wynne (W. H. Freeman, 1993).

Animals—Caves; Caves; Exploration; Geology— Caves; Plant Life—Caves

Scientific information about cave exploration, equipment requirements and safety rules, and the flora and fauna in caves is presented. Bibliography. Index. Map.

Caves exist all over the world. If possible, take a trip to one in your area. For a list of U.S. caves that are open to the public contact Gurnee Guide to American Caves, NCA Books, Route 9, Box 106, McMinnville, TN 37110. Further information on cave exploration can be obtained from the National Speleological Society, Cave Avenue, Huntsville, AL 55810.

533. Sis, Peter. **Follow the Dream: The Story of Christopher Columbus** (Alfred A. Knopf, 1991).

Adventure; Biographies; Columbus, Christopher (1451-1506); Dreams; Explorers; Maps; Navigation; Ships' Logs

Sis uses a pictorial retelling to recount Columbus' adventures and explain how he overcame obstacles to follow his dream.

Sis provides his version of how ancient maps may have looked in Columbus' time. Look at these and other versions of the world from historic times. Is anything on them still accurate today? How would a mapmaker from the 1400s depict your town or state?

534. Sis, Peter. **A Small Tall Tale from the Far Far North** (Alfred A. Knopf, 1993).

Adventures; Czechoslovakia; Eskimos; Folk Heroes; Heroes— Folk; Storytelling; Survival; Tall Tales

Embellishing on story memories from his childhood, Sis shares a telling of Jan Welzl, a Czechoslovakian folk hero. Welzl's adventure takes him to the Arctic, where Eskimos befriend him and he, in turn, plans to save them and their land from destructive gold seekers. Prologue. Epilogue.

In this book storytelling is both a written and visual experience. Use the illustration and story on the page "Later I learn the songs and tales that were whispered to me while I was coming back to life" to pique student interest.

 = Extraordinary!   = Idea   = Further Reading   = Writing $\frac{2}{4}$ = Math   = Science   = History

The prologue and epilogue explain the various things people believe about Jan Welzl. Compare and contrast these stories with those of other folk heroes.

535. Sis, Peter. **The Three Golden Keys** (Doubleday, 1994).

Autobiographies; Books—Editors; Czechoslovakia; Editors; Geography; Legends—Czechoslovakia; Memoirs; Prague; Social Studies

A cat leads readers on a magical tour through the cultural landmarks of Prague (Sis' childhood home) in search of keys to open the doors to the family house. Within this story are three legends of Prague.

This is the last book Jacqueline Onassis edited before her death. In 1989, shortly after Czechoslovakia was freed from Communist rule, Onassis asked Sis to create a book for children about his homeland. Sis says, "As an editor, Mrs. Onassis gave me complete artistic freedom but was able to lead me at the same time." Although she discouraged authors from dedicating books to her, Sis included a note, "Thank you for a dream, J.O.!," just before the book went to press. Learn more about book editors and what they do. If possible, invite an editor to your class.

The legends and the cultural landmarks of Prague make this book ideal to include in a unit on Czechoslovakia.

536. Skira-Venturi, Rosabianca. **A Weekend with Van Gogh** (Rizzoli, 1994).

Artists; Biographies; History of Art; Impressionists; Painting Techniques; Van Gogh, Vincent (1853-1890)

This book about Van Gogh weaves art explanations, factual information, photographs, and reproductions into a weekend visit with the artist as the guide. Chronology. Museum and illustration directory.

Books such as Bruce Bernard's *Van Gogh* (Dorling Kindersley, 1992) and Richard Muhlberger's *What Makes a Van Gogh a Van Gogh?* (Metropolitan Museum of Art/Viking, 1993) will complement a study of Van Gogh's life or a study of the Impressionists.

537. Smith, Lane. **The Happy Hocky Family** (Viking, 1993).

Basal Readers; Humor; Jokes; Read-Aloud; Reading Education; Satire; Student Teachers; Teacher Education

This offbeat satire of the old "Dick and Jane" basal readers has an ageless appeal.

Share this book with prospective teachers during their training. (If they don't enjoy the humor perhaps they should think about another career!) Also student teachers working with beginning readers shouldn't miss the opportunity to use the book with their students. They will all enjoy the humor that was missing from the original basal series.

538. Smucker, Anna Egan. **No Star Night**. Paintings by Steve Johnson (Alfred A. Knopf, 1989).

Air Pollution; Environment; Factories; Historical Fiction; Mill Towns; Pollution; Steel Industry; West Virginia—1950s

The author tells of her childhood growing up in the steel mill town of Weirton, West Virginia, during the 1950s.

From the title to the last page, Smucker focuses on the environment, especially air pollution and slag. Students can investigate industrial pollution, past and present, answering these questions: What is the general impact of industry on the environment? What is being done to lessen the impact in your area?

In a study of business and labor display a collection of books featuring life in factory and mill towns since the advent of the Industrial Revolution. Feature Judith Hendershot's *In Coal Country* (Alfred A. Knopf, 1987) and David Macauley's *Mill* (Houghton Mifflin, 1983). As there are numerous titles with this theme, it won't be hard to match readers with appropriate books such as the nonfiction *Kids at Work* by Russell Freedman (Clarion Books, 1994) or novels like Gloria Skurzynski's *Goodbye, Billy Radish* (Bradbury Press, 1992).

 = Geography   = Art   = Music   = Drama   = Speech   = Research   = Read-Aloud

Art; Art—Indians of North America; Indians of North America—Poetry; Lullabies; Oral Traditions; Poetry

539. Sneve, Virginia Driving Hawk. **Dancing Teepees: Poems of American Indian Youth**. Art by Stephen Gammell (Holiday House, 1989).

Recognizing the importance of oral tradition to Native American culture, Sneve has collected in this volume historic and contemporary poetry including lullabies, prayers, and chants. Gammell's illustrations feature aspects of Indian life.

 Along with this book use poetry written by Native American youth. *Rising Voices: Writings of Young Native Americans* selected by Arlene B. Hirschfelder and Beverly R. Singer (Charles Scribner's Sons, 1992) is an excellent example of how the history of a culture can be eloquently reflected in the writings of their young people. Another poetry book of interest is *Dancing Moons* by Nancy Wood (Doubleday Books for Young Readers, 1995).

Courage; Dungeons and Dragons; Enchantment; Games; Greed; Magic; Mazes; Royalty; Wizards

540. Snyder, Zilpha Keatley. **The Changing Maze**. Ill. by Charles Mikolaycak (Macmillan, 1985).

Long ago an evil wizard king created a magic maze that knowing folks shun. But when a shepherd boy's lamb wanders into the maze, the boy must resist the magic that makes the maze shift and change in order to rescue his pet.

Develop a maze similar to the one in this book. Students may want to create a game that includes dragons, wizards, witches, spells, and other fantasy elements. As a reference consult Ray J. Marran's *Table Games: How to Make and How to Play Them* (A. S. Barnes, 1976) and Walter Shepherd's *Big Book of Mazes and Labyrinths* (Dover, 1973).

"Dungeons and Dragons" aficionados often create mazes within their games. If a class member is a D & D player, invite that person to demonstrate this popular role-playing game.

Disasters; Journeys; Shipwrecks; Spedden, Daisy Corning Stone (1872-1950); Teddy Bears; Titanic; Toys

541. Spedden, Daisy Corning Stone. **Polar the Titanic Bear**. Ill. by Laurie McGaw (Little, Brown, 1994).

This true story, told in the first-person by Polar the bear, describes the lifestyle of a wealthy American family and their journeys, including their voyage on the ill-fated *Titanic*. Photographs. Introduction. Epilogue.

Polar, the teddy bear, was made by the famous Steiff company of Germany and purchased at F.A.O. Schwarz in New York City. The Steiff company is still considered to be one of the foremost teddy bear manufacturers in the world. Use this book as a springboard for further study of this stuffed toy, perhaps inviting students to bring in a favorite or historic teddy for display. Books with more information include *How Teddy Bears Are Made: A Visit to the Vermont Teddy Bear Factory* by Ann Morris (Scholastic, 1994), *The Ultimate Teddy Bear Book* (Dorling Kindersley, 1991) and *The Teddy Bear Encyclopedia* by Pauline Cockrill (Dorling Kindersley, 1993), and *Teddy Bears: The Collectors Guide to Selecting, Restoring, and Enjoying New and Vintage Teddy Bears* (Courage Books, 1994).

This amazing story was written for Douglas Spedden, owner of Polar, by his mother, Daisy Spedden. It is not only an excellent chronicle of privileged life in the early 1900s, but it also provides an interesting perspective on the fascinating tragedy of the *Titanic*. Provide other books about the *Titanic* for an always fascinated readership. These may include Robert D. Ballard's *Exploring the Titanic* (Scholastic, 1988), Jonathan Rawlinson's *Discovering the Titanic* (Rourke, 1988), Frank Sloan's *Titanic* (Franklin Watts, 1987), and *Titanic: An Illustrated History* by Donald Lynch (Hyperion, 1992).

 = Extraordinary!   = Idea   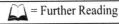 = Further Reading   = Writing $\frac{2}{4}$ = Math   = Science   = History

542. Spier, Peter. **The Erie Canal** (Doubleday, 1970).

Canals; Erie Canal; History—United States; Music; Songs; Transportation

The words to Thomas S. Allen's song are brought to life with detailed illustrations. Note. Lyrics and music.

For further information, students can read books such as Len Hilts' *Timmy O'Dowd and the Big Ditch: A Story of the Glory Days on the Old Erie Canal* (Harcourt Brace Jovanovich, 1988) and Cheryl Harness' *The Amazing Impossible Erie Canal* (Macmillan, 1995).

The 14 most frequent questions (and answers) asked of the staff at the Canal Museum in Syracuse, New York, follow the text. The information is fascinating and provides a plethora of data to complement a historical study.

543. Spier, Peter. **Tin Lizzie** (Doubleday, 1975).

Antique Cars; Assembly Lines; Automobiles; History— Automobiles; Inventions; Model-T Fords; Transportation

Follow a Model-T Ford from its assembly in 1909 to its place in an antique car collection.

Antique car buffs, especially Model-T Ford fans, will enjoy reading the history of this car. Students have a fascination with cars, including many of the classic antique models. Invite a member of a local antique car club to share information and enthusiasm with students. Consider taking a field trip to see vintage automobiles and the restoration process.

Why was it significant that 56 Model-Ts were produced on the same day in 1909? Use this book to begin studying assembly lines and their impact on history.

544. Spier, Peter. **We the People: The Constitution of the United States of America** (Doubleday, 1987).

Bill of Rights; Citizenship; Civil Rights; Constitution— United States; Ethnic Diversity; Government— Democratic; United States— History—Revolution

This tribute to the U.S. Constitution (including the Bill of Rights and the Amendments) visually traces U.S. history in relation to its most important document. The country's diversity is seen through panels depicting the growth and changes of the nation since its birth.

We the People is a great book for introducing students to the Constitution and how it relates to the American people.

For reluctant readers, this is a nonthreatening visual introduction to the history of the United States.

545. Spinelli, Eileen. **Somebody Loves You, Mr. Hatch**. Ill. by Paul Yalowitz (Macmillan, 1991).

Belonging; Feelings; Friendship; Loneliness; Love; Self-Esteem; Valentines

After receiving a huge box of chocolates from an unknown admirer, the lonely and reclusive Mr. Hatch becomes part of the neighborhood life.

Use this story to begin a discussion with middle schoolers on self-esteem and helping others. Many of them will feel compassion for Mr. Hatch.

546. Spohn. Kate. **Broken Umbrellas** (Viking, 1994).

Homeless; Mental Illness; Outcasts; Social Issues—Homeless; Street People

Something changes the woman's regular life. She begins worrying about money and picking up and saving old things (including her favorite— broken umbrellas). Gradually she becomes dysfunctional.

Evocative paintings and a sensitive text take the reader into the life of a street person. This book is perfect for sparking discussions on the homeless and dysfunctional people living on the streets.

 = Geography   = Art   = Music   = Drama   = Speech   Q = Research   = Read-Aloud

547. Stanley, Diane. **The Gentleman and the Kitchen Maid**. Ill. by Dennis Nolan (Dial Books for Young Readers, 1994).

Art—Coming to Life; Artists; History of Art; Museums; Paintings

An art student, practicing painting in a museum, notices the love between two portraits hanging across from each other and cleverly unites them. Illustrator note.

A perfect companion book is *The Girl with a Watering Can* by Eva Zadrzynska (Chameleon Books, 1990), in which characters in paintings at the National Gallery of Art come to life.

This book is truly a celebration of paintings by masters ranging from Rembrandt to Picasso. The illustrator's note identifies the 19 master artists included. Although Nolan did not copy particular paintings, he used the styles and elements commonly associated with those artists. In addition to the artists, many schools of art are represented including Dutch Masters, Little Dutch Masters, Dutch Baroque, Impressionism, Post-Impressionism, and Abstraction. Use *The Gentleman and the Kitchen Maid* to introduce a study of these specific masters and/or schools of art.

548. Stanley, Diane. **Peter the Great** (Four Winds Press, 1986).

Discoveries; History— Russia (1672-1725); Monarchs; Peter the Great (1672-1725); Russia; Shipbuilding; Tsars

Peter was the Russian tsar who Europeanized his country during the late 17th and early 18th centuries, even though his fellow Russians were reluctant to do so. Peter traveled the world and brought home amazing inventions and modern discoveries that he applied to Russian life.

This lavishly illustrated biography is a good introduction to Peter the Great, one of Russia's most interesting and influential tsars.

Peter the Great's reforms influenced his country for the next 200 years and partially caused the 1917 revolution. Students can study more about the historic split between the classes.

549. Stanley, Diane and Peter Vennema. **Bard of Avon: The Story of William Shakespeare**. Ill. by Diane Stanley (Morrow Junior Books, 1992).

Biographies; Drama; Elizabethan Theater; England; History—England; Language—English; Set Design; Shakespeare, William (1564-1616)

The great playwright William Shakespeare was the son of a glove maker and grew up in a small English town. This biography traces Shakespeare's life through his days as an actor to his relationships with Queen Elizabeth and other notables of the Elizabethan period. The authors discuss many of Shakespeare's plays as well as the variety of characters he created. Afterword.

A good companion volume for middle schoolers is Geraldine McCaughrean's *Stories from Shakespeare* (Margaret K. McElderry, 1994).

The physical design of the theater in Shakespeare's time was quite different from traditional theaters today. The buildings were circular with an open courtyard in the middle. For a penny people could stand in the courtyard and watch the performance. Others with more money could sit in one of three galleries surrounding the courtyard. Design a set and stage a play using the historic design of an imagined theater or the famous Globe Theatre. For an extensive list of books, videos, recordings, and activities consult "Meeting the Bard" by Andrew W. Frew [*Book Links* 3(4):41-44, March 1994]. Be sure to include the use of *Shakespeare and Macbeth: The Story Behind the Play* by Stewart Ross (Viking, 1994).

Shakespeare's effect on the English language was significant. The afterword notes that he invented more than 2,000 new words. Discuss where new words come from today. What examples can students suggest? Consult Janet Klausner's *Talk About English: How Words Travel*

 = Extraordinary! 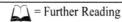 = Idea = Further Reading = Writing = Math = Science = History

and Change (Thomas Y. Crowell, 1990), for information about the history of English, the *Oxford English Dictionary* for specific changes to words throughout history, and a current slang dictionary for words that might someday get into the *Oxford English Dictionary,* the definitive dictionary.

550. Stanley, Diane and Peter Vennema. **Charles Dickens: The Man Who Had Great Expectations**. Ill. by Diane Stanley (William Morrow, 1993).

This famous Victorian novelist led an intriguing life. The authors combine the melodrama of Dickens' life with his literary world, making connections between his real life, people he knew, and his writings.

Authors; Biographies; Dickens, Charles (1812-1870); Public Policy; Social Action; Social Issues; Travel; Victorian Literature

Dickens never stopped working to help the poor. What projects can your students or school become involved with in your community?

According to Stanley, Dickens "became the mirror in which England was reflected. And the people were shocked and moved by what they saw. They began to pass reform laws, to build better houses and even schools for the poor." Students can discover which other authors or illustrators have tried to create change and/or influence public policy. For examples consult *The Greatest Table: A Banquet to Fight Against Hunger* (Harcourt Brace Jovanovich, 1994) and *Speak* (Harcourt Brace Jovanovich, 1993), both edited by Michael J. Rosen. Also review Ann Durell and Marilyn Sachs' *The Big Book for Peace* (E. P. Dutton, 1990). These books address the issues of hunger, humane treatment for pets, and world peace.

551. Stanley, Diane and Peter Vennema. **Cleopatra**. Ill. by Diane Stanley (Morrow Junior Books, 1994).

The brilliance and ambition of Cleopatra's life are captured in text and art. Included are details about her political aspirations as well as her romantic relationships with Julius Caesar and Mark Antony. Notes. Maps. Epilogue. Bibliography.

Ambition; Antony, Mark (d. 31 B.C.); Biographies; Caesar, Julius (d. 44 B.C.); Cleopatra (d. 30 B.C.); Egypt— History; Greed; History— Egypt—1st Century B.C.; Love; Politics; War; Women Rulers

The information offered in *Cleopatra* will easily spark interest in further investigation of this often misrepresented woman and her powerful political relationships. For further reading provide *Cleopatra: Goddess of Egypt, Enemy of Rome* by Polly Schoyer Brooks (Harper-Collins, 1995).

552. Stanley, Diane and Peter Vennema. **Good Queen Bess: The Story of Elizabeth I of England**. Ill. by Diane Stanley (Four Winds Press, 1990).

This biographical account of Elizabeth I tells of a queen who won the hearts of her people with her strong will, religious tolerance, shrewd diplomacy, and great love for her subjects.

Biographies; Elizabeth I (1533-1603); Elizabethan England; Great Britain; History—England—1533-1603; Monarchs; Queens

Students can read this book as an introduction to the Elizabethan period and prior to reading some of Shakespeare's plays.

With the information given concerning King Henry VIII and his many wives, students can learn more about the history of the English monarchy.

553. Stanley, Diane and Peter Vennema. **Shaka: King of the Zulus**. Ill. by Diane Stanley (Morrow Junior Books, 1988).

Banished from their tiny Zulu clan, Shaka and his mother sought refuge with another village. There Shaka grew up to become a military genius and king of a successful Zulu nation. Bibliography. Map.

Africa—History; Biographies; Courage; History—Zulus; Military Strategy; Shaka, Zulu Chief (1787?-1828); War; Zulus— History (1700s)

Shaka was an innovative leader, developing new weapons and fighting methods. Compare and contrast his military skill with that of other famous leaders. Some books like Albert Marrin's *Napoleon and the*

 = Geography = Art = Music = Drama = Speech = Research = Read-Aloud

Napoleonic Wars (Viking, 1991) focus on the military genius of an individual. Students might also be interested in learning about other military tacticians such as Robert E. Lee and Alexander the Great. General military science and weapons information can be found in books like *The Visual Dictionary of Special Military Forces* (Dorling Kindersley, 1993) and *The Visual Dictionary of Military Uniforms* (Dorling Kindersley, 1992).

554. Stanley, Fay. **The Last Princess: The Story of Princess Ka'iulani of Hawai'i**. Ill. by Diane Stanley (Four Winds Press, 1991).

Biographies; Government—Hawaiian; Hawaii—History; Ka'iulani, Princess (1875-1899); Language—Hawaiian; Missionaries; Monarchies; Sovereignty

When the Hawaiian monarchy was abolished in 1893, members of the Hawaiian royal family were no longer involved in running their country. This biography of Princess Ka'iulani tells of her childhood, education, and eventual heartbreak. Map. Notes. Bibliography.

In 1994, many Hawaiians commemorated the 100-year anniversary of the loss of their sovereignty. The movement to regain sovereignty is very much alive as native Hawaiians strive to reclaim their religion, culture, and language. Students can view the television documentary *Act of War: The Overthrow of the Hawaiian Nation* (Center for Hawaiian Studies, 1994) and research current periodicals to determine what is happening with this movement today.

Stanley includes a note on the Hawaiian language at the end of this book. Interested students can practice the complicated pronunciations and learn to speak some of this lyrical language.

Two picture books in particular can add to student understanding about the history of Hawaii. *To Find the Way* by Susan Nunes (University of Hawaii Press, 1992) features a Tahitian navigator who used his knowledge of the sea and stars to guide his companions aboard a great canoe to the unknown island of Hawaii. *In the Night Still Dark* by Richard Lewis (Atheneum, 1988) is an adaptation of a traditional Hawaiian creation chant, which served as a genealogical record of the Hawaiian Kings. It portrays a concept of evolution by an indigenous people and helps bond the life of a newborn child to all living things.

555. Stevens, Janet. **Coyote Steals the Blanket: A Ute Tale** (Holiday House, 1993).

Art—Navajo Blankets; Drama; Indians of North America—Legends; Legends—Ute Indians; Navajo Indians; Read-Aloud; Trickster Tales; Ute Indians—Legends; Weaving

Despite a warning, Coyote steals a blanket and then is pursued, to the point of exhaustion, by "the ancient spirit of the great desert."

Blankets and rugs made by Navajo weavers are treasures collected by museums and individuals. If you do not have access to a museum with such a collection, find an individual who can bring samples of these blankets and/or rugs to show to your students. Study the weaving process and historic designs that are often associated with different areas such as Two Gray Hills, Wide Ruins, and Crystal.

Write and produce a play featuring tricksters from different cultures. Note that there are many trickster tales highlighted in this book.

---

556. Stolz, Mary. **Zekmet, the Stone Carver: A Tale of Ancient Egypt**. Ill. by Deborah Nourse Lattimore (Harcourt Brace Jovanovich, 1988).

Ancient Egypt; Codes; Communication; Hieroglyphics; Historical Fiction; Sphinx

Chosen to design and carve a monument to honor a pharaoh, Zekmet ends up working on the Sphinx that everyone today associates with ancient Egypt.

The hieroglyphics on the endpapers are from the borders adorning the pages and retell the story. Students interested in learning more about hieroglyphics will find the following materials fascinating: *Egyptian Hieroglyphics for Everyone* by Joseph Scott and Lenore Scott (Thomas Y. Crowell, 1990) *Hieroglyphs from A to Z: A Rhyming Book with Ancient Egyptian Stencils for Kids* by Peter Der Manuelian (Rizzoli, 1993), *Hieroglyphs: The Writing of Ancient Egypt* by Norma J. Katan and Barbara Mintz (Margaret K. McElderry, 1981), *Pepi and the Secret Names* by Jill Paton Walsh (Lothrop, Lee & Shepard, 1995), *Croco'nile* by Roy Gerrard (Farrar, Straus & Giroux, 1994), and the boxed rubber stamps and booklet entitled *Fun with Hieroglyphs* by Catherine Roehrig (Metropolitan Museum of Art/Viking, 1990).

557. Strauss, Gwen. **Trail of Stones**. Ill. by Anthony Browne (Alfred A. Knopf, 1990).

Art; Fairy Tales— Novelizations; Munch, Edvard (1863-1944); Perspective; Poems; Portraits

In an examination of the lasting power of fairy tales, Strauss and Browne have combined talents to form a collection of poetry and portraits that approach familiar tales from a slightly different perspective.

Reworking fairy tales is not an original idea, but it continues to be an interesting way to extend stories that have a timeless appeal. For further reading provide students with novelizations of fairy tales such as Donna Jo Napoli's retelling of the Hansel and Gretel story from the witch's perspective, *The Magic Circle* (Dutton Children's Books, 1993); Robin McKinley's *Beauty: A Retelling of the Story of Beauty & the Beast* (Harper & Row, 1978); and for older readers McKinley's *Deerskin* (Ace Books, 1993); *Black Thorn, White Rose* edited by Ellen Datlow and Terri Windling (Avon Books, 1994); and a young adult trilogy set in modern times by Adele Geras which includes *The Tower Room, Watching the Roses,* and *Pictures of the Night* (Harcourt Brace Jovanovich, 1992).

The first poem in the book, entitled "Their Father," describes with words and art the helpless anger suffered by Hansel and Gretel's father. Hanging on the wall of the father's house is a replication of Edvard Munch's famous painting *The Scream*. Provide background information on Munch's art to spark a discussion or writing experience based on what is found.

558. Supree, Burton with Ann Ross. **Bear's Heart**. Ill. by Bear's Heart (J. B. Lippincott, 1977).

Art—Primitive; Bear's Heart (1851-1882); Biographies; Cheyennne Iindians; Indians of North America—Cheyenne; Primitive Art; Prison; Reservations

Bear's Heart was a Cheyenne Indian who was imprisoned, along with 71 other Indians, in a Florida prison in the late 1880s. While in prison, Bear's Heart drew the pictures that illustrate this book. Afterword by Jamake Highwater.

This glimpse at the lives of Native Americans in the late 1880s is poignant. Use this book with others such as *This Land Is My Land* by George Littlechild (Children's Book Press, 1993) that explain the circumstances and feelings that existed as these people were forced to leave their land and move to reservations. Another book about these transitional times is *White Bead Ceremony* by Sherrin Watkins (Council Oak Publishing, 1994).

Primitivism, popularly known as primitive art, is a style that seems childlike ("fresh and fanciful") and is often done by untrained artists. Famous artists who have painted in this style include Grandma Moses (1860-1961), Henri Rousseau (1844-1910), and Edward Hicks (1780-1849). Introduce students to this art style by sharing reproductions by these artists and books such as Mattie Lou O'Kelley's *From the Hills of Georgia: An Autobiography in Paintings* (Little, Brown, 1983) in addition to those by Bear's Heart.

559. Swope, Sam. **The Araboolies of Liberty Street**. Ill. by Barry Root (Potter, 1989).

Debate; Diversity; Fable; Government; Individualism; Neighbors; Political Issues; Tolerance

General Pinch (who likes to have everything orderly and looking the same) becomes overwrought when the Araboolies move to the quiet conventional Liberty Street. Their colorful skin and noncomformist ways bring happiness to all the residents except the mean-spirited Pinches.

This modern fable addresses some weighty political issues—the role of the military in modern society and the rights of individuals versus the government. Use the book along with real examples, such as the Randy Weaver standoff in Idaho with the FBI in 1992 and the government assault on the Branch Davidian compound near Waco, Texas, in 1993, to launch a class discussion. A debate concerning the rights of individuals versus the government could be staged by students after adequate research and preparation.

T

560. Talbott, Hudson. **We're Back! A Dinosaur's Story** (Crown, 1987).

Allusions; Creative Writing; Dinosaurs; Humor; Literary Devices; Museums; Paleontology; Prehistoric Animals; Read-Aloud; Science

A group of dinosaurs are treated to "Brain Grain" and experimentation by a strange group of aliens. Their ultimate reward is a trip to the 20th century where they create excitement at a parade and at the Museum of Natural History in New York City.

Sophisticated scientific allusion is used in this funny story grounded in paleontology. Examples include a reference to someone who "used to hang out at the tar pit" and the museum curator, who reads a bedtime story about a little trilobite who just wants to climb up out of the ocean. As a creative writing assignment, students can write other stories using allusion as a literary device. Making sure their allusions are scientifically plausible will add to the fun.

561. Taylor, Clark. **The House That Crack Built**. Ill. by Jan Thompson Dicks (Chronicle Books, 1992).

Cocaine; Crack; Crack Babies; Drug Abuse; Drug Education; Drugs—Illegal; Gangs; Social Issues—Drugs; Victims

The cumulative verse structure of the well-known "This Is the House That Jack Built" nursery rhyme and a hip-hop beat are used to present a chilling look at crack cocaine and its impact on society. Resource list.

This book is a perfect discussion starter for drug education classes or seminars for all but the youngest child. Because it transcends ages, it is effective when used with multiage groups. The list of national organizations that provide help for and education about drug abuse should be viewed as a supplement to what is available locally.

562. Tejima, Keizaburo. **Fox's Dream** (Philomel, 1987).

Art—Woodcuts; Dreams; Forests; Foxes; Life Cycle; Winter; Woodcuts

A lone fox wanders though a winter forest looking for food. The icy trees evoke images of a pleasant past; the new dawn brings hope for the future when he spies a vixen in a snowy field.

 = Extraordinary!   = Idea   = Further Reading   = Writing $\frac{2}{4}$ = Math   = Science   = History

Perfect companion books about a fox's life are Cherie Mason's *Wild Fox: A True Story* (Down East Books, 1993) and Allison Blyler's *Finding Foxes* (Philomel, 1990).

 Have students do research to find information about traditional methods of Japanese woodcuts so they will have a background for studying Tejima's work. *Fox's Dream* was a *New York Times* Best Illustrated Children's Book.

563. Tejima, Keizaburo. **Owl Lake** (Philomel, 1987).

564. Tejima, Keizaburo. **Swan Sky** (Philomel, 1988).

565. Tejima, Keizaburo. **Woodpecker Forest** (Philomel, 1989).

Birds; Death; Flight; Life Cycle; Nature; Science— Wildlife; Woodcuts

These companion books feature woodland animals and their life cycles. *Owl Lake* follows an owl family through the night; *Woodpecker Forest* follows a family making a nest and raising their young; and despite the encouragement of other swans, the young sick swan in *Swan Sky* refuses to go on the annual migration.

 Have students read and investigate several of Tejima's books. Then discuss the following: Tejima's books have two main characteristics: stunning woodcuts combined with a simple, powerful story. Why and how does this combination work so well?

 Use Tejima's books as a starting point for an in-depth study of the natural habits of animals. A look at migration might include the migration routes nearest to your locale. What type of wildlife uses these routes? What are some scientists doing to help birds alter their migration routes because of human infringement on the areas within the traditional routes?

566. Tennyson, Alfred. **The Lady of Shalott**. Ill. by Charles Keeping (Oxford University Press, 1986).

Arthurian Legends; Death; Lancelot; Legends— Arthurian; Love; Poetry

Keeping illustrates Tennyson's classic poem about the lady of Shalott, a maiden of Arthurian legends who falls in love with Sir Lancelot of the Lake and dies because her love is not returned.

 Tennyson's classic poem and Keeping's gothic style of illustration elegantly combine to create this picture book. First read the poem in its entirety and then read it again, this time showing Keeping's illustrations. Discuss the poem's impact after each reading. Do students prefer to hear the poem and see the illustrations, or hear it without seeing the illustrations? Does seeing the illustrations change the experience of hearing the poem for the students? Discuss individual preferences.

 567. Thayer, Ernest Lawrence. **Casey at the Bat: A Centennial Edition**. Ill. by Barry Moser (Godine, 1988).

Baseball; Creative Writing; Essays; Libraries; Poetry; Read-Aloud

Thayer presents a centennial edition of this popular poem about the baseball player who struck out at the crucial moment. Afterword.

 Moser's illustrations are based on famous historic photographs and drawings from the archives of the National Baseball Library in Cooperstown, New York. There are special library collections throughout the United States. Are any of them near you? Does your local library maintain any special collections—local history, science fiction, business, etc.? Take a field trip or invite the curator or librarian to visit your classroom and discuss the library's collection.

 = Geography   = Art   = Music   = Drama   = Speech   = Research   = Read-Aloud

Use the edition of this poem illustrated by Gerald Fitzgerald (Atheneum, 1995) along with Jack Norworth's *Take Me Out to the Ballgame* (Four Winds Press, 1992) to add more perspective to the historical facts and popular culture of baseball.

 Have students read Donald Hall's afterword, which celebrates the poem, its hero, and those times when each of us inevitably strikes out in life. Students can write their own essays inspired by, or modeled after Hall's thoughts and comments.

568. Thompson, Colin. **The Paper Bag Prince** (Alfred A. Knopf, 1992).

Ecology; Outcasts; Pollution; Recycling

A wise elderly man moves into an abandoned train in the town dump and watches as nature reclaims the polluted land that had been his farmland more than 40 years ago.

 Some communities have excellent recycling programs which include making and selling compost and wood chips, and selling garbage for trash-to-energy plants in addition to recycling the standard aluminum, glass, metal, and plastic. Students can become more involved in the recycling efforts of their school, homes, or community. Chris Van Allsburg's *Just a Dream* (Houghton Mifflin, 1990) is a great companion book for a project concerning recycling and student involvement.

569. Tompert, Ann. **Grandfather Tang's Story**. Ill. by Robert Andrew Parker (Crown, 1990).

China; Fairies; Folklore— Chinese; Foxes; Friendship; Puzzles; Storytelling; Tangrams

As Grandfather Tang tells a story about the shape-changing fox fairies, each new character in the story tries to get the best of the others. Character designs. Puzzle pattern.

 Tangrams are the ancient Chinese puzzles made up of seven traditional pieces. Students can make tangrams by following the directions in the book or by purchasing a commercially produced tangram. After practicing with their own tangrams, students can create their own stories based on the Chinese tradition of the puzzle pieces being rearranged as new characters or story elements are introduced. *The Tangram Magician* (Harry N. Abrams, 1990) by Lisa Campbell Ernst and Lee Ernst contains three sets of stick-on tangrams.

570. Towle, Wendy. **The Real McCoy: The Life of an African-American Inventor**. Paintings by Wil Clay (Scholastic, 1993).

African Americans; Biographies; Black History Month; Inventions; Legends; McCoy, Elijah (1844-1929); Phrases; Trains

The origin of the expression "the real McCoy" comes from Elijah McCoy's invention of a superior lubricating machine for trains.

 Although the exact origin of the phrase "the real McCoy" cannot be authenticated, one legend indicates it can be attributed as it is in this book. Students might be interested in the origins of other phrases. Provide books such as *Morris Dictionary of Word and Phrase Origins* by William Morris (Harper & Row, 1988), *Mad as a Wet Hen! And Other Funny Idioms* by Marvin Terban (Clarion Books, 1987), and *Cleopatra's Nose, The Twinkie Defense & 1500 Other Verbal Shortcuts in Popular Parlance* by Jerome Agel (Prentice-Hall, 1990).

571. Tripp, Wallace. **Marguerite, Go Wash Your Feet** (Houghton Mifflin, 1985).

Humor; Nonsense; Poetry; Satire

This is a collection of funny verses by a variety of poets (Emily Dickinson, William Shakespeare, Groucho Marx, and others) juxtaposed with equally funny and/or odd illustrations and caricatures.

This collection has a sophisticated appeal because of the spoofs Tripp includes. Older students who don't like poetry might be pleasantly surprised if they are willing to take the time to explore this book. What funny elements can students find?

 572. Trivizas, Eugene. **The Three Little Wolves and the Big Bad Pig**. Ill. by Helen Oxenbury (Macmillan, 1993).

Creative Writing; Folktales—Fractured; Fractured Folktales; Humorous Stories; Plays— Script Material; Read-Aloud; Reader's Theater

The tables are turned when the three little wolves are harassed by the big bad pig. When neither bricks, concrete, nor an armor-plated house keep them safe from the pig, they change their tactics.

Be sure to share Jon Scieszka's *The True Story of the 3 Little Pigs by A. Wolf* (Viking Kestrel, 1989) as a companion to this book. Working in groups, students should easily be inspired to create their own fractured folktales.

 Students can adapt this story to a script to perform.

573. Tsuchiya, Yukio. **Faithful Elephants: A True Story of Animals, People and War**. Ill. by Ted Lewin (Houghton Mifflin, 1988).

Animal Rights; Elephants; Japan—History—World War II; Read-Aloud; War; World War II—Japan; Zoos

During the last days of World War II, the potentially dangerous animals in the Tokyo Zoo had to be killed for fear they might escape during an air raid.

Faithful Elephants provides the perfect springboard for discussion or further research on the impact of warfare on animal species and the environment.

Of interest will be *Hanna's Cold Winter* by Trish Marx (Carolrhoda Books, 1993), the story of how the citizens in Budapest kept their zoo's beloved hippopotamus from starving during World War II. Students can research newspaper and magazine articles about what happened to the animals in the Kuwait Zoo during and after the U.S. military's Operation Desert Storm.

574. Turner, Ann. **Dakota Dugout**. Ill. by Ronald Himler (Macmillan, 1985).

Diaries; Historical Fiction; Journals; Pioneer Life; Sod Houses; Survival; Westward Expansion; Women Pioneers

A woman describes what it was like living on the Dakota prairie in a sod house in the late 19th century.

Numerous women pioneers kept diaries, journals, or photographic records about their experiences. Create a classroom library with materials such as *Emily, the Diary of a Hard-Working Woman* by Emily French and Janet Lecompte (University of Nebraska Press, 1987), *Lizzie: The Letters of Elizabeth Chester Fisk, 1864-1893* by Elizabeth Chester Fisk and Rex C. Myers (Mountain Press, 1989), and the books by Elinore Pruitt Stewart: *Letters of a Woman Homesteader* (Houghton Mifflin, 1982) and *Letters on an Elk Hunt* (University of Nebraska Press 1915, 1979). Another picture book diary on this subject is *The Way West: Journal of a Pioneer Woman* by Amelia Stewart Knight (Simon & Schuster, 1993). Use the topic "women pioneers" to find regional heroines in library searches.

For a complete pictorial history about the sod houses built in the 19th century consult Glen Rounds' *Sod Houses on the Great Plains* (Holiday House, 1995) and *Prairie Visions: The Life and Times of Solomon Butcher* by Pam Conrad (HarperCollins, 1991). Other picture books about pioneer settlements include *Aurora Means Dawn* by Scott Russell Sanders (Bradbury Press, 1989), which features the settling of a new community in Ohio by pioneers who traveled there from Connecticut in 1800, and *West by Covered Wagon: Retracing the Pioneer Trails* by Dorothy Hinshaw Patent (Walker, 1995). Another great source is *Atlas of Western Expansion* by Alan Wexler (Facts on File, 1995).

 = Geography = Art = Music = Drama = Speech = Research = Read-Aloud

575. Turner, Ann. **Heron Street**. Paintings by Lisa Desimini (Harper & Row, 1989).

Boston; Changes; City Planning; Ecology; Environmental Issues— Urban Growth; Read-Aloud; Science—Ecology; Urban Growth; Wetlands

The marsh and nearby sea, once home to many birds and animals, disappear as Boston grows from an early settlement to a modern metropolis.

Thomas Locker's *The Land of Gray Wolf* (Dial Books for Young Readers, 1991) is a good companion book from a historical perspective. It features a sensitive portrayal of ecologically balanced Indian land use versus the destruction of the forests and the development of farms by the New England white settlers.

Development on the edges of towns and cities continues to put a strain on the environment. Communities are faced with problems concerning adequate water supplies, available landfill space, loss of wildlife habitat, population density, and pollution, among others. Have students review your community's planning and development strategy and evaluate its strengths and weaknesses.

576. Turner, Ann. **Katie's Trunk**. Ill. by Ronald Himler (Macmillan, 1992).

Children and War; Courage; Fear; Historical Fiction; History—United States—Revolutionary War; Revolutionary War—United States; United States— History—Revolution (1775-1783); War

Katie's family is loyal to the British Crown so they abandon their home when American rebel soldiers invade. All but Katie, that is. She hides under the clothes in her mother's wedding trunk in this story based on a true incident that happened to Turner's ancestors.

What happened to families or individuals who were on the losing side of the Revolution? Students can examine historical conflicts and look at the other side of victory.

577. Turner, Ann. **Nettie's Trip South**. Ill. by Ronald Himler (Macmillan, 1987).

Abolitionists; Compassion; Cruelty; Historical Fiction; History—Pre-Civil War; Letters; Slavery; Social Life and Customs—Southern States—Pre-Civil War

Ten-year-old Nettie writes letters to her friend about the horrors of slavery she encounters when she visits Richmond, Virginia, and sees a slave auction.

Benjamin Banneker was an astronomer, mathematician, and the author of the first published almanac by a Black man. He was born free when most Blacks were still enslaved, and slavery troubled him. He began a correspondence with Secretary of State Thomas Jefferson telling him exactly what he felt about Jefferson owning slaves. The picture book *Dear Benjamin Banneker* by Andrea Davis Pinkney (Harcourt Brace Jovanovich, 1994) details the story of their amazing correspondence. Provide this book to students for another perspective of slavery.

Using a letter format like that used by Nettie, students can write about significant experiences in such a way that the reader learns important details about events and times. Topics can include current social injustices.

The author notes that Nettie is inspired by her own great-grandmother, who became a committed abolitionist. Study some of the famous abolitionists of the Civil War era. This eloquent book is a fine beginning.

578. Turney-Zagwÿn, Deborah. **Long Nellie** (Orca, 1993).

Cats; Conservation; Ecology; Friendship; Outcasts; Recycling; Scavengers; Social Concerns

Long Nellie lives by herself in a decrepit trailer and survives by searching through dumpsters and garbage. When young Jeremy finds a stray cat, he is determined to provide Long Nellie with a friend.

Pair this book with Kate Spohn's *Broken Umbrellas* (Viking, 1994) and Colin Thompson's *The Paper Bag Prince* (Alfred A. Knopf, 1992) to generate discussions about compassion and the need to reach out to individuals living on society's fringe.

---

579. Twain, Mark. **The Stolen White Elephant**. Ill. by Robert Ingpen (P.I.C. Pty Ltd., 1987).

Only Inspector Blunt can solve the crime when a white elephant, bound for England as a gift from the King of Siam, is stolen. For three weeks detectives search for clues, only cracking the case when the award is raised to $100,000.

Crime; Detectives; Elephants; Gifts; Humor; Kings; Short Stories; Theft; Twain, Mark (1835-1920)

 This story is classic Mark Twain with its droll and hilarious plot line and remarkable characters. The short prologue states that this story was left out of Twain's *A Tramp Abroad* "because it was feared that some of the particulars had been exaggerated, and that others were not true." Use this story as an excuse to collect a variety of Twain's short stories, essays, and overlooked novels for student reading.

U

580. Uchida, Yoshiko. **The Bracelet**. Ill. by Joanna Yardley (Philomel, 1993).

After losing the bracelet given to her by her best friend, a Japanese American girl in an internment camp during World War II learns that the most important gift can simply be a memory. Afterword.

Civil Rights; Friendship; Government—United States; Internment Camps (1942-1945); Japanese Americans; Memories; World War II

 The afterword of this book focuses on the civil rights issues concerning the internment of Japanese Americans. Students can investigate more completely the 1976 statement by President Ford, the work of the commission established by President Carter in 1982, and the 1988 government apology and symbolic restitution.

 Other picture books on the internment of Japanese Americans are Sheila Hamanaka's *The Journey: Japanese Americans, Racism, and Renewal* (Orchard, 1990) and Ken Mochizuki's *Baseball Saved Us* (Lee & Low Books, 1993) and *Heroes* (Lee & Low Books, 1995).

581. UNICEF. **A Children's Chorus: Celebrating the 30th Anniversary of the Declaration of the Rights of the Child**. Ill. by various artists (E. P. Dutton, 1989).

Eleven acclaimed international illustrators joined forces to celebrate the anniversary of the Declaration of the Rights of the Child. The document, unanimously adopted on November 20, 1959, includes 10 fundamental rights each child should have such as education, food, medical care, and safe shelter.

Artists; Celebrations; Children; Equality; Hope; Public Policy; Rights—Of Children; UNICEF; United Nations

After a discussion of the 10 Rights of the Child, students can focus on how well those rights are being met in their community, in the United States, and in selected other countries.

This book can spur students to learn more about the role and accomplishments of UNICEF and/or the United Nations.

V

582. Van Allsburg, Chris. **Ben's Dream** (Houghton Mifflin, 1982).

Lulled to sleep by the rain, Ben dreams he and his house are floating past the half-submerged great monuments of the world, which, in reality, he had been studying about for a test.

Arts and Crafts; Dream Catchers; Dreams; Fantasy; Floods; Geography; Indians of North America; Monuments

---

 = Geography　　 = Art　　 = Music　　 = Drama　　 = Speech　　 = Research　　 = Read-Aloud

According to some Indian legends, good and bad dreams float though the night air. Members of the Ojibwa tribe began hanging dream catchers in their homes and lodges years ago to help catch the bad dreams and let the good dreams through. Recently, other Indian tribes and non-Indians as well have adopted the custom. Invite someone to your school who can teach this craft of making dream catchers and discuss the symbolism behind them. Display the results.

This largely wordless book can easily become a geography game. Using the "Who? What? Why? Where? and When?" approach, center a geography project on monuments around the world, including others not in Ben's dream. Be sure to have a world map and globe to pinpoint each location. Provide students with a video version of *Ben's Dream,* titled with *Ben's Dream and Other Stories and Fun* (Made-to-Order Productions, 1990).

 583. Van Allsburg, Chris. **Jumanji** (Houghton Mifflin, 1981).

 584. Van Allsburg, Chris. **The Stranger** (Houghton Mifflin, 1986).

 585. Van Allsburg, Chris. **The Sweetest Fig** (Houghton Mifflin, 1993).

586. Van Allsburg, Chris. **The Wreck of the Zephyr** (Houghton Mifflin, 1983).

Autumn; Dreams;
Enchantments; Fantasy;
Games; Magic; Read-Aloud;
Seasons; Weather

The plain-looking board game *Jumanji* (Caldecott Medal, 1982) turns a quiet house into a jungle adventure land. During *The Stranger*'s stay, the farmer is perplexed about the unusual seasonal change from autumn to winter. *The Sweetest Fig* makes dreams come true, but not in the way the sadistic dentist intended. Unless you believe in enchantments it seems impossible for *The Wreck of the Zephyr* to be so high on the cliff above the water.

 Your students can adapt the *Jumanji* game idea into an original magical "Van Allsburg Adventure." Combine Van Allsburg stories in different ways to create traditional board games, videos, etc. Students can also see the movie *Jumanji* (Tri-Star, 1995), starring Robin Williams.

 Along with *The Stranger,* provide *Peboan and Seegwun* by Charles Larry (Farrar, Straus & Giroux, 1993), an Ojibwa legend about Old Man Winter and the Spirit of Spring.

587. Van Allsburg, Chris. **The Mysteries of Harris Burdick** (Houghton Mifflin, 1984).

Analysis; Creative
Writing; Imagination;
Mystery and Detective
Stories; Perspectives;

Fourteen mysterious and evocative drawings are accompanied by a title and one or two provocative sentences.

 The selected captions in this book complement the drawings while challenging the viewer to look at them from different perspectives. Other books that challenge the viewer are Mitsumasa Anno's *The Unique World of Mitsumasa Anno: Selected Works (1968-1977)* (Philomel, 1980), with 41 unusual texts juxtaposed with illustrations, and Guy Billout's *Journey: Travel Diary of a Daydreamer* (Creative Education, 1993). Students can select a picture and speculate on what they think it communicates in a story or essay.

The illustration of "The Third-Floor Bedroom" shows a transfer from two to three dimensions. Let students explore books featuring M. C. Escher's art such as *M. C. Escher: His Life and Complete Graphic Work* (Harry N. Abrams, 1992) and *M. C. Escher: 29 Master Prints* (Harry N. Abrams, 1983) to find examples of similar drawings.

 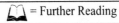

588. Van Allsburg, Chris. **The Polar Express** (Houghton Mifflin, 1985).

Christmas; Fairy Tales—Modern; Fantasy; Imagination; Read-Aloud; Santa Claus; Trains; Wishes

A boy takes a magical train ride to the North Pole on Christmas Eve and is granted a wish from Santa Claus—a bell from the reindeer harness. Caldecott Medal, 1986.

Upon publication, this book immediately captured the imagination of adults and children alike, becoming a classic to share across generations. Whether or not the audience members are Santa "believers," it's an excellent selection for a Christmas read-aloud. According to the story, only believers can hear the ringing sound of the broken bell. A new edition, published in 1996, contains a letter from Van Allsburg, purportedly an explanation of how he received a silent bell.

589. Van Allsburg, Chris. **The Widow's Broom** (Houghton Mifflin, 1992).

Art—Visual Literacy; Fantasy; Good Versus Evil; Halloween; Literary Devices; Loneliness; Magic; Personification; Read-Aloud; Supernatural Tales; Visual Literacy; Witches

The old broom, discarded by a witch, still has enough magic to please the widow Minna Shaw. However, the broom's independent doings (sweeping, chopping wood, fetching water, and even playing the piano) bring trouble from the neighbors and villagers.

The villagers decide the broom is evil and must be burned at the stake. Van Allsburg's setting, portrayed through the illustrations and text, bring to mind the Witchcraft Trials of Salem in 1692. Students can consult books such as Laurel Van Der Linde's *Devil in Salem Village* (Millbrook, 1992) and Shirley Jackson's *The Witchcraft of Salem Village* (Random House, 1962) for more information.

The sepia-toned illustrations set the mysterious mood underlying this story. Collect Van Allsburg books illustrated with black pencil, charcoal, and/or sepia tones [*The Garden of Abdul Gasazi* (Houghton Mifflin, 1979), *Jumanji* (Houghton Mifflin, 1981), *The Mysteries of Harris Burdick* (Houghton Mifflin, 1984), etc.)] to study these types of illustrations and the moods they create. Art students might want to experiment with blending carbon or graphite dust with a brush as well as using traditional pencil lines and shading in their own drawings.

590. Van Allsburg, Chris. **The Wretched Stone** (Houghton Mifflin, 1991).

Fantasy; Literary Devices; Magic; Media Literacy; Metaphor; Ships' Log; Supernatural; Television Management; Violence—Television

Writings in the ship's log indicate the glowing rock taken aboard transfixed the crew for days.

The glowing rock and its effect on the crew are an obvious metaphor for the way television absorbs many viewers. The illustration of the transfixed crew with the light shining on them can begin a discussion of media literacy. The United States is the only industrialized nation that does not have media literacy included in school curricula. Discuss the effects (negative and positive) of television. Invite a media literacy expert (e.g., librarian, community access television staff member) to talk about managing and analyzing television, and becoming critical viewers and consumers as a result.

Secondary students will also enjoy the strange shipboard happenings in Paul Fleischman's short story "The Binnacle Boy" in *Graven Images* (Harper & Row, 1982).

591. Van der Rol, Ruud and Rian Verhoeven. **Anne Frank: Beyond the Diary** (Viking, 1993).

Biographies; Courage; Diaries; Frank, Anne (1929-1944); Holocaust; Jews; Nazis; Netherlands

Using photographs, illustrations, maps, diary excerpts, and interviews the compilers provide insight into the world of Anne Frank.

Use this interesting and easy-to-read biography in conjunction with the many excellent novels set in Europe during World War II.

 = Geography   = Art   = Music    = Drama   = Speech   = Research   = Read-Aloud

592. Viorst, Judith. **The Alphabet from Z to A (With Much Confusion on the Way)**. Ill. by Richard Hull (Atheneum, 1994).

Alphabet Books; Book Games; Games; Languages—English; Literary Recreations; Reading; Spelling

Witty verses going backward through the alphabet demonstrate the maddening inconsistencies in spellings and sounds of the English language.

 Older struggling spellers will be delighted to know that adults (including the one who gave them this book) have a sense of humor and can acknowledge the idiocy of English.

 The humorous detailed illustrations include many hidden objects that start with the featured letter. All the answers are listed in "A Challenge," found on the last pages of the book.

593. Volavková, Hana, ed. **I Never Saw Another Butterfly: Children's Drawings and Poems from Terezin Concentration Camp, 1942-1944**, 2nd ed. (Schocken Books, 1993).

Art—Children's; Children and War; Concentration Camps; Czechoslovakia; Holocaust; Jews; Nazis; Poetry—Children's; War; World War II—Holocaust

Approximately 100 children out of the 15,000 who lived in the Terezin ghetto lived; the rest were sent to Auschwitz. This collection of poetry and art, created by some of those children, reflects their hopes and fears, and honors their memory. Foreword. Catalogs of drawings and poems. Epilogue. Afterword. Chronology.

 An earlier English language edition of this book was published by McGraw-Hill in 1964. That edition includes some other poems, drawings, and catalog notes. The two books together double the impact and enhance any study of the Holocaust.

 Use this book along with poetry written by youth from other cultures. *Rising Voices: Writings of Young Native Americans* selected by Arlene B. Hirschfelder and Beverly R. Singer (Charles Scribner's Sons, 1992) is an excellent example of how the history of a culture can be eloquently reflected in the writings of its young people.

594. Von Tscharner, Renata and Ronald Lee Fleming. **New Providence: A Changing Cityscape**. Ill. by Denis Orloff (Harcourt Brace Jovanovich, 1987).

Architecture; Economic Changes; History—United States—20th Century; Population; Social Commentary; Urban Development

The growth of American cities in the 20th century is mirrored in this tale of a mythical city's evolution during the changing times of the 20th century.

 Excellent companion books include Jorg Muller's *The Changing City* (Margaret K. McElderry, 1977) and John S. Goodall's wordless *The Story of Main Street* (Margaret K. McElderry, 1987). *New Providence* is also available as a set of seven posters with a 32-page teaching guide from Dale Seymour Publications, P.O. Box 10888, Palo Alto, CA 94303-0879.

 The social, cultural, and economic changes of society are reflected in the city's growth during the featured years: 1910, 1935, 1955, 1970, 1980, and 1987. Using the information as a springboard for further study, students can select one of the featured time periods.

 New Providence is the perfect introduction to American architecture. Students can become amateur architectural historians by learning more about the styles depicted here and then creating a photographic (or illustrated) display of buildings in their community that exemplify various styles.

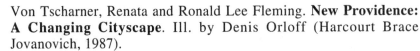

W

595. Walker, Alice. **To Hell with Dying**. Ill. by Catherine Deeter (Harcourt Brace Jovanovich, 1967, 1988).

African Americans; Alcoholism; Death; Friendship; Intergenerational Relationships; Love; Loyalty; Social Issues—Alcoholism

Nostalgically, Walker tells of old Mr. Sweet, a lovable alcoholic always on the verge of dying. However, he was nearly always revived by the loving attention she and her brother lavished on him.

This short, illustrated story is an excellent introduction to one of America's most noted authors. Provide high school students with more of Walker's works, such as *The Color Purple* (Harcourt Brace Jovanovich, 1992), *Possessing the Secret of Joy* (Harcourt Brace Jovanovich, 1968, 1992), *Temple of My Familiar* (Harcourt Brace Jovanovich, 1980), and *Her Blue Body Everything We Know: Earthling Poems, 1965-1990* (Harcourt Brace Jovanovich, 1991).

596. **We Are All in the Dumps with Jack and Guy: Two Nursery Rhymes with Pictures**. Ill. by Maurice Sendak (HarperCollins, 1993).

Allegory; Homeless—Children; Mother Goose Rhymes; Newspapers; Nursery Rhymes; Poetry; Read-Aloud; Social Issues—Homeless

Two homeless ragamuffins rescue a kidnapped baby and some kittens from an evil band of rats. Two separate (little-known) Mother Goose rhymes, connected by Sendak, are given new meaning through his provocative illustrations.

We Are All in the Dumps with Jack and Guy is a good springboard for launching a study on the historical origins (and meanings) of some Mother Goose rhymes. Historical notes on seven Mother Goose rhymes are found at the end of Stephen Krensky's *The Missing Mother Goose: Original Stories from Favorite Rhymes* (Doubleday, 1991). Some critics disapprove of Sendak's use of these two rhymes, which along with his illustrations, deal with a disheartening social issue. What do your students think?

Provide "We Are All in the Dumps with Jack and Guy: Two Nursery Rhymes with Pictures by Maurice Sendak" by Peter F. Neumeyer [*Children's Literature in Education* 25(1):29-40, March 1994] for an in-depth presentation concerning the book's art, sources, and allusive references.

The newspaper headlines featured in Sendak's illustrations provide ample grist for discussions on a variety of social concerns in addition to the homeless.

597. Wegen, Ronald. **Where Can the Animals Go?** (Greenwillow Books, 1978).

Africa; Balance of Nature; Black Market; Conservation Organizations; Environmental Action; Poachers; Trade Sanctions; Wildlife Conservation; Zoology

The impact on the wildlife of the African plains when humans overtake the land and overuse its resources is depicted in this deceptively simple book.

The extent to which poachers are killing animals for specific body parts or hunting endangered species has reached a crisis point in many countries. Students can research select topics such as the trade in elephant tusks or rhinoceros horns or the hunting of whales, including the role of the United Nations, trade sanctions, endangered species, and other aspects.

Use this book to help launch a study on the status of wildlife conservation from a world perspective. Include endangered species, which international organizations are involved in their protection, and the political and economic implications of international actions. Other heavily illustrated books that focus on endangered animals include Patricia Mullin's *V for Vanishing: An Alphabet of Endangered Animals*

(HarperCollins, 1994), Holly Keller's *Grandfather's Dream* (Greenwillow Books, 1994), Helen Cowcher's *Tigress* (Farrar, Straus & Giroux, 1991), Lisa Lindblad's *The Serengeti Migration: Africa's Animals on the Move* (Hyperion, 1994), and Margery Flacklam's *And Then There Was One: The Mysteries of Extinction* (Little, Brown, 1990).

598. Wegman, William. **ABC: William Wegman** (Hyperion, 1994)

Alphabet Books;
Animals—Ethical Treatment;
Art—Photography; Debate;
Dogs; Ethical Treatment of
Animals; Photography;
Weimaraners

This sophisticated alphabet book features Wegman's famous weimaraners photographed in dramatic, costumed poses.

Some people are opposed to Wegman's art, calling it inhumane to the dogs. What do your students think? Are their feelings passionate enough to stage a debate?

Wegman's other unusual picture books include *Man's Best Friend* (Henry N. Abrams, 1982), *Cinderella* (Hyperion, 1993), and *Little Red Riding Hood* (Hyperion, 1993).

Taking photos of animals without dressing them up is difficult enough. Challenge students to take photographs of animals and display the results in a gallery.

599. Weller, Frances Ward. **I Wonder If I'll See a Whale**. Ill. by Ted Lewin (Philomel, 1991).

Charitable Organizations;
Environmental Action;
Foundations; Humpback
Whales; Music; Whale
Watching; Whales

Readers share a girl's anticipation and excitement in spotting a humpback during a whale-watching excursion off the New England coast. Note.

It's evident from the popularity of whale-watching tours and the Save the Whale foundation that many people are fascinated with whales. Student research concerning the mission and activities of the Save the Whale foundation can help them learn about investigating and evaluating charitable organizations from the consumer perspective.

The Whales' Song (Dial Books for Young Readers, 1991) by Dyan Sheldon, a companion picture book with a younger protagonist, focuses on the mysterious whale songs. Play recordings of these songs from *Songs of the Humpback Whale* (Capitol Records, 1970) and *Whales Alive* by Paul Winter and Paul Halley (Living Music, 1985).

600. Wells, Ruth. **A to Zen: A Book of Japanese Culture**. Ill. by Yoshi (Picture Book Studio, 1992).

Alphabet Books; Art—
Batik; Batik; Cultures—
Japanese; Japan;
Languages—Japanese

This sophisticated travelogue presents Japanese life through 20 words that highlight their customs, art, geography, and history while showing both the differences and the similarities between their culture and that of the United States. The traditional Japanese book design, beginning on the back page, immediately captures the attention of readers.

A cultural study about Japan might include materials such as *Festival in My Heart: Poems by Japanese Children* selected and translated by Bruno Navasky (Harry N. Abrams, 1993), *Commodore Perry in the Land of Shogun* by Rhoda Blumberg (Lothrop, Lee & Shepard 1985), *The Tale of the Mandarin Ducks* by Katherine Paterson (Lodestar Books/Dutton Children's Books, 1990), and the videotape *Japan* by Peter Spry-Leverton and Jane Seymour (MPI Home Video, 1992), among others.

❗ = Extraordinary!   💡 = Idea   📖 = Further Reading   ✍ = Writing $\frac{2}{4}$ = Math   = Science   = History

These batik illustrations offer an opportunity to introduce this interesting art form to students. Invite an artist to discuss and demonstrate the process. Patricia MacCarthy's illustrations for *17 Kings and 42 Elephants* (Dial Books for Young Readers, 1987) by Margaret Mahy are also interesting batiks.

601. Werner, Vivian. **Petrouchka: The Story of the Ballet.** Ill. by John Collier (Viking Penguin, 1992).

Ballet; Dance—Ballet; Drama; Fairs; Folklore—Russia; Plays; Puppets; Russia—Folklore; Stravinsky, Igor (1882-1971); Tragedy

The classic ballet by Russian composer Igor Stravinsky is told here in picture book format. The tragic clown puppet Petrouchka longs to be alive and be loved by the beautiful ballerina. Introduction.

Like the classic Pinocchio story, Petrouchka goes through several stages before he can truly come to life. Students can read versions of the Pinocchio story and compare Pinocchio with Petrouchka.

Fashioned after the Punch and Judy puppet shows popular in fairs, this story exemplifies this important folk theater. Drama students can develop and perform their own plays, using puppets or actors posing as puppets. See Alice Provensen's *Punch in New York* (Viking, 1991).

602. Wheatley, Nadia and Donna Rawlins. **My Place: The Story of Australia from Now to Then** (Collins/Dove, 1987).

Australia; Changes; Drawing; History—Australia; Mapping; Maps; Neighborhoods; Social Life and Customs—Australia

The history of an Australian city neighborhood is revealed decade by decade, beginning in 1988 and traveling back in time to 1788.

Companion picture books include Lilith Norman's *The Paddock: A Story in Praise of the Earth*, also about Australia (Alfred A. Knopf, 1993), John S. Goodall's wordless *The Story of Main Street* (Margaret K. McElderry, 1987), and Renata Von Tscharner and Ronald Lee Fleming's *New Providence: A Changing Cityscape* (Harcourt Brace Jovanovich, 1987).

Using *My Place* as a model (focusing on specific events, clothing styles, inventions, etc.), students can draw maps of "their place" now and in the past. Futuristic-minded artists may wish to predict what "their place" will look like decades from now.

603. White Deer of Autumn. **The Great Change.** Ill. by Carol Grigg (Beyond Words, 1992).

Cultures; Death; Grandmothers; Indians of North America; Intergenerational Relationships; Traditions

A wise Indian grandmother explains the meaning of death, or "the Great Change," to her granddaughter.

Reading works by Indian writers will give students a better understanding of the cultural past and the contemporary concerns of these first Americans. A book collection might include *This Land Is My Land* by George Littlechild (Children's Book Press, 1993), *Lakota Woman* by Mary Crow Dog and Richard Erdoes (HarperCollins, 1990), *Dancing Teepees: Poems of American Indian Youth* edited by Virginia Driving Hawk Sneve (Holiday House, 1989), *Raven Tells Stories: An Anthology of Alaskan Writing* edited by Joseph Bruchac (Greenfield Review Press, 1991), *Dancing Moons* by Nancy Wood (Doubleday, 1995), and *Rising Voices: Writings of Young Native Americans* edited by Arlene B. Hirschfelder and Beverly R. Singer (Charles Scribner's Sons, 1992).

Against Borders: Promoting Books for a Multicultural World by Hazel Rochman (American Library Association, 1993) and *Through Indian Eyes: The Native Experience in Books for Children* edited by Beverly Slapin and Doris Seale (New Society, 1992) will be helpful reference books for finding other recommended titles.

 = Geography   = Art   = Music   = Drama   = Speech   Q = Research   = Read-Aloud

Aging; Alzheimer's Disease; Birthdays; Grand-daughters; Grandmothers; Love; Memories; Social Issues—Aging

604. Whitelaw, Nancy. **A Beautiful Pearl**. Ill. by Judith Friedman (Whitman, 1991).

Even though her mind is deteriorating from the effects of Alzheimer's disease, Grandma presents Lisa with a special gift on her birthday. Note.

Provide other picture books dealing with aging and memory loss such as *The Memory Box* by Mary Bahr (Whitman, 1992) and *Wilfrid Gordon McDonald Partridge* by Mem Fox (Kane/Miller, 1989).

The cause(s) of Alzheimer's disease are not fully understood. Intermediate students can use Laurie Beckelman's *Alzheimer's Disease* (Macmillan, 1990) and articles in current journals to learn more about it.

Diaries; Frontier Life— 1900; Historical Fiction; History—United States— 1900; Nature; United States— History; Whiteley, Opal (d. 1992)

605. Whiteley, Opal. **Only Opal: The Diary of a Young Girl**. Selected by Jane Boulton, ill. by Barbara Cooney (Philomel, 1994).

Selections from what many believe is the real diary of six-year-old Opal Whiteley (circa 1903), along with Cooney's illustrations, comprise this description of life in an Oregon logging camp at the turn of the century through the eyes of a child.

The fascinating story of Opal Whiteley's childhood and her later attempts to publish children's stories will interest many students. Her diary was originally serialized in a magazine in 1920 and rediscovered and republished as verse by Jane Boulton in 1976. A complete version of the diary is *The Singing Creek Where the Willows Grow: The Mystical Nature Diary of Opal Whiteley* with a biography and an afterword by Benjamin Hoff (Penguin Books, 1994).

Chess; Composition— Movement; Creative Writing; Dreams; Fantasy; Maps; Subconscious; Surrealism; Wordless Books

606. Wiesner, David. **Free Fall** (Lothrop, Lee & Shepard, 1988).

Clutching an atlas and some chess pieces, a young boy falls asleep and into a dreamland where aspects of reality merge with his subconscious into a fantastic trip. Caldecott Honor, 1989.

Have students write about any of the characters or objects and then share the stories aloud. They each will discover elements that they had never noticed and will be curious to look at the book again to find what their classmates saw that they missed.

Wordless books provide an excellent opportunity for students to write narratives to accompany the illustrations. In addition to the other wordless books cited in the index to this book, provide Lane Smith's *Flying Jake* (Macmillan, 1988) and invite students to write the text.

Flying; Humor; Imagination; Languages— Study of; Science— Experiments; Science Fiction; Surrealism

607. Wiesner, David. **June 29, 1999** (Clarion Books, 1992).

608. Wiesner, David. **Tuesday** (Houghton Mifflin, 1991).

On June 29, 1999, Holly's ambitious science experiment ("to study the effects of extraterrestrial conditions on vegetable growth and development") becomes more than she imagined. Meanwhile, frogs float through a community on *Tuesday* as the residents sleep. They disappear by dawn, leaving behind a hint of what's to come. *Tuesday,* Caldecott Medal, 1992.

Help students develop observational and analytical skills by comparing the similarities (the visual angles and perspectives, the contemporary scenes, the atmospheric conditions, and the plot twists at the end) between these two books.

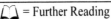

Use wordless and almost wordless books in foreign language or English as a Second Language (ESL) classes. For example, introduce students to all the words for the vegetables in *June 29, 1999* in the appropriate language. Then students can use the words in either oral or written activities related to the book.

 Introduce the next science project unit by sharing *June 29, 1999* aloud with students. A great companion book is Brian Wildsmith and Rebecca Wildsmith's *Jack and the Meanstalk* (Alfred A. Knopf, 1994).

 609. Wilbur, Richard. **A Game of Catch**. Ill. by Barry Moser (Harcourt Brace Jovanovich, 1994).

Anger; Baseball; Feelings; Friendship; Interpersonal Skills; Magazines; Outsiders; Read-Aloud; Short Stories

A game of catch between two seventh-grade friends is interrupted by a boy without a glove. Feeling left out, Sacho attempts to interact with the boys, but the results aren't satisfactory for anyone.

 This story would be wonderful for reading aloud and then discussing with middle school and junior high students in a class on interpersonal skills.

 This short story was originally published in a 1953 *New Yorker* magazine. A collection of books with short stories for high school students can include *Traveling on into the Light: And Other Stories* by Martha Brooks (Orchard, 1994), *Am I Blue? Coming Out from the Silence* (HarperCollins, 1994) edited by Marion Dane Bauer, and *Athletic Shorts: Six Short Stories* by Chris Crutcher (Greenwillow Books, 1991). Middle school and junior high students will enjoy collections such as *Oddly Enough* by Bruce Coville (Harcourt Brace Jovanovich, 1994), *Teller of Tales* by William J. Brooke (HarperCollins, 1994), and *The Stinky Cheese Man and Other Fairly Stupid Tales* by Jon Scieszka (Viking, 1992).

610. Wild, Margaret. **Let the Celebrations Begin!** Ill. by Julie Vivas (Orchard, 1991).

Children and War; Concentration Camps; History—World War II; Holocaust; Jews; Nazis; Toys; War; World War II

The women in Hut 18 are making toys from scraps in anticipation of the soldiers liberating their concentration camp at the end of World War II.

 Consult the note preceding the story and the paragraphs following the story to further enhance study and discussions on the Holocaust and concentration camps.

 The history of handmade toys can be explored by interested art or history students. Further study can focus on antique toys using books like *Discovering Toys & Museums,* 2nd edition, by Pauline Flick (Legacy Books, 1977). Students can also make rag toys like the residents in Hut 18 and give them to charities for distribution. Helpful books include *Folk Toys Around the World & How to Make Them* by Virginie Fowler (Prentice-Hall, 1984).

611. Wild, Margaret. **The Very Best of Friends**. Ill. by Julie Vivas (Harcourt Brace Jovanovich, 1990).

Cats; Death; Farm Life; Friendship; Grieving; Love; Relationships

Jessie never much cared for her husband's cat, William. But after James dies suddenly, William eventually wins Jessie's heart and helps her begin the grieving process.

 This evocative story is a perfect discussion starter about death and, especially, the grieving process. Invite a counselor or hospice staff member to lead a discussion about death and dying. Refer to books such as *Living with Death and Dying* by Elisabeth Kubler-Ross (Macmillan, 1981) and *Teenagers Face to Face with Bereavement* by Karen Gravelle and Charles Haskins (Messner, 1989).

 = Geography　　 = Art　　 = Music　　 = Drama　　 = Speech　　 = Research　　 = Read-Aloud

612. Wildsmith, Brian. **Professor Noah's Spaceship** (Oxford University Press, 1980).

Animals; Bible Stories; Creative Writing; Floods; Literary Devices; Metaphor; Noah's Ark; Pollution; Science Fiction; Time Travel

All the animals board Professor Noah's spaceship to escape from a doomed Earth. The incorrectly repaired "time-zone guidance fin" sends the ship's inhabitants backwards through time back to Earth before it became polluted.

 Wildsmith uses the traditional Bible story of Noah's ark to make a statement about the earth's environment. Many picture book authors and artists use this medium to metaphorically address serious topics in an appealing, nonthreatening format. Provide students with other picture books such as Dr. Seuss' *The Butter Battle Book* (Random House, 1984) as well as Bill Peet's *The Wump World* (Houghton Mifflin, 1970) and Barbara Emberley's *Drummer Hoff* (Prentice-Hall, 1967) for thought-provoking reading and discussion. In the same fashion students can write about current issues using imaginary characters and places in a metaphorical sense.

Many cultures have flood stories in their folklore and traditional literature. Provide books such as *The Tree That Rains: The Flood Myth of the Huichol Indians of Mexico* by Emery Bernhard and Durga Bernhard (Holiday House, 1994) for students to enjoy.

Student writers can create their own contemporary or futuristic Noah stories. For a list of other Noah books and suggested activities consult "Noah's Continuing Voyage" by Kathy Piehl [*Book Links* 3(2):35-38, November 1993].

613. Willard, Nancy. **An Alphabet of Angels** (Blue Sky Press/Scholastic, 1994).

Alphabet Books; Angels; Folk Art; Poetry

Using an alphabetical framework, Willard combines rhyming couplets with photographs featuring her three-dimensional folk art creations of angels in unique settings.

This celebration of angels introduces fans of Willard's books to her folk art talents. Use this book as an introduction to folk artists in your community. Identify and invite a variety of folk artists to your school to discuss and exhibit their work.

614. Willard, Nancy. **The Ballad of Biddy Early**. Ill. by Barry Moser (Alfred A. Knopf, 1989).

Ballads; Early, Biddy (1798-1874); Historical Fiction; Ireland—19th Century; Legends—Irish; Prophesies; Supernatural; Witchcraft

Poems, limericks, and songs celebrate the 19th-century wise Irish woman who was well known for her magical cures and prophesies.

Books featuring both real and fanciful witches include Monica Furlong's *Wise Child* (Alfred A. Knopf, 1987) and *Juniper* (Alfred A. Knopf, 1991); *The Scarlet Letter* by Nathaniel Hawthorne (Everymans Library/Alfred A. Knopf, 1992); *Enter Three Witches* by Kate Gilmore (Houghton Mifflin, 1990); *Rosemary's Witch* by Ann Turner (Harper-Collins, 1991); and *The Witch of Blackbird Pond* by Elizabeth Speare George (Houghton Mifflin, 1958).

615. Willard, Nancy. **Pish, Posh, Said Hieronymus Bosch**. Ill. by Leo Dillon, Diane Dillon and Lee Dillon (Harcourt Brace Jovanovich, 1991).

Art; Bosch, Hieronymus (1450s-1516); Calligraphy; Creative Writing; Medieval Period; Paintings; Poetry; Sculpture

Bosch's imaginary creatures drive his housekeeper wild. Note.

The Dillons' version of Bosch's imaginary creatures rivals the legendary imagination of the 15th-century painter. According to the note, the artists (Diane and Leo Dillon) and author Willard have long been fascinated by Bosch's paintings. Filled with the bizarre, they are bound

---

! = Extraordinary!   💡 = Idea   📖 = Further Reading   ✎ = Writing   ²⁄₄ = Math   ⚛ = Science   📚 = History

to spark the curiosity of students. Give them the opportunity to look at Bosch's art and surmise their meanings, which he never explained. In addition, note the gilt wood frame made by the Dillons' son Lee.

Students can select one of Bosch's (or the Dillons') creatures and write a story about it.

616. Willard, Nancy. **The Sorcerer's Apprentice**. Ill. by Leo Dillon and Diane Dillon (Blue Sky, 1993).

Apprentices; Environment; Fables; Fantasy; Literary Devices; Magic; Magicians; Personification; Problem Solving; Stealing

Sylvia, the adolescent apprentice sewing clothes for the Magician Tottibo's fantastic menagerie, steals a magic potion, loses control of the ancient sewing machine, and creates havoc only the magician can stop.

Students may be more familiar with the popular Disney version of *The Sorcerer's Apprentice*. Compare and contrast this tale to Disney's.

Students may wish to learn more about apprenticeships. What were their role in history, and what kind of apprenticeships exist today? Are there apprenticeships in any of the fields these students wish to pursue?

617. Willard, Nancy. **A Visit to William Blake's Inn: Poems for Innocent and Experienced Travelers**. Ill. by Alice Provensen and Martin Provensen (Harcourt Brace Jovanovich, 1981).

Art—Painting and Drawing; Blake, William (1757-1827); Engraving; Inns; Poetry; Printmaking; Reader's Theater; Travel

An illustrated collection of 18 original lyrical and nonsensical poems written as a tribute to William Blake (1757-1827), the English poet and artist. Newbery Medal and Caldecott Honor, 1982.

Compare the similarity of the tone Willard used to that in Blake's *Songs of Innocence and Experience*.

Use the idea of enhancing poetry through illustration to inspire students to select (or write) and illustrate other poems.

Blake engraved 31 copperplates for his first "illuminated book," *Songs of Innocence and Experience*. The poetry and designs were intermingled, and each copy of the book was color-washed by hand. Invite an engraver to your classroom for a demonstration.

618. Willard, Nancy. **The Voyage of the Ludgate Hill: Travels with Robert Louis Stevenson**. Ill. by Alice Provensen and Martin Provensen (Harcourt Brace Jovanovich, 1987).

Animals—Poetry; Letters; Nonsense; Ocean Voyages; Poetry; Sea—Poetry; Ships; Stevenson, Robert Louis (1850-1894)

Inspired by Robert Louis Stevenson's letters, Willard's poem describes how the author and his wife survived a stormy ocean voyage with a shipload of exotic animals.

Use this book to inspire students to further study the works of Robert Louis Stevenson. Include novels as well as poetry.

619. Williams, Kit. **Masquerade** (Schocken Books, 1980).

Adventure; Book Games; Games; Literary Recreations; Mysteries; Picture Puzzles; Treasure Hunts

Hidden in the illustrations are clues to a buried treasure.

This illustrated fantasy set off an international treasure hunt for the real gold filigree rabbit with the ruby eye, buried in England. Although the treasure has been found, students can try to solve the mystery and then consult *Masquerade: The Complete Book with the Answer Explained* (Workman, 1983) to discover everything hidden in the book. Williams designed another treasure hunt published by Alfred A. Knopf in 1984. For cataloging purposes, it was called *Book Without a Name,* but the secret was to discover the book's real name.

 = Geography   = Art   = Music = Drama = Speech Q = Research   = Read-Aloud

For another picture/puzzle book, take a look at *The Egyptian Jukebox,* a conundrum created by Nick Bantock (Byzantium Books, 1993). Bantock presents an intricate variety of clues in photographs, text, and drawings designed to provide the answer to a riddle for a canny reader.

620. Williams, Sherley Anne. **Working Cotton**. Ill. by Carole Byard (Harcourt Brace Jovanovich, 1992).

African Americans; California; Child Labor; Families; Historical Fiction; Migrant Labor; Poetry

In this story, based on the author's childhood experiences, the young narrator tells of the daily events in her family's migrant life as cotton pickers in California. Caldecott Honor, 1993.

The text of this book is based on poems written by the author and published in *The Peacock Poems* (Wesleyan University Press, 1975), a National Book Award nominee. Obtain a copy of this book for a further look at Williams' work.

Detailed information about Byard's art can be found in "Four African American Illustrators" by Dilys Evans [*Book Links* 2(3):26-29, January 1993].

Use the author's note (which in part says, "In environments characterized by minimums—minimum wages, minimum shelters, minimum food and education—individual character, the love of a family, can only do so much; the rest is up to the country.") to focus student research on migrant labor. For more information provide books such as S. Beth Atkin's *Voices from the Field: Children of Migrant Farm Workers Tell Their Stories* (Little, Brown, 1993), Russell Freedman's *Kids at Work: Lewis Hine and the Crusade Against Child Labor* (Clarion Books, 1994), and Milton Meltzer's *Cheap Raw Material* (Viking, 1994). Related picture books are *Amelia's Road* by Linda Jacobs Altman (Lee & Low Books, 1993) and *Lights on the River* by Jane Resh Thomas (Hyperion Books for Children, 1994).

621. Williams, Vera B. **"More More More," Said the Baby: 3 Love Stories** (Greenwillow Books, 1990).

Child Development; Love; Parenting Classes; Self-Esteem

Three babies are playfully picked up by their loving father, grandmother, or mother and given kisses. Caldecott Honor, 1991.

Clearly intended for toddlers, this book is ideal for sharing in child development and parenting classes.

622. Williams, Vera B. **Stringbean's Trip to the Shining Sea**. Ill. by Vera B. Williams and Jennifer Williams (Greenwillow Books, 1988).

Creative Writing; Geography; Postcards; Stamps; Travel; Vacations; Western United States

Stringbean and his uncle chronicle their trip from Jeloway, Kansas, to the West Coast, sending postcards that Grandpa puts in an album with "photographs" and notes.

Students can use the postcard format, a variation on journal writing that requires additional creativity, for a writing/art project featuring real or imagined travel. For additional examples provide *Postcards from Pluto: A Tour of the Solar System* by Loreen Leedy (Holiday House, 1993), *The Armadillo from Amarillo* by Lynne Cherry (Harcourt Brace Jovanovich, 1994), and *The Jolly Postman* by Janet Ahlberg and Allan Ahlberg (Little, Brown, 1986). High school students would also be interested in the "extraordinary correspondence" of postcards and letters in the "Griffin & Sabine" books by Nick Bantock (Chronicle Books) for a more sophisticated perspective on this idea.

❗ = Extraordinary!　💡 = Idea　📖 = Further Reading　✍ = Writing　$\frac{2}{4}$ = Math　 = Science　 = History

The Williams designed the stamps for the postcards. Students can explore more about the business of stamp design, production, and collection. Collecting guides are in abundance, but encourage students to go beyond with items like various U.S. Postal Service guides to stamps, visits to stamp collecting sites on the Internet, the current edition of *The Postal Service Guide to U.S. Stamps,* available from stamp dealers or the philatelic counter at larger post offices, and *Stamps! A Young Collector's Guide* by Brenda R. Lewis (Dutton Children's Books, 1991). *Book Links* [2(3):17-20, January 1993] has an article "Stamps with Spirit: Human Endeavors in Postal Art" by Glenn E. Estes, which focuses on Black Americans featured in the Postal Service's collection *I Have a Dream: A Collection of Black Americans on U.S. Postage Stamps.*

623. Winter, Jannette. **Follow the Drinking Gourd** (Alfred A. Knopf, 1988).

African Americans; Astronomy; Celestial Navigation; Folk Songs; Freedom; Historical Fiction; History—United States—19th Century; Music; Science—Astronomy; Slavery; Underground Railroad; United States—History—19th Century

Runaway slaves journey north along the route of the Underground Railroad, following the directions (an actual map to freedom) hidden in the song "Follow the Drinking Gourd." Author note. Words and music.

There are numerous books to complement a study of this time period. Be sure to include Ann Turner's *Nettie's Trip South* (Macmillan, 1987), which includes another reaction to a slave auction as well as Jacob Lawrence's *Harriet and the Promised Land* (Simon & Schuster, 1993) and *The Freedom Riddle* retold by Angela Shelf Medearis (Lodestar Books, 1995). Others are listed in the subject index in this book.

The Big Dipper, pointing to the North Star, has led travelers (fugitive slaves and explorers alike) to their destinations. Invite someone skilled in celestial navigation to your class for a presentation. Provide students with appropriate astronomy and navigation books for preparation and follow-up study.

The words and music to "Follow the Drinking Gourd" are on the last page of this book. Obtain some folk recordings and teach this song to your students as part of a unit, perhaps during February (Black History Month). Also share the gospel music by Sweet Honey in the Rock who sing about the history of African Americans in their recording *Still on the Journey: The 20th Anniversary Album* (Earthbeat, 1993).

624. Winter, Jonah. **Diego**. Ill. by Jeannette Winter (Alfred A. Knopf, 1991).

Artists; Bilingual Books; Biographies; History of Art; Languages—Spanish; Murals; Paintings; Rivera, Diego (1886-1957)

The life and talent of Mexican muralist Diego Rivera is related in both English and Spanish.

Spanish language students can practice their skills with this book, which offers the text in both English and Spanish. Many picture books are available in Spanish such as *Flecha al Sol: Un Cuento de los Indios Pueblo (Arrow to the Sun)* by Gerald McDermott. These are perfect to use in a literature-based Spanish reading program.

Provide this title for art students who are studying murals. Rivera's murals told the story of the Mexican people. Students can select a story to convey through this artistic medium for temporary or permanent display. For a further look at Hispanic art provide students with *Here Is My Kingdon: Hispanic-American Literature and Art for Young People* edited by Charles Sullivan (Harry N. Abrams, 1994).

Is there an available wall in your school or community upon which students can create an appropriate mural? For how-to instructions, provide the video *How to Paint a Mural Step-by-Step* (Double Diamond Corporation, 1994), which provides information on the location, function, and purpose of potential murals.

 = Geography   = Art   = Music   = Drama   = Speech   = Research   = Read-Aloud

625. Wisniewski, David. **Elfwyn's Saga** (Lothrop, Lee & Shepard, 1990).

626. Wisniewski, David. **Rain Player** (Lothrop, Lee & Shepard, 1991).

627. Wisniewski, David. **Sundiata: Lion King of Mali** (Clarion Books, 1992).

628. Wisniewski, David. **The Warrior and the Wise Man** (Lothrop, Lee & Shepard, 1989).

Africa—Mali; Art—Cut-Paper; Biographies; Disabilities; Emperors; Fairy Tales; Games; Good Versus Evil; Iceland—Legends; Indians of Central America; Japan—Fairy Tales; Kieta Soundiata (d. 1255); Kings; Legends—Africa; Legends—Iceland; Mali—History; Mayas; Northern Lights; Paper Cuttings; Quests; Vikings

Although blind because of a curse placed on her by the jealous Gorm, Elfwyn breaks the spell and saves her family in *Elfwyn's Saga*. In hopes of ending a drought, Pik challenges the rain god to a game in *Rain Player*. *Sundiata: Lion King of Mali* tells the story of a Mali prince who overcame physical disabilities, social disgrace, and strong opposition to rule Mali in the 13th century. In *The Warrior and the Wise Man*, twin brothers, one a warrior and one a wise man, are sent on a quest to see who will rule the kingdom.

For the Inuit culture's explanation of the Northern Lights see *Northern Lights: The Soccer Trails* by Michael Arvaarluk Kusugak (Annick Press, 1993).

The intricate cut-paper illustrations are fascinating. Wisniewski, who has a background in shadow puppetry, used between 800 and 1,000 X-Acto blades to illustrate each book. Invite a skilled paper cutter to demonstrate his or her skills. Be sure to share *The Amazing Paper Cuttings of Hans Christian Andersen* by Beth Wagner Brust (Ticknor & Fields, 1994) to show the work of another artist who excelled at this art form.

Elfwyn's Saga and *The Warrior and the Wise Man* are set in approximately the same time period in different parts of the world. Begin a study of the Viking and Japanese cultures starting with the detailed information Wisniewski provides. As students work, they can create charts and time lines for comparing and contrasting these two cultures.

629. Wood, A. J. **Errata: A Book of Historical Errors**. Ill. by Hemesh Alles, historical consultant William Crouch (Green Tiger Press, 1992).

Civilization—Ancient; History—World; Literary Recreations; Picture Puzzles

Twelve scenes from history depict great civilizations of the past. However, each picture has 10 deliberate errors or anachronisms that readers are challenged to find. Answers and explanations are included.

Use this book with students of all ages in history, sociology, and anthropology studies. The errors are fun and challenging to find, and the explanations reveal interesting information about cultures of the past.

630. Wood, Douglas. **Old Turtle**. Watercolors by Cheng-Khee Chee (Pfeifer-Hamilton, 1992).

Conservation; Ecology; Fables; God; International Understanding; Peace; Science—Ecology

Old Turtle is a poetic fable about the nature of God and humans' disregard for the Earth.

This is a perfect selection for environmental awareness workshops or classes. Although spiritual in nature, it is ecumenical in delivery.

! = Extraordinary! 💡 = Idea 📖 = Further Reading ✍ = Writing $\frac{2}{4}$ = Math ⚛ = Science 📖 = History

631. Woolf, Virginia. **Nurse Lugton's Curtain**. Ill. by Julie Vivas (Gulliver Books, 1991).

Animals; Fantasy;
Literature—American;
Woolf, Virginia (1882-1941)

The animals on the fabric Nurse Lugton is sewing come alive while she dozes.

Although not published until 1965, Woolf's story was probably written in the fall of 1924 for her visiting niece. It was found among the pages of Woolf's manuscript for her well-known novel *Mrs. Dalloway*. Use this picture book as an interesting aside when commencing a study of Woolf.

Y

632. Yee, Paul. **Roses Sing on New Snow: A Delicious Tale**. Ill. by Harvey Chan (Macmillan, 1991).

Chinatowns; Cooking;
Home Economics; Lies;
Social Life and Customs—
Chinese Americans—1900

The Old World traditions are already changing when Maylin cooks the food in her father's turn-of-the-century Chinese restaurant. When her father lies and claims his sons are the cooks, disaster nearly occurs.

Many Chinese were brought to the United States for cheap labor. They developed their own communities within cities and towns throughout the country. They maintained the traditions they brought with them, but inevitable changes took place as people found themselves part of two cultures. Books on this topic that would be of interest for high school students include Maxine Hong Kingston's *The Woman Warrior* (Alfred A. Knopf, 1976), Amy Tan's *The Joy Luck Club* (Putnam, 1989), and Gus Lee's *China Boy* (NAL, 1991). Younger students will enjoy Bette Bao Lord's *In the Year of the Boar and Jackie Robinson* (HarperCollins, 1984), Lensey Namioka's *Yang the Youngest and His Terrible Ear* (Little, Brown/Joy Street Books, 1992), and Paul Yee's *Tales from Gold Mountain: Stories of the Chinese in the New World* (Macmillan, 1990).

Students in home economics classes will enjoy learning how to cook some Chinese dishes. Be sure to include some wok cooking, which is often fast, inexpensive, and easy.

633. Yerxa, Leo. **Last Leaf First Snowflake to Fall** (Orchard, 1994).

Art—Collage; Canoes;
Changes; Collage; Indians
of North America; Nature;
Poetry—Free Verse;
Read-Aloud; Seasons

Evocative free verse tells of the seasonal change from the end of autumn to the beginning of winter.

This sophisticated and timeless story—with its minimal punctuation, organization of lines, and poetic language—can serve as an excellent example of free verse.

Yerxa created an unusual variation of collage with the use of dyed tissue paper combined with paintings from different perspectives. Compare and contrast Yerxa's illustrations with other collage illustrations highlighted in this book. Students can experiment with various techniques.

634. Yolen, Jane. **Encounter**. Ill. by David Shannon (Harcourt Brace Jovanovich, 1992).

Columbus, Christopher
(1451-1506); Explorers;
Historical Fiction; Indians
of the West Indies; Point of
View; Taino Indians; World
History—1492

A Taino Indian boy tells his story of the landing of Columbus on the island of San Salvador in 1492. Notes.

Encounter provides a look at the world Columbus invaded and changed forever. Use the following to get a more complete picture of the Tainos: *The Tainos: The People Who Welcomed Columbus* by Francine Jacobs (Putnam, 1992) and *Morning Girl* by Michael Dorris (Hyperion, 1992).

 = Geography   = Art   = Music   = Drama   = Speech   = Research   = Read-Aloud

Prior to the numerous publications that came out in 1992 to celebrate the quincentenary anniversary of Columbus' arrival in the New World, almost all of the books about Columbus had been written from the European point of view. Discuss point of view and how it can affect historical accounts. Let students survey this time period from varied points of view. Consult *The Log of Christopher Columbus: The First Voyage: Spring, Summer and Fall 1492* edited by Steve Lowe (Philomel, 1992), *I, Columbus: My Journal, 1492-3* edited by Peter Roop and Connie Roop (Walker, 1990), and the many books listed by Barbara Elleman in "The Columbus Encounter" [*Book Links* 1(1):6-13, September 1991] and in "The Columbus Encounter—Update" [*Book Links* 2(1):31-34, September 1992].

Bird Calls; Families; Fathers and Daughters; Forests; Hope; Nature; Owls; Read-Aloud; Winter

 635. Yolen, Jane. **Owl Moon**. Ill. by John Schoenherr (Philomel, 1987).

Under the full moon on a cold winter's night, a father and daughter go in search of the great horned owl. Caldecott Medal, 1988.

 To enhance this poetic story, dedicated to Yolen's husband, "who took all of our children owling," read selected poems from *If the Owl Calls Again: A Collection of Owl Poems* selected by Myra Cohn Livingston (Margaret K. McElderry, 1990) and *The Man Who Could Call Down Owls* by Eve Bunting (Macmillan, 1984). Invite a guest to demonstrate owl calling, or use the audiocassette from the National Geographic Society, "Guide to Bird Sounds." For more books about the great horned owl consult Barbara Juster Esbensen's *Tiger with Wings: The Great Horned Owl* (Orchard, 1991) and Bernd Heinrich's *An Owl in the House: A Naturalist's Diary* (Joy Street, 1990).

636. Yolen, Jane. **Piggins**. Ill. by Jane Dyer (Harcourt Brace Jovanovich, 1987).

637. Yolen, Jane. **Piggins and the Royal Wedding**. Ill. by Jane Dyer (Harcourt Brace Jovanovich, 1988).

638. Yolen, Jane. **Picnic with Piggins**. Ill. by Jane Dyer (Harcourt Brace Jovanovich, 1988).

Allusions; Animals; Birthdays; Creative Writing; Deductive Thinking; Literary Devices; Mysteries; Pigs

This trio of picture book mysteries features the enigmatic pig butler Piggins and his amazing capacity for solving mysteries. Using deductive powers, Piggins locates a stolen necklace, discovers a surprise birthday party, and reveals who stole the queen's wedding ring.

 The literary device *allusion* is aptly employed here. Yolen uses the names of the characters to correspond to the animals they are. Use these books to explain this device to students and invite similar creative writing endeavors.

Cave Dwellers; Humor; Inventions; Parodies; Prehistoric Times; Read-Aloud

639. Yorinks, Arthur. **Ugh**. Ill. by Richard Egielski (Farrar, Straus & Giroux, 1990).

Ugh, the Cinderfella of the cave people, has a miserable time until he capitalizes on the invention of the wheel and rides off to a new and happy life.

Aside from serving as a read-aloud, this humorous story may prompt students to further research the beginnings of such important tools as the wheel.

---

640. Young, Ed. **Lon Po Po: A Red-Riding Hood Story from China** (Philomel, 1989).

China; Folklore—China; Obedience; Wolves

The three sisters, left alone while their mother goes to visit their grandmother, are stalked by a hungry wolf, disguised as the grandmother. Caldecott Medal, 1990.

Have students find other variations of "Little Red-Riding Hood," such as the version illustrated by Beni Montresor (Doubleday, 1991), and bring them to class for sharing.

The dedication of this book ("To all the wolves of the world for lending their good name as a tangible symbol for our darkness") and the accompanying illustration are perfect for launching a discussion, and possibly research, into the reality behind this quote.

Z

641. Zadrzynska, Ewa. **The Girl with a Watering Can**. Ill. by Arnold Skolnick (Chameleon Books, 1990).

Art—Coming to Life; Artists; Fantasy; History of Art; Impressionists; Museums; Paintings; Renoir, Auguste (1841-1919)

The girl in Renoir's famous painting steps out of the frame and visits 10 other famous paintings on display in the National Gallery of Art in Washington, D.C.

Perfect companion books are Diane Stanley's *The Gentleman and the Kitchen Maid* (Dial Books for Young Readers, 1994) and Johnny Alcorn's *Rembrandt's Beret: Or the Painter's Crown* (Tambourine Books, 1991).

Provide this book as a springboard for a study of some of the world's most famous artists. Included in this book are works by Auguste Renoir, Henri Fantin-Latour, Henri Rousseau, Edouard Manet, Joseph Mallord, William Turner, Judith Leyster, Winslow Homer, W. H. Brown, and Giovanni Belleni. Rosabianca Skira-Venturi's *A Weekend with Renoir* (Rizzoli, 1990) weaves art explanations, factual information, photographs, and reproductions into a weekend visit with the artist as your guide. Use this with *The Girl with a Watering Can* to begin or supplement a study on Renoir. However, don't limit your students; let them learn more about any of the other artists whose works are featured in this book.

642. Zelver, Patricia. **The Wonderful Towers of Watts**. Pictures by Frané Lessac (Tambourine Books, 1994).

Art; Buildings and Structures; Construction; Government; Rhodia, Simon; Sculptures; Storytelling; Towers

Zelver writes a true story about an Italian immigrant who built three unusual towers in his backyard, located in the Watts neighborhood in Los Angeles, California.

Compare and contrast this story with Eve Bunting's *Smoky Night* (Harcourt Brace Jovanovich, 1994). Both take place in the same neighborhood. What happened to the Watts Towers during the Los Angeles riots? What has happened to the neighborhood since?

Simon Rhodia isn't the only artist who uses a large palate. Interested students can delve further into this sort of art by researching Christo, the world's best-known site-specific artist. His creations include yellow umbrellas in southern California and floating pink skirts in Miami's Biscayne Bay.

Ramon Ross' modern tale "Paco," found in his *Storyteller,* 2nd edition (Charles E. Merrill, 1980), is based on the origin of the Watts Towers of Los Angeles. It is written as a flannel board story (with helpful drawings for potential storytellers) and is delightful for even sophisticated audiences.

Artifacts; Battles; Friendship; Gilgamesh; Mythology

643. Zeman, Ludmila. **Gilgamesh the King** (Tundra Books, 1992).

Based on the story of Gilgamesh, one of the oldest written stories in the world, this book recounts the battle between the gods Gilgamesh and Enkidu.

Use Zeman's version as an introduction to more complex Gilgamesh stories.

Artist-filmmaker Ludmila Zeman based her illustrations on various artifacts, bas reliefs, and tablets found in Syria, Iraq, and eastern Turkey—ancient Mesopotamia. Interested students can study further about existing artifacts of this era.

Autobiographies; China— History; China—Politics; History—China; Zhang, Song Nan (1943-)

644. Zhang, Song Nan. **A Little Tiger in the Chinese Night: An Autobiography in Art** (Tundra Books, 1993).

This autobiography traces the life of author and artist Song Nan Zhang as he becomes a student, an artist, a husband, a father, and finally an exile. Fifty years of Chinese history is also unveiled through the incidents at Tiananmen Square.

Students can write and illustrate their own autobiographies using Song Nan Zhang's technique of linking his own upbringing to historical events.

Thousands of students gathered in Tiananmen Square in 1989 to mourn the death of former Communist Party leader Hu Yaobang and demand a greater degree of democracy, free expression, and government accountability. Students can trace the beginnings of the political movements that led to that uprising and the Chinese government's reaction.

Art—Criticism and Interpretation; Artists; Biographies; Child Prodigy; Chinese Paintings; Creative Writing; Legends; Painting— Chinese; Wang, Ya-Ni (1975-)

645. Zhensun, Zheng and Alice Low. **A Young Painter: The Life and Paintings of Wang Yani—China's Extraordinary Young Artist**. Photographs by Zheng Zhensun (Scholastic, 1991).

The "young painter" is Wang Yani, a Chinese artist who started painting remarkable pictures of monkeys and cats at age three and, as a teen, was the youngest artist ever to have an art show at the Smithsonian Institution.

Use *The Boy Who Drew Cats* by Arthur A. Levine (Dial Books for Young Readers, 1993), a Japanese legend of a young boy's mysterious journey and his love for drawing cats, as a companion book. This story is based on the legend of Sesshu Toyo, the 15th-century Japanese artist, whose animal ink drawings were so vivid they could come alive. Discuss legends and their origins. Could Wang Yani become the basis for a legend? Have the students write a contemporary legend about her.

❗ = Extraordinary!   💡 = Idea   📖 = Further Reading   🖌 = Writing $\frac{2}{4}$ = Math   ⚛ = Science   📓 = History

Numbers refer to entries, not pages. The letter "n" following an entry number refers to an author or illustrator mentioned in the annotation.

Numbers refer to entries, not pages. The letter "n" following an entry refers to a title mentioned in the annotation.

Subject Index

Abandonment, 524
Abolitionists, 149, 577
Aborigines, 396, 424
Abstract thinking, 32
Accidents, 410
Activism, 348
Actors, 213
Adages, 8, 281, 300
Adam (biblical figure), 285, 428
Adaptation, 272
Addition, 38
Adjectives, 261
Adventure, 44, 47, 152, 164, 309-10, 373, 449, 501, 506, 533-34, 619
Adverbs, 261
Advertisements, 166, 422
Aesop's Fables, 443
Africa, 10, 105, 154, 419, 597
  East, 406
  Ethiopia, 510
  folklore, 14
  history, 553
  Mali, 628
  North, 397
African American poetry, 230
African Americans, 114, 149-50, 155, 216, 228, 247, 273, 279, 301-2, 338, 399, 420, 447, 471, 478-80, 509, 570, 595, 620, 623
  biographies, 339
  history, 149
Aging, 39, 81, 151, 176, 492, 511, 604
Ailey, Alvin (1931-1989), 447
Air pollution, 538
Airplanes, 98, 312, 351
  designs, 463
Airports, 89
Alamo, 298
Alaska, 508
Alcoholism, 595
Allegory, 72, 94, 367, 404, 468, 521, 596
Alliteration, 377
Allusion, 470, 560, 638
Almanacs, 63
Alphabet, 27, 79, 280
Alphabet books, 154, 279-80, 403, 413, 419, 444, 469, 592, 598, 600, 613
Alzheimer's disease, 39, 604
Amazon, 108, 390
  rain forest, 307
Ambition, 75, 551
America, poetry, 430
American dream, 45, 505

American history, 302
American literature, 292
American Revolution, 362
American Sign Language, 469
Amish, 453
Analogy, 213
Analysis, 587
Anamorphic art, 27
Anasazi, 299
Ancient civilization, 331, 629
  Egypt, 459, 556
  Greece, 333
  Rome, 498
Andersen, Hans Christian (1805-1875), 412
Andromeda, 289
Angels, 382, 613
Anger, 93, 609
Animals, 41, 85, 94, 108, 120, 238, 267, 279, 313, 320, 403, 432, 444, 474, 504, 612, 631, 638
  adaptation, 272
  Australia, 48
  behavior, 325
  caves, 532
  characteristics, 325
  endangered, 101
  ethical treatment, 598
  folklore, 300
  foxes, 381
  habitats, 325
  habits and behavior, 70, 325
  jungle, 306-7
  mythical, 122, 437
  nocturnal, 500
  poetry, 618
  rights, 573
  tracks, 70
  treatment, 524
  whales, 101
Anthropology, 266, 418
Antique cars, 392, 543
Antiquities, 327
Antony, Mark (d. 31 B.C.), 551
Anxiety, 82
Apache Indians, 525
Apartheid, 295
Apes, 88
Appalachia, 262, 277, 495
Apprentices, 355, 616
Archeology, 299, 372-73, 426
Architecture, 80, 92, 167, 226, 265, 278, 293-94, 369, 371, 386, 417, 449, 451, 517, 594
Arctic, 405, 520

X

Anderson County Library
202 East Greenville Street
Anderson, South Carolina 29621
(864) 260-4500

Belton Honea Path Iva
Lander Regional
Pendleton Piedmont
Powdersville Bookmobile

DEMCO